DALITS AND HUMAN RIGHTS (IN 3 VOLUMES)

DALIT
THE
BROKEN FUTURE

Volume 3

DALITS AND HUMAN RIGHTS (IN 3 VOLUMES)

DALIT THE BROKEN FUTURE

Volume 3

Editor
Prem K. Shinde

ISBN : 978-81-8205-240-6 (Set)

ISBN : 978-81-8205-274-1

Published, 2018

Published by

Isha Books
D-69, New Gupta Colony,
Near DDA Market
Delhi — 110009

Contents

Preface

Over years, more than one-sixth of India's population, some 240 million people, live a precarious existence, shunned by much of society because of their rank as 'untouchables' or dalits—literally meaning 'broken' people—at the bottom of India's caste system. Dalits are discriminated against, denied access to land, forced to work in degrading conditions, and routinely abused at the hands of the police and of higher-caste groups that enjoy the state's protection. In what has been called India's 'hidden apartheid', entire villages in many Indian states remain completely segregated by caste. National legislation and constitutional protections serve only to mask the social realities of discrimination and violence faced by those living below the 'pollution line'.

Despite the fact that 'untouchability' was abolished under India's constitution in 1950, the practice of 'untouchability'—the imposition of social disabilities on persons by reason of their birth in certain castes— remains very much a part of rural India. 'Untouchables' may not cross the line dividing their part of the village from that occupied by higher castes. They may not use the same wells, visit the same temples, drink from the same cups in tea stalls, or lay claim to land that is legally theirs.

The plight of India's "untouchables" elicits only sporadic attention within the country. Public outrage over large-scale incidents of violence or particularly egregious examples of discrimination fades quickly, and the state is under little pressure to undertake more meaningful reforms. Laws granting Dalits special consideration for government jobs and education reach only a small percentage of those they are meant to benefit. Laws designed to ensure that dalits enjoy equal rights and protection have seldom been enforced. Without a serious and sustained commitment to implementing constitutional safeguards and other national and international legal protections, human rights abuses in their most degrading forms will continue against scheduled-caste community members.

This book covers the burning issues of dalits —the broken people—who have depressed, oppressed and discriminated for centuries on the basis of the old, dilapidated system of caste, which was made by the elite groups for their own sake. It calls for a campaigned action of the government, NGOs and people to eradicate all kinds of discrimination and violence against dalits and to make them the part of nation-building process. It is hoped that this book will be highly useful for researchers, academicians, planners and human rights activists.

Editor

1

Racism and Cast-based Discrimination

Racism

The concept of racism will be meant in the entirety of its broad scope and polysemy (plurality of meaning). 'Racist' can be a description of attitudes (mental states of individuals or groups), ideologies (sets of socially constructed and politically functional ideas of whole societies, classes, cultures etc.), social practices, institutions, etc.

Human rights practitioners and international organisations have addressed issues of racism mostly in respect to social practices. This is understandable. While racist beliefs and attitudes can be present in a person's mind with varying degrees of conviction, awareness, scope and intensity, we can define less vaguely (and prohibit by law) racist acts as acts which contribute, more or less directly, to ethnic or racial inequality in society.

Critical race theory, one of the recent legal philosophies among American lawyers, which can be traced back to a 1989 workshop in Madison, Wisconsin, understands racism broadly. "Racism is viewed not only as a matter of individual prejudice and everyday practice, but as a phenomenon that is deeply embedded in language and perception.

Racism is a ubiquitous and inescapable feature of modern society, and despite official rhetoric to the contrary, race is always present even in the most neutral and innocent terms. Concepts such as 'justice', 'truth', and 'reason' are open to questions that reveal their complicity with power. This extraordinary pervasiveness of unconscious racism is often ignored by the legal system."There exists a large body of literature on research and measurement of racist attitudes, in the wake of the classical study of Theodor Adorno and others, The Authoritarian Personality, identifying and measuring ethnocentrism, anti-Semitism, fascist attitudes, and susceptibility to anti-democratic propaganda in the United States during the 1940s.

The so called high-scorers, who score high on the ethnocentric and fascist scales, were found to comprise about 90% of the population. Can we talk of racism in a trans-historic sense; in other words, was there 'racism' in slave owning society, or in feudalism? Or is racism a phenomenon of modern history? Having accepted a very broad definition of racism, we should understand racism as present throughout history, i.e. at least since the beginning of 'written history'.

In ancient Greece and Rome, racism was typical of the treatment of slaves and 'metekoi' and reached extreme forms of expression on such places as the Greek ergasterion - which was a special prison for slaves, in which slaves - as a rule ethnically different from the locals - were engaged in hard labour. In the orthodoxy of Stalinist Marxist textbooks, racism was regarded under the rubric "Nature and Society."

Racism was denounced as a reactionary doctrine whose theoretic defect consisted in the naturalisation of social phenomena, processes, and properties.Race itself was regarded as a biological concept, while discrimination on racial grounds was denounced. Politically, the concept applied to cases such as the treatment of coloured people in the United States, apartheid in South Africa, etc., but it was not applicable to socialist society. Thus, the societies of post-communist Central and Eastern Europe were unprepared to accept the more general definition of race discrimination as found in international law, especially in the United Nations Convention on the Elimination of All Forms of Racial Discrimination, and to agree to describing prevailing attitudes to Roma as 'racist'. In the first half of the 1990s, the governments and the political classes of the region were scandalised at the very suggestion that one can speak of anti-Roma racism in Eastern Europe.

On October 30, 1995, non-Romani persons on a train in the Czech Republic threatened to beat up and throw from the train four Romani passengers. Perpetrators were subsequently prosecuted and charged with, inter alia, racially motivated violence. On 20 November 1996, the District Court in Hradec Kralove acquitted the defendants stating that the Romani victims were not a distinct racial group and "belong(ed) to the same race" as the defendants (ethnic Czechs). In so holding the Court relied on a narrow biologically rooted definition of race according to which Roma, like Czechs, are members of the same 'Indo-European' race.

The Court declined to impose punishment on either defendant.Cognitively, there can be different grades of consciousness or awareness of racism: from totally explicit clear awareness to hidden assumptions and merely lived experience or habit. For instance, people may be unable to formulate general racist or ethnocentric principles as such, but they know

that they disapprove of facilitating immigration, or preferential job allocation to minorities. Levels of awareness of racist attitudes can also be dependent on whether such attitudes form part of a dominant ideology. Some notes Whereas oppositional ideologies by definition will tend to be more explicit and conscious among group members, dominant ideologies will precisely tend to be implicit and denied, or felt to be 'natural' by their members. Such group members may indeed be unaware of their ideologies until they are challenged by members of the other group.

Denial of racism is a reaction to the existing sanction of racism as a socially unacceptable opinion.Most people who share racist opinions and act accordingly, would vigorously deny that they are racists - because racism is officially and culturally condemned; it is a negative qualification in societies in which tolerance, equality and democracy are dominant official ideological values. Thus, racism is rarely a self-description; it is mostly an ideology applying to a 'group as defined by others.'

The Freedom Party led by Heider in present day Austria does not consider its platform racist in character; it is seen as 'racist' by the political opponents of that platform both at home and abroad. With time, at least in Western cultures, racist prejudice has sunk deeper into the layers of the prepredicative judgement and has metamorphosed into a set of more subtle assumptions. Most forms of contemporary racism are no longer biologically based, but take a more 'acceptable' form of "cultural racism," though the latter label is denied by its proponents.

A prominent example of this development is the work of Dinesh D'Souza. In his book The End of Racism we find a forceful rejection of any form of affirmative action; repudiation of egalitarian values; extensive blaming the victim; and emphasis on the 'pathologies' of black culture. His views have also been characterised as 'symbolic racism'. Thus, at the academic and intellectual-ideological level, 'cultural racism' is a form of denial, insofar as its proponents are trying to avoid the stigmatisation of being called 'racists', while at the same time holding views that perpetuate or worsen race inequality.

An illustration of the way in which racism manifests itself in seemingly race-neutral policies is the policy of the European Union (EU) and other Western countries on immigration restrictions. The West has been pushing marketisation, and with it the free movement of capital and goods. However, it has balked at the idea of a free movement of labour and has an increasingly strict definition for the movement of people across borders. At face value, the current policy of increased obstacles to immigration created by the EU is race neutral, and its justification may sound legitimate from the point of view of protecting domestic labour, national security, etc.

However, this policy operates on the foundation of deeper lying, unchallenged racist presumptions, and is applied in a racist way. The latter becomes evident in the case of seekers of political asylum who come from countries with civil and political unrest, in which whole ethnic groups are denied their basic rights. These people, even though they may also be potential economic migrants on account of worse living conditions back home, are often genuine victims of persecution in the sense of the Geneva conventions. But if their numbers are 'significant' by Western standards, they are rejected and categorised as economic migrants.

What is wrong with the prospect of persecuted ethnic groups from outside Europe being allowed to remain in the calm and clean cities of the West? At first glance, the claims that they would bring down the fortifications of social welfare by offering cheap labour may seem convincing to those who are unwilling or unable to think beyond the trivialities of mass politics.

Given sufficient political will, this can be of course be prevented by social policy instruments. The less 'sublimated' claim that such ethnic immigrant groups would disintegrate the national culture since they will not be able to integrate meets with the immediate sympathy of the large sections of Western society. But this is a strange point in many cases, when it certainly would be possible to accommodate such groups. Finland, not very densely populated, might have accommodated several hundred Roma escaping racist persecution in their native Slovakia. Nor would it be impossible for Canada to take even much larger groups. But even if it is the case that an influx of immigrants would really threaten to deteriorate some aspects of life in the host country, there remains a small question. Why is a citizen of Western

Europe more anxious about her compatriots' wellbeing, than about the threats to life and physical safety of foreign nationals?

The very frame of reference of our responsibility (the community, the nation) that is giving shape to opinions is fraught with assumptions of racist superiority. Most of us take for granted that we should contribute mostly to "our" community/city/nation, even though we would - at second thought - admit that 'outsiders' have suffered more severe violations of human rights than our neighbour.

The priority list of the Western majority's concerns is thus not the same as the priority list that would occur if the sole basis of judgement were humanitarian and related to the seriousness of human rights violations. This is possible exactly because racism interferes with our judgement.Considering 'racism' from the point of view of its 'denial' is relevant at this point of the struggle against racism, since it immediately conveys the paradigmatic limitations of the Enlightenment weltanschauung.

The discussion of denial leaves behind any illusion that knowledge alone is sufficient as a motive of action, whether at the individual or collective level. Even if people clearly know the facts of racial abuse, they do not take prompt or adequate action. Why? The problematic of 'denial' seeks the answer in the direction of justifications and rationalisations of the racist status quo.

Moreover, the concept of denial questions 'knowledge' as such, showing that the options "They knew" and "They did not know" are neither simple nor exhausting. The discussion of 'denial' should be accompanied by the following strong caveat: it is possible that racist prejudice is clearly present in an actor, it is not denied or masked in any way, but the actor admits that s/he is simply not good enough and/or strong enough to deal with racism: "Racism is definitely a shame; and I/we have absolutely no excuse not to address it promptly and adequately. We, people, are fallible, and why not accept ourselves as such. No one is perfect, and we do not live in a perfect world". This position of full acknowledgement combined with an acceptance of our being 'evil' or 'week' is rare, potentially very dangerous, and falls outside the analysis of denial. A separate attention should be given to the practical and political implications of 'acknowledgement'.

Forms of Denial of Racism

Many of the types of denial identified by Stanley Cohen in his 1995 Denial and Acknowledgement are highly relevant to the case of denial of racism. Cohen talks of denial in the sense of "how people react to the suffering of others". Denial of racism is meant below in the sense that

(a) the suffering of victims of racism,

(b) the existence of attitudes in oneself or society which makes this suffering possible, and/or

(c) the existence of practices and institutions of racism, are denied.

Following Cohen's distinctions, we can differentiate between different forms of denial with respect to the truth-value awareness of the subject/s:

(i) denial in good faith, when the subject honestly thinks s/he is telling the truth;

(ii) denial as outright lying, when the truth about racist abuse is clearly known but denied, as in deliberate deception at the individual level and disinformation, manipulation, or cover-up at the political level; and

(i) all other cases of "partly" knowing, when the denying subject is in neither of the above mental states.

Needless to say, the most challenging case, both in theory and in practice, is the third case: several philosophical and social science schools of thought have addressed the experience of "knowing without knowing that you know", the lack of the Kantian 'transcendental apperception', or selfconsciousness accompanying the mental possession of the 'object'. The psychoanalytic metaphor of the 'sub-consciousness', the phenomenological theories of perception as constitution of the object, the existential idea of the self are all possible frameworks of discussing the transcendental possibility of 'denial'. Cohen's distinction between literal, interpretative and implicatory denialis highly relevant to the denial of racism issues as well.

Interpretative denial is at work when the facts are not disputed, but their interpretation disguises their racist aspect. Example: "This police action was not a punitive expedition as such and such human rights advocate called it; it was a legitimate arrest of suspects in the Roma neighbourhood; it is true that force was used, but police acted in self-defence, etc." would like to highlight implicatory denial as the toughest challenge in dealing with racist denial. In this case, the subject - individual or collective - inserts a shield of rationalisations between the facts and the moral responsibility that they suggest.

A further useful classification contained in Cohen is that of individual, official (sponsored by the state) and cultural denial. The latter is again the most serious challenge in addressing the issue of racist denial: society members, without being told what to think, share a consensus about what can be publicly acknowledged. For example, there is a broad consensus in EU countries that tightening of immigration controls is good and therefore it cannot be described as 'racist'. Further, "the mass media coverage of wars, atrocities and human rights stories is the most important arena to observe the mutual dependency between official and cultural denial". We saw this interdependency in the case of the anti-Serb bias of the West in the Kosovo war of the Spring 1999, and also in the coverage of the ethnic cleansing of the Serbs and Roma from Kosovo in the aftermath of the bombing.

The way in which the destruction of the Kosovo Roma was presented in the mainstream media was a case of wholesale official and cultural denial. Rather than presenting the process as reversed ethnic cleansing, the media stressed the 'understandable' aspect of revenge due to Roma alleged complicity with 'the Serbs'. In conclusion, we will briefly list several rhetoric forms of racist denial:

Denial One - Recasting race difference as mental disability: A brief case study of this form might be the denial by the Czech majority of the de facto segregation of Roma children in the schooling system in the Czech Republic, by sending them to so called 'special' schools for the mentally handicapped. The policy is built on the underlying stereotype that Roma are inferior, and "Romani children are not ready for normal school". The result has been a denial of equal educational opportunity for most Romani children.

The evidence documented by the European Roma Rights Centre (ERRC) shows that, in the city of Ostrava, for example, a Romani child is over 27 times more likely than non-Romani children to be enrolled in a 'special school'. Although Roma represent fewer than 5% of all primary school-age students in Ostrava, they constitute 50% of the special school population. Nation-wide, as the Czech government itself concedes, approximately 75% of Romani children attend special schools, and more than half of all special school students are Roma. This extraordinary racial disparity constitutes what the United Nations Committee on Elimination of Racial Discrimination has condemned in 1998 as "de facto racial segregation" in the field of education, which is inconsistent with the government's obligations under international law.

Many Czech politicians and educationalists deny vehemently that sending of Roma to special schools is a racist policy. However, race-neutral factors fail adequately to explain the gross racial disparity. Thus, few openly maintain the fiction that Roma, as a race, are genetically less intelligent. Those who do are confronted with a virtual consensus among government officials and acknowledged experts that many Roma assigned to special schools are not, in fact, mentally deficient. Evidence built by ERRC demonstrates that the evaluation mechanisms employed to assess "intelligence" are flawed and unreliable. Many of the tests have been selected, and their results continue to be used, although they have previously been shown to generate racially disparate effects.

Denial Two - Recasting race difference as behavioural disorder as in the case of Roma "private student" arrangement in Hungary; or that of the Black Caribbean boys in the UK: Black Caribbean boys are around six times more likely to be permanently excluded from UK schools than white boys, according to Department for Education and Employment Statistics. While there has been a lot of media interest in soaring school exclusion rates in England and Wales, the statistic no longer appears to shock. Yet for black Caribbean families it amounts to a crisis in the education of their children. With an estimated 10,000 - 14,000 permanent exclusions during 1995-96, schools are dumping the population of a small town each year. This suggests bad practice and possible unlawful discrimination in managing behaviour in schools. Exclusion from school often means the denial of the child's right to education; once excluded a pupil has only a 15% chance of returning to mainstream schooling.

Denial Three - Presenting race/ethnicity problems as only a social and economic problem. Several governments (e.g. Bulgaria and Romania) have been saying: "We are not racist, and do not discriminate, we have no problem with the race or ethnicity of the Roma, but this group is economically and socially weak, and the fact that its members are of the same, namely Romani ethnicity, is unimportant/arbitrary." In this case, the government has an excuse for not dealing with race discrimination as an urgent issue. The government's obligation is reduced to slowly improving the material conditions, educational status, etc., depending on the availability of resources. "We can't solve entrenched social problems overnight." That the ethnic group is also socially disadvantaged, excluded or marginalised is true, but this partial truth is used to deny the racist side of reality.

Denial Four - The 'legal equality' argument. Somewhat opposite to denial by presenting race problems as solely socioeconomic problems, this one is a stress on legal equality. As has been noted, sometimes there is a conflict between legal equality and social justice with respect to ethnic minorities, which might require a special program for a particular group to compensate the disadvantage. The stress on legal equality as sufficient to guarantee race equality can be, in certain contexts, a highly legitimate form of denial of a racist status quo. The claim is: "Racial minorities are equal before the law, or are entitled to equal protection by the law, and anything that would favour them over others is unfair."

Denial Five - The 'equal opportunity' (meritocratic) argument. This denial is similar to the 'legal equality' argument, but in this case the claim sounds like this: "The members of the Roma ethnic group enjoy equal opportunities with everyone else in our society, because it is a society where everyone is free. How they use these opportunities is up to them. The fact that they do not make good use of their opportunities is not anyone's fault. People ultimately get what they deserve." This form sometimes verges on blaming the victims: "The Roma must have done something wrong, if not the current then previous generations; otherwise they would not have ended up in such misery/in prison/in the street, etc."

Denial Six - Reduction of the struggle against racism to prohibition and penalisation. Many people think that they have essentially challenged racism in society by outlawing race discrimination and providing access to justice and adequate legal remedy to victims of race discrimination. Such is also in essence the anti-racism strategy of the United Nations to date, according to the major United Nations covenants and conventions. While this strategy of making race discrimination illegal and bringing lawsuits in cases of abuse is indispensable, it cannot alone eradicate, or even substantially reduce racist attitudes or practices in any society. As the removal or reduction of crime can't be accomplished only via the criminal justice system, no mater how well developed the latter is, so the removal or reduction of racism is impossible if policy is limited to prohibiting its damaging expressions, by declaring them illegal. Those who believe that litigation is the universal answer to racism, both miss the point, and create for themselves a moral complacency, which ultimately legitimates the racist status quo.

Denial Seven - Emphasis on duties as pre-condition for the enjoyment of rights. "If Roma do not fulfil their duty X, they can't claim their right Y." Such was also the communist approach to rights: rights were seen as conditioned on the fulfilment of corresponding duties. The respective chapters in the communist constitutions were usually titled "Rights and Duties of the Citizen". One often hears that the high drop out rate of Roma from primary school is due to the fact that Romani parents do not fulfil their parental duties. Absent in this case is the inability and/or unwillingness to understand rights as entitlements, not dependent on past, present or future behaviour of the subject.

Denial Eight - Denial by 'the positive example' argument. "Look at those minority members who made it to the top of society, the company, etc." In social practice, a policy of tokenism is often used to fight back allegations of racism and discrimination.

Denial Nine - Denial by disclaimer. "Some of my best friends are Roma/blacks/Jews"; "Of course there are exceptions, but most X are Y." The personal disclaimer is so typical of most contemporary racist discourses that it can be seen as an ideological marker. Actually, it was one of the statements already in Adorno's 1950 inquiry into prejudice, and produced clear clustering in the answers of high scorers and low scorers.

Denial Ten - Individualisation and self-exclusion from the mainstream. "I love my black neighbour and her friendship is more dear to me than that of others; and such personal links are more important than race relations in the larger society".

"I can't be racist, because in my building there lived a Roma family, and I had very good relationships with them."

Denial Eleven - The romanticising stereotype: A romantic stereotype almost surely will be found to accompany the negative one for an ethnic group, e.g. the Roma, the blacks and native Americans in the United States, the Australian indigenous people, etc. The romantic stereotype of Roma includes such elements as musical and dancing genius, capability of passionate love, free spirited nature, magical relatedness to nature, ability to enjoy themselves, etc.

Denial Twelve - The overstatement of historic optimism and the reference to historical progress in race relations: "Compare and consider how much has changed in the last 20 years; see how much the situation of minority X has improved."

Denial Thirteen - The normalisation shrug: On visiting a Romani ghetto, somewhere in Europe, "That's just what it is like in places like that."

Denial Fourteen - Interpretative denial by downplaying of injury: "No serious damage has taken place; Roma were indeed treated not very gently by the police, but they don't feel abused or humiliated, because they are used to violence; they understand only the language of coercion". Denial Fifteen - Condemning the condemners. We have heard from Central European politicians presently in office: "The western governments are condemning us only because they want to create trouble and to put pressure on us. They are pressing their agenda on us. They are not really concerned with ethnic equality and their criticism is a geopolitical game".

Almost none of the above statements, taken in isolation, would be sufficient to describe a racist attitude. Racist statements are contextual. We can describe an attitude as racist only if we can identify a set of opinions, a more or less clear bias or stereotype. Otherwise, we would have difficulty in differentiating racism from innocent, morally neutral remarks, such as "The Italians are bad drivers".

Most forms of denial are characterised by a deceptively easy availability, when needed as comments on the causes of racially based disadvantage, which, at the level of non-reflective everyday discourse, are never in short supply. For example, "Roma drop out of school because they are poor". Yet, the same person will say a minute later, "They are poor because they don't study well." Like in all 'ideological' thoughts, being 'logical' is not among their qualities. Only upon reflection, it is revealed that racist 'explanations' usually rotate in a vicious circle.

Cast-based Discrimination

The Universal Declaration of Human Rights states "All human beings are born free and equal in dignity and rights. They are endowed with reason and conscience and should act towards one another in a spirit of brotherhood" (art. 1). In article 2 it is expressly stated that everyone is entitled to all the rights and freedoms without distinction of any kind "such as race ... national or social origin, property, birth or other status".

Like other forms of discrimination, therefore, any distinction, exclusion, restriction or preference based on work and descent which has the purpose or effect of nullifying or impeding the recognition, enjoyment or exercise by all persons, on an equal footing, of all rights and freedoms contravenes the spirit and letter of international human rights law.

The International Covenant on Civil and Political Rights recognizes that all persons are entitled to the equal protection of the law "without any discrimination" (art. 26). The International Convention on the Elimination of All Forms of Racial Discrimination specifically prohibits discrimination based on "descent" which the Committee on the Elimination of Racial Discrimination (CERD) has interpreted to mean not solely race but tribal or caste distinctions as well. In its General Recommendation No. XIV CERD stated that "in seeking to determine whether an action has an effect contrary to the

Convention, it will look to see whether that action has an unjustifiable disparate impact upon a group distinguished by race, colour, descent or national or ethnic origin" (HRI/GEN/1/Rev.4, p. 144(E), para. 2).

The International Covenant on Economic, Social and Cultural Rights recognizes the right of everyone "to gain his living by work which he freely chooses or accepts". (art. 6, para. 1).

The International Labour Organisation Discrimination (Employment and Occupation) Convention, 1958 (No. III) calls on States to "eliminate discrimination based on race ... national extraction or social origin", in the matter of employment or occupation. The UNESCO Convention against Discrimination in Education of 1960 asserts the principle of non-discrimination in education based on "race ... national or social origin, economic condition or birth".

Discrimination based on work and descent is a long-standing practice in many societies throughout the world and affects a large portion of the world's population. Discrimination based on descent manifests itself most notably in caste - or tribe - based distinctions. These distinctions, determined by birth, result in serious violations across the full spectrum of civil, cultural, economic, political and social rights. Likewise, the nature of a person's work or occupation is often the reason for, or a result of, discrimination against the person. Persons who perform the least desirable jobs in a society are often victims of double discrimination, suffering first from the nature of the work they must perform and suffering again by the denial of their rights because they perform work that is unacceptable. In most cases, a person's descent determines or is intimately connected with the type of work they are afforded in the society. Victims of discrimination based on descent are singled out, not because of a difference in physical appearance or race, but rather by their membership in an endogamous social group that has been isolated socially and occupationally from other groups in the society.

Instances of discrimination based on work and descent have been identified in many different social and cultural contexts. The manifestations of such discrimination commonly include prohibitions on intermarriage between socially or occupationally defined groups; physical segregation of communities; restrictions upon access to resources including land, water and other means of production; social prohibitions regarding physical contact such as sharing food or utensils; restrictions on access to education or segregation in educational facilities; restrictions on access to religious buildings and restrictions on participation in religious ceremonies. The most widespread discrimination on the basis of work and descent occurs in societies in which at least a portion of the population is influenced by the tradition of caste, including the Asian countries of Bangladesh, India, Nepal, Pakistan and Sri Lanka.

Cast-based Discrimination in India

In 1937, Dr. B.R. Ambedkar, a learned and respected Indian leader and advocate of the rights of untouchables – or Dalits, as he called them – and himself an untouchable, announced that he had made a momentous decision to renounce the religion of his birth, Hinduism, because he traced a great social injustice in contemporary Indian society, namely the caste system, to Hindu scriptures. Mahatma Gandhi, the spiritual leader of India, who was moved by the plight of the untouchables, was himself not prepared to blame Hinduism for the appalling discrimination against millions of Indians by other Indians. In a response to Dr. Ambedkar, the Mahatma said:

> "Caste has nothing to do with religion. It is a custom whose origin I do not know and do not need to know for the satisfaction of my spiritual hunger.... The law of Varna teaches us that each one of us earns our bread by following the ancestral calling. It defines not our rights but our duties. It also follows that there is no calling too low and none too high. All are good, lawful and absolutely equal in status."

The Mandal Commission on the reservation of government jobs for Scheduled Tribes and other Backward Classes in its 1980 report said of the caste system: "The social ranks and their respective duties, ordained by God for humanity, were intended to remain fixed and unmovable. Like the limbs of the body they cannot properly exchange either their place or function".

The debate as to whether caste is or is not derived from Hindu scriptures need not detain us because 85 per cent of India's 1 billion people remain Hindu. Only a few million followed Dr. Ambedkar and became Buddhists. Lesser numbers became converts to Christianity and Islam. India is a stratified or compartmental society not based on class but on descent or occupation. It has been so for many thousand years. Dr. Ambedkar, as Minister of Law and Chairman of the Drafting Committee of the Constituent Assembly, was responsible for the many provisions in the Constitution intended to fulfil the promise in the preamble to secure to all citizens justice and equality of status and opportunity.

Besides untouchables, there are other underprivileged segments of Indian society who are grouped as Scheduled Tribes and Other Backward Classes and they number many millions. Scheduled Tribes are distinguished by tribal characteristics such as social, religious, linguistic and cultural distinctions. In addition, they are concentrated in certain geographical areas. While they are officially recognized as deserving of special treatment, the policy towards them is to effect improvements of their conditions while at the same time preserving their distinctiveness and giving them a measure of autonomy. In the case of Other Backward Classes there is the initial difficulty of identifying the persons who fit the description.

They appear to include all religious minorities who are economically poor and lacking in educational opportunities. The Mandal Commission report found 3,743 sub-castes as being socially and educationally backward, and that Other

Backward Classes constituted 52 per cent of the population. That was in addition to the Scheduled Castes/Tribes, which constituted a separate category of 22.5 per cent of the population. Dalits estimate that they constitute 19 per cent of the population, or 160 million people. The present study does not include Scheduled Tribes and Other Backward Classes as the discrimination against them, where it exists, cannot strictly be said to be based on work or descent.

Those who suffer discrimination based on descent or work have received different names. Official terms were "untouchables", "depressed classes" or "scheduled castes". For Gandhi, they were "Harijans" or "people of God" rather than "untouchables". Today they are known as Dalits, or "oppressed people" or "broken people".

Hindu society recognizes a caste hierarchy of four classes or varnas: Brahmins (priests and scholars); Kshathriyas (rulers and soldiers); Vaishyas (merchants and farmers); and Sudras (servant class). The Sudras, the lowest caste, are seen as persons who exist to serve the higher castes or "twice born". Servility is their badge and with it loss of dignity. According to some researchers there were upper Sudras and lower Sudras, depending on the work they performed.

Artisans, carpenters, barbers, washermen and the like belonged to the former while those engaged in unclean work such as sweepers, scavengers, cobblers, cremation workers, hide and leather workers, agricultural labourers, toddy tappers belonged to the latter. Those considered to be at the lower end of the Sudras are not in fact Sudras but are untouchables who are outside the caste system or "outcastes", or they constitute a distinct fifth caste.

In the mind of the upper castes untouchables are polluted by their work and polluting to others by contact which must therefore be avoided at all costs. A corollary is pointed out by the Mandal Commission: "The real triumph of the caste system lies not in upholding the supremacy of the Brahmin, but in conditioning the consciousness of the lower castes in accepting their inferior status in the ritual hierarchy as part of the natural order of things".

Untouchability conveys "a sense of impurity and defilement. It implies certain socio-religious disabilities. It includes customs, practices sanctioned by the rigid Indian caste system whereby persons belonging to the Scheduled Castes were debarred from entering Hindu temples, public places, streets, public conveyances, eating places, educational institutions, etc." There are other disadvantages – segregation in colonies in the village, denial of land rights, low wages for manual work, denial of access to services, e.g. by barbers and washermen, to health care and education. Untouchables belong to castes which have the lowest ritual standing and often the most depressed economic condition.

In the course of time occupations may have changed and many Dalits are now engaged in agriculture as landless labourers, as this activity has been opened to all. But this is not so in the case of other occupations to which access is not permitted by caste traditions. It is not merely the indignities heaped on Dalits that make them an oppressed people. Because of the social ostracism and economic deprivation they suffer, they often fall prey to the most serious forms of persecution in their society, including killings, mutilation, rape, arson, destruction of property and other forms of violence (sometimes regrettably by State agents) when they assert their rights.

The Government of India has taken several steps to prohibit the practice of untouchability. First, and most importantly, the Government has recognized the existence of the problem. Second, the Government has made determined efforts to deal with it. The Constitution of India in its Bill of Rights (Part III), besides guaranteeing to all citizens the basic civil and political rights and fundamental freedoms has special provisions that are directed at the practice of caste discrimination:

(a) Article 15 prohibits subjection to a disadvantage based on caste with respect to access to shops, public restaurants, etc. or to the use of wells, roads and public places maintained out of State funds;

(b) Article 16 prohibits discrimination on the ground of caste or descent in respect of employment under the State;

(c) Article 17 abolishes untouchability and prohibits its practice in any form;

(d) Article 23 prohibits forced labour and discrimination on the ground of caste when imposing compulsory service for public purposes;

(e) Article 29(2) prohibits denial of admission to any educational institution on the ground of caste;

(f) There are also positive duties imposed on the State to redress imbalances due to past injustices against untouchables. Article 15(4) permits the State to make special provisions for the advancement of any socially and educationally backward class of citizens, including Scheduled Castes;

(g) Article 16(4) permits the State to reserve appointments for members of backward class not adequately represented in the State services.

Articles 15(4) and 16(4) recognize beneficial discrimination or protective/compensatory/preferential discrimination, or simply affirmative action. Indeed, in the governance of the country the State is enjoined by a directive principle of State policy (art. 46) to "promote with special care the educational and economic interests of the weaker sections of the people, and in particular of the Scheduled Castes and the Scheduled Tribes, and to protect them from social injustice and all forms of exploitation". But it is important to note that in the implementation of these provisions the efficiency of the administration is not to be sacrificed (art. 355).

Other provisions in the Constitution addressing caste discrimination are:

(a) Article 325 which prohibits disfranchisement on ground of caste;

(b) Articles 330 and 333 which provide for reserving of seats for members of the Scheduled Castes and Scheduled Tribes in Union and state legislatures according to the Scheduled Caste population in each constituency;

(c) Article 338 which mandates the appointment of a National Commission for Scheduled Castes and Scheduled Tribes. The Commission has been appointed and investigates and monitors all matters relating to the safeguards provided for Scheduled Castes;

(d) Article 341 which makes possible the legal identification of Scheduled Castes or untouchables by means of lists prepared for each state and union territory. The list, when published by the President, is final as to the castes or groups within castes deemed to be Scheduled Castes. The current state and union lists, when totalled, contain more than 1,000 castes but, given the fact that the same castes appear in the different state lists, the estimate given of 76 Scheduled Castes is probably correct.

To bolster the constitutional provisions, India has passed several laws:

(a) The Protection of Civil Rights (Anti-Untouchability) Act, 1955, strengthened by an amendment in 1973, punishes offences that amount to the observance of untouchability, such as prohibiting entry to temples or insulting someone on the basis of his caste;

(b) The Bonded Labour (Abolition) Act, 1976 aims at the release of labourers (usually Dalits) who work in slave-like conditions in order to pay off a debt due to a high caste employer, by cancelling any outstanding debt and prohibiting the creation of new bondage agreements;

c) The Scheduled Castes and Scheduled Tribes (Prevention of Atrocities) Act, 1989. This important law was needed because of the high incidence of recurrent acts of violence against helpless Dalits throughout the country. Eighteen atrocities are listed, including violence against women, dispossession of a Dalit of his land, mischief by fire and destruction of property. Penal Code offences carrying a punishment of 10 years' imprisonment if committed against a member of a Scheduled Caste are punishable by imprisonment for life. The offences are cognizable and non-bailable. There are special courts to provide speedy trials and special prosecutors to conduct cases. In 1999 rules were enacted under the Act to strengthen the investigation process and make provision for payment of compensation to victims;

d) The Employment of Manual Scavengers and Construction of Dry Latrines (Prohibition) Act, 1993. A special law was considered necessary to deal with the most distressing discrimination based on work and descent. There are an estimated 800,000 people, mainly women, who are engaged in cleaning dry latrines using the most primitive methods. The law itself describes this as a "dehumanizing practice" and is intended to make it obligatory to convert dry latrines into water-seal latrines. For the implementation of the Act the National Commission for Safai Karamcharis was appointed. In its 1997 report the Commission found that manual scavengers are "totally cut off from the mainstream of progress and are still subjected to the worst kind of oppression and indignities". What is more pathetic is the fact that manual scavenging is still largely a hereditary occupation. Safai karamcharis are no doubt the most oppressed and disadvantaged section of the population. There is unfortunately evidence that manual scavengers are considered untouchable by other untouchables;

e) Land reform laws to redistribute land to the landless.

It is an impressive list of the actions that have been taken by the Government of India. That improvements have taken place cannot be doubted and credit should probably go to the National Human Rights Commission, the National Commission for Women, the Scheduled Castes and Scheduled Tribes Commission and the National Commission for Safai Karamcharis. A micro-level study in the States of Karnataka, Gujerat, Andra Pradesh and Orissa has led a scholar to conclude that:

> "Like other institutions, caste- and untouchability-based discrimination in the Indian society has undergone change. The practice of untouchability and resultant discrimination has reduced in the public sphere, like panchyat offices, schools, use of public roads, public transport, health and medical services, services of shops (for buying goods) and services rendered by the tailor, barber, eating places and tea shops in large villages and urban areas. But even here discrimination in various subtle forms prevail".

If in urban areas it is more the hidden or invisible discrimination that a Dalit would encounter, in rural areas where three fourths of the Dalits live open discrimination in all its forms is fairly widespread. The overall picture is depressing. In school education there is a marked literacy gap between the Scheduled Castes and the rest of the population. It is reported that reserved quotas in the universities are not filled, especially in the technical and professional courses.

There is reportedly poor representation of Scheduled Castes in teaching posts and caste clustering. There has been inadequate distribution of lands among the Scheduled Castes promised under the Ceiling of Land Acts. The shame of bonded labour remains for millions, including a large number of children. The hideous occupation of manual scavenging continues except in a few states. If reports are to be believed no real effort has been made to improve the conditions of work for these wretched people who out of sheer necessity find that it is their lot to clean dry latrines.

The Reservation of quotas in government employment and education has run into the vexed problem of having to determine whether caste alone should be the test or whether caste should be combined with economic need. Quota reservations in state employment are being filled in lower category jobs such as sweepers, peons and clerks. In the absence of quotas there is hardly any representation in the defence forces, scientific establishments and judiciary. The Scheduled Castes have not benefited from the economic progress made in the country in the 50 years since independence because there has been no policy in the allocation of resources. In the rapidly growing private sector there does not seem to be any opportunities for advancement for members of Scheduled Castes.

At the same time atrocities are being committed almost daily against Dalits and they go unpunished. These have been researched and documented, mainly by Dalit organizations, in several publications in horrifying detail. The laws are there, but there is a clear lack of will on the part of law enforcement officers to take action owing to caste prejudice on their part or deference shown to higher-caste perpetrators.

The Supreme Court in *State of Kerala vs. Appu Balu* said: "More than 75 per cent of the cases under the (SC/ST) Act are ending in acquittal at all levels". What is frightening is that the atrocities committed – murder, rape, mutilation, arson etc. – are not only isolated acts but could even be acts of mass savagery committed by militia groups employed by the higher castes. The inability of the police and courts to deal with these crimes has had a backlash effect on young Dalits who also themselves have formed armed groups or Naxalites.

The present situation in India could not have been better expressed than in the words of the National Scheduled Caste and Scheduled Tribes Commission:

> "The task ahead is clearly, therefore, to focus on the basic needs and requirements of SCs/STs and give them the social dignity and the economic capability to come at par with other sections

of the society and become part of the mainstream which had been the charter visualized by the Constitutional makers 50 years ago. Such a strategy would not only control the feeling of alienation, frustration and rising military and civil strife but would also make the SCs/STs active partners in nation building".

Cast-based Discrimination in Sri Lanka

In Sri Lanka there are two caste systems, one for the Sinhalese and the other for the Tamils. Although they both have their origin in India, the Sinhalese caste system is not linked to the Hindu varna. It was an aspect of a feudal society which divided people "according to Descent and Blood" or according to their hereditary roles and functions. The caste system was a secular hierarchy.

The stratification took into account as many caste and sub-caste groups as there were feudal services and functions or temple services to perform in a disputed hierarchical order. There were no non-untouchables in the Indian sense. Social distance was practised but the notion of pollution hardly existed. As an American scholar concluded, "The absence of the Hindu concept had rendered the Sinhalese caste system mild and humanitarian when judged by Indian standards".

The exception is the caste of Rodiyas or Rodi (meaning 'filth") from very early times. Many legends surround their origin, all agreeing that they were banished for a heinous crime and condemned to a life of begging or, more accurately, soliciting for alms. They were denied land and work and subjected to many disadvantages and degrading treatment. They were a despised lot; even in the middle of the nineteenth century they suffered "untouchability with a vengeance". They were always a small community of about 500 families living mainly in the central highlands in their own colonies of huts devoid of amenities.

During 150 years of British rule when caste distinctions were not officially recognized, there was a high degree of mobility from low caste groups to positions of social standing through entry into professions, business and politics. Desertions from traditional caste occupations were easily achieved through education, and caste became a status concept.

In the case of the Rodi the process has been much slower. Through the efforts of the Backward Communities Development Board, Rodi children were able to attend village schools. Government land was given to them for cultivation. While official sympathy was shown to the Rodi the prejudices of villagers were not easily overcome; however, there is no evidence of any atrocities committed against the Rodi. Farming and casual labour have provided some opportunities but they have not been completely emancipated from the economic point of view: for many Rodi the old life outside the social system has continued.

The caste system of the Tamils, who are mostly Hindus, is also occupation based. Tamils have high and low caste groups which show a stronger concept of pollution and social distance. At the bottom of the caste hierarchy are three castes of untouchables who suffer social disadvantage more than others. While Pallas and Nalavas (descendants of former slaves) can work on upper caste land for wages or rent garden land from them, Paraiyars engage mainly in so-called unclean work.

While the numerically powerful Vellala or farmer caste is not inclined to loosen its dominant position in society over all other castes, upward mobility could not be prevented after American missionary schools were established in the nineteenth century and education was opened to all without caste distinction. Descent is still important in Tamil society and prejudice is more openly shown. It is manifested publicly in acrimonious disputes over temple entry. Only a small number of temples are open to non-Vellala worshippers.

Recognizing that social disadvantages were imposed on people based on the accident of birth or the work they perform, the Prevention of Social Disabilities Act, 1957 was passed in 1957. The Act made it an offence for any person to discriminate against another on the ground of his caste in the matter of access to shops, public eating houses and hostels, public wells, hairdressing salons, laundries, cemeteries, places of worship, or for purposes of education and employment.

In 1971 the Act was amended to strengthen its priorities and to impose heavier punishment. Initially there were some prosecutions in the North but there was a tendency for the police not to take action against violations. In a celebrated temple-entry case, the Act was challenged as interfering with customs and ancient usages that prohibited defilement of a Hindu temple by the entry of law caste persons. This argument was rejected by the Supreme Court and Privy Council.

The 1978 Constitution prohibits discrimination on the ground of caste (art. 12(2)) and prohibits subjecting a person by reason of his caste to any disadvantage with regard to access to shops, public restaurants, etc. and places of public worship of his own religion. There are no affirmative action provisions as in India. Discrimination based on descent and work may not have disappeared, but there are no signs that it is a problem.

A recent allegation of discrimination based on descent is that made by Tamils of Indian origin employed mainly as tea estate workers in the hill country. With regard to wages, housing, sanitation, health and educational facilities, they were an oppressed group. Improvements have slowly been made as a result of government policies and powerful trade union action. Integration with the rest of society is more difficult owing to prejudice, but this is breaking down. There are signs of upward mobility through education and non-discriminatory laws. Caste distinctions exist among themselves and complaints have been made that workers (mostly Dalits) are kept out of trade union offices by high caste supervisors.

The citizenship laws enacted after independence rendered Indian Tamils, who numbered about 1 million, stateless, and they were denied voting rights. Subsequent laws based on agreements between the Governments of India and Sri Lanka have enabled them to acquire citizenship by registration without any distinction being made between them and others who are citizens by descent.

Cast-based Discrimination in Nepal

Nepal has a predominantly Hindu population and a caste system similar to that of India. About 21 per cent of the population of 22 million constitute the service castes (untouchables/Dalits) who are engaged in traditional occupations with low status value. They range from artisans and singers to castes doing unclean work like scavenging and removing dead animals. What unites them is that they are subject to hurtful discrimination - segregation, exclusion from public institutions such as hostels, restaurants and milk cooperatives, or denied free access to water, schools and temples, on the one hand, and deprived of rights, facilities and opportunities given to others to improve their conditions, on the other.

Untouchability was declared illegal in 1963 but the practice was not made punishable until the onset of multi-party democracy in 1990. The Constitution of 1990 guarantees the fundamental rights of the people and makes any discrimination against untouchables punishable by law. The National Code that prohibited Dalits from entering temples and religious sites was declared invalid by the Supreme Court in 1993. The Government is committed to implementing policies aimed at the advancement of Dalits. Thus, the "Independent Downtrodden and Oppressed Community Council" was formed in 1998 with the objective of coordinating policies and supervising programmes to benefit Dalits. The Ninth Five-Year Plan adopted several specific policies and programmes for the socio-economic development of the Dalits, including in education, health, sanitation, training and capability enhancement, and employment.

While these winds of change are appreciated, Dalits complain that untouchability has not been eliminated, that there is unequal distribution of resources, that many of them lack agricultural land and that they remain economically and socially depressed. The Government has acknowledged that "for an overwhelming majority of people the caste system continues to be an extremely salient feature of personal identity and social relationships and, to some extent, determines access to social opportunities". At the Asian Regional Preparatory Meeting for the World Conference against Racism, Racial Discrimination, Xenophobia and Related Intolerances, held in Teheran in February 2000, the Government, whilst again admitting the problem of caste discrimination, declared that the issue should be addressed at the World Conference.

Cast-based Discrimination in Japan

Japanese feudal society, which started 400 years ago and lasted till 1867, left a class structure that placed "humble people" at the bottom. They consisted of eta (extreme filth) and hinin (non-human). The eta were assigned such duties as disposing of dead cattle, leather production, being security guards and sweeping while hinin made their living as security guards, executioners and performers.

The Buraku, as they are now known, were subjected to intense prejudice and discrimination, forbidden to marry or have physical contact with common people as such contact was seen as "polluting" the higher classes. They were an outcast population confined to living in hamlets, now officially classified as Dowa districts. The people of a Dowa district consist of the original eta and hinin people and others who have moved there. The official figures are 4,442 Dowa districts with a total population of 1.2 million Burakumin, but the unofficial figures are 6,000 and 3 million, respectively. The discrimination is not only against those who work in traditional occupations.

Beginning with the Emancipation Edict, 1871, many laws have been enacted addressing the Buraku issue. Article 14 of the Constitution of 1946 states: "All people are equal under the law and there shall be no discrimination in political, economic or social relations because of race, creed, sex, social status or family origin". But a government report in 1965 conceded that the Burakumin are "placed in such an inferior position economically, socially and culturally that their fundamental human rights are grossly violated even in present-day society and that, in particular, their civil rights and liberties which are assured to all people as a principle of modern society are not guaranteed in reality".

The State's responsibility to solve the Buraku problem was accepted and special laws were passed in 1969, 1982 and 1987. The Law for the Measures for Promotion of Human Rights Protection, 1996, established a committee to analyse the extent of Buraku discrimination and make recommendations for human rights education and relief measures for victims. The Law on the Promotion of Human Rights Education and Human Rights Awareness - Raising, 2000 was the result of a national campaign for the enactment of a fundamental law for Buraku liberation.

It is admitted that the living standard of Buraku people has improved, but discrimination in marriage and employment continues. Particularly hurtful is the use of derogatory terms in speech and writing. Also a matter of concern in the printing of lists of Buraku households with the names of the occupants, drawn up after private investigation and made available to big companies to prevent the employment of Burakumin. Government has enacted laws against such activities but the practice continues.

Cast-based Discrimination in Pakistan

Swat is an area of northern Pakistan which had a system of stratification of unequal social groups (qoum) that can be compared to the Hindu caste system, except that the people are Sunni Muslims. The concept of ritual pollution is absent, its place taken by notions of privilege and shame. The population of the area is about 500,000 and the people are dependent on subsistence agriculture. The groups are such as are to be found in an agricultural community, and at the bottom are despised people - sweepers, washermen, barbers and those who work with the guts of animals. There is pollution by occupation but caste status by birth does not prevent change of occupation. In ritual activities there is equality but in everyday situations a distinction exists.

In Sindh Province there are about 1.8 million persons living in bondage as agricultural workers, the majority of whom are Dalits originally from India. A large number of Dalit families work in the brick kiln industry, also under conditions of total bondage. Bonded families are virtual prisoners and not permitted to leave until the debt is paid. In 1992 the Bonded Labour (Abolition) Act was passed but observers note that even when the national police take action state prosecutors fail to file charges. In addition to suffering discrimination on the basis of work and descent, Dalit women and girls also suffer gender discrimination. Women in Dalit communities in Asia are poorly educated and subjected to gruelling labour and many forms of violence, including trafficking and prostitution. Dalit women are consistently subjected to physical abuse and sexual exploitation by higher caste landlords. Women are raped, mutilated and murdered during caste violence. Dalit women do not regularly report incidents of sexual assault because of entrenched biases at every stage of the process.

Most girls and women in India's and Nepal's urban brothels are from lower caste, tribal or minority communities. The practice of devadasi involves the marriage or dedication of a pre-pubescent low caste girl to a deity or temple. Once dedicated, the girls are unable to marry; their role is to serve as prostitutes to the higher caste men in the village. Some states in India have passed laws prohibiting the practice of dedication but they are reportedly not well enforced.

India has tried to remedy discrimination against women by adopting a constitutional amendment in 1993 that provided for one third of all panchyat or village council, seats and village chief positions to be reserved for women and also reserved a percentage of those for women from the lowest rungs of the caste system. In Nepal the Constitution requires that 5 per cent of candidates put up by national parties be women, and in local government 5 per cent of the seats are reserved for women. It would appear, however, that Dalit women are not represented at the national or local level.

The people suffering from cast-based discrimation have inherited a life of burdens and few rights, a life of continuous discrimination, a life without dignity. What wrongs have they committed? The world may have changed around them but not for them. They are ruled by traditions which are hundreds, and sometimes even thousands of years old, traditions that cannot be justified today. It is sometimes said that they are not a race as understood in the international instruments. But they are in fact a race of broken people with commonalities that bring them together. They speak in many tongues and with one voice to ask for social justice and good governance that will end the miseries in their daily lives. They are a people subject to violations of their human rights. It is the responsibility of the respective States to endeavour, not merely the passing of remedial laws, but by positive State action, to ensure that these violations do not go unpunished. The strict enforcement of the law can assist the other ongoing educational processes in society to bring about attitudinal changes in the direction of tolerance, compassion and justice.

Final Declaration of the Global Dalits Conference against Racism and Caste-based Discrimination

The Global Conference Against Racism and Caste-based Discrimination was convened in New Delhi, 1-4 March 2001, and included representatives and victims from India, Nepal,

Bangladesh, Pakistan, South Africa, Japan, Sri Lanka, the Netherlands, Denmark, Germany, Hong Kong SAR, the United Kingdom, and the United States. The participants of the Global Conference strongly condemn caste (occupation and descent based) discrimination and the practice of untouchability, which is the source of immense human suffering and the cause of gross human rights violations and of dehumanising and degrading treatment of 240 million people.

We, the participants of the Global Conference, have listened to disturbing testimonies from victims of caste-based discrimination who have suffered extreme violence, abhorrent conditions of work, degradation, exclusion and humiliation. We have also heard from experts, activists, academics, and grassroots leaders about their work to end caste-based discrimination. We appeal to governments and the international community to end this crime against humanity, and we strongly endorse the following declaration.

Preamble

1. Taking note of the concluding observation of the United Nations Committee on the Elimination of All Forms of Racial Discrimination (CERD) "that the situation of scheduled castes and scheduled tribes falls within the scope of the Convention on the Elimination of All Forms of Racial Discrimination," and that the term "descent" contained in Article 1 of the Convention does not refer solely to race, and encompasses the situation of scheduled castes and scheduled tribes, as cited on September 17, 1996, in the document CERD/C/304/Add.13,
2. Affirming that caste as a basis for the segregation and oppression of peoples in terms of their descent and occupation is a form of apartheid and a distinct form of racism affecting victims equally irrespective of religion.
3. Asserting that Untouchability is a Crime against Humanity,

4. Recognizing that caste-based practices - distinction, exclusion and restrictions on social and occupational mobility - which lead to a negation of humanity and the inability to exercise all human rights are affecting at least 240 million persons in South Asia and millions of others in East Asia and West Africa,
5. Recognizing that the 52 United Nations Sub-Commission on Human Rights, given their concerns over caste-based discrimination, passed a unanimous resolution calling for a working paper on occupation- and descent-based discrimination,
6. Recalling conclusions drawn by the Committee on the Elimination of All Forms of Discrimination Against Women (CEDAW), the Committee on the Rights of the Child (CRC), the United Nations Special Rapporteur on racism, racial discrimination, xenophobia and related intolerance and the Human Rights Committee that Dalit men, women and children endure severe forms of discrimination, violence and exploitation because of their caste status,
7. Committed to the inclusion of caste-based discrimination on the agenda, the declaration and the programme of action of the World Conference Against Racism, Racial Discrimination, Xenophobia, and Related Forms of Intolerance (WCAR), to be held at Durban, South Africa, from August 31-September 8, 2001,
8. Calling attention to the proceedings of the Bellagio Consultation, the European NGO preparatory meeting, and the Asian and African expert meetings in preparation for the WCAR which specifically address the problem of caste discrimination,
9. Encouraged by the solidarity expressed by non-governmental organizations in the WCAR preparatory and expert meetings and taking note of the consensus reached in the Asia-Pacific NGO Declaration in Tehran

for inclusion of caste-based discrimination in the agenda of the WCAR and the Declaration and Programme of Action,

10. Taking note of governments' obligations to uphold universal standards of human rights under the UN treaties and covenants,

11. Commending those governments that are supporting the inclusion of discrimination based on caste on the agenda of the WCAR,

12. Noting that many countries have recognized that certain communities, such as Dalit peoples in India, Nepal, Pakistan, Sri Lanka, and Bangladesh, Buraku people in Japan, and other communities in Senegal, South Mauritania and other countries, face caste-based discrimination,

13. Recognizing that governments have undertaken constitutional, legislative, and policy initiatives, as well as set up administrative bodies to combat discrimination based on caste and race, but also that, due to lack of political will, these efforts have been insufficient and are being diluted, subverted, and not properly implemented,

14. Noting that women - especially Dalit women - represent the most oppressed sections of all societies, and that they face multiple forms of discrimination, including caste-based, religious and patriarchal ideology and practices;

15. Taking note of the support of some public leaders, the media, non-governmental organizations, and concerned citizens from various walks of life who have condemned the existence and perpetuation of caste-based discrimination,

16. Strongly condemning the attempts of the government of India to oppose the inclusion of caste-based discrimination in the agenda of the WCAR, and urging other governments to support the inclusion of caste-based discrimination in the WCAR agenda,

17. Denouncing governments - particularly India- that refuse to comply with or recognize their legal obligations as defined by the CERD,

The participants of the Global Conference adopt the following:

Programme of Action

The participants of the Global Conference Against Racism and Caste-based Discrimination call upon Governments to:

I. Measures at the national level

1. Enforce and implement an effective and time-bound program to abolish untouchability and similar practices in all spheres.
2. Enact and enforce laws related to compulsory primary education and the elimination of child labour, bonded labour, manual scavenging, caste-bound free labour, the decades system or temple prostitution, and other similar practices.
3. Ensure that all necessary constitutional, legislative, and administrative measures, including appropriate forms of affirmative action, are in place to prohibit and redress discrimination on the basis of caste, and that such measures - including those in Japan and India - are continued until discrimination is eliminated.
4. Monitor and publicize the extent to which existing laws have been implemented.
5. Monitor and analyse educational syllabi and textbooks that perpetrate caste-based oppressions and exclusion, and glorify worldviews that have contributed to the continued existence of a system of "hidden apartheid." Implement alternatives that emphasize human rights education at the school and university levels.
6. Allocate adequate funds for and effectively implement programs for the socio-economic empowerment of

communities discriminated against on the basis of caste or descent.

7. Ensure full proportional representation based on percentage of national population size of Dalits, Buraku, and other groups excluded on the basis of caste in all sections of society including police, judiciary, public service, media, and private industry.
8. Urge statutory and constitutional bodies such as national human rights commissions, on women, race, minorities, and other relevant groups, as well as the Asia-Pacific Coordinating Committee of National Institutions, the African Coordinating Committee of National Institutions, and the International Coordinating of National Institutions, to take up the issue of caste-based discrimination and to support its inclusion in the WCAR.
9. Urge national and state governments to take all measures to combat caste-based discrimination against women.
10. Urge governments not to deny passports to people wishing to attend the WCAR in Durban, particularly Dalit activists.

II. Measures at the United Nations level

11. Demand that the WCAR agenda specifically address caste-based discrimination and that the WCAR Platform for Action identifies concrete measures for ending this form of discrimination;
12. Demand that the caste system be included in the WCAR documents as a major source of discrimination.
13. Call upon the WCAR to underline the necessity for States to adopt immediate concrete measures to eradicate the widespread discrimination and persecution targeting Dalits, Burakumin, and other communities facing discrimination on the basis of caste or descent.

14. Call upon CERD and the Special Rapporteur on Racism, Racial Discrimination, Xenophobia, and Related Forms of Intolerance to reaffirm their position that caste-based discrimination comes under the purview of the CERD and to state that caste should be addressed in the WCAR.
15. Call for a declaration by the United Nations that untouchability constitutes a crime against humanity.
16. Call for intensified efforts at educating the public about the extent of caste discrimination and about the contributions of Dalit culture and history.
17. Urge the appointment of a United Nations Special Rapporteur on caste discrimination.
18. Declare April 14 (Dr. B. R. Ambedkar's birthday) as the International Day of Dalit Solidarity.
19. Recommend that United Nations development agencies pay particular attention to caste violence and caste discrimination, assess the impact of their existing programs with regard to caste, and develop programs and strategies designed to curb abuse and encourage accountability.

[1] Untouchability is the subjugation and denial of the basic human rights of people labelled as "impure," a practice sanctified by religious tradition.

[2] The Human Rights Commission of Sri Lanka does not subscribe to this section of the declaration.

[3] The Human Rights Commission of Sri Lanka does not subscribe to this section of the declaration.

2

Indian Dalits: The Agony of Living

More than one-sixth of India's population, some 160 million people, live a precarious existence, shunned by much of society because of their rank as "untouchables" or Dalits—literally meaning "broken" people—at the bottom of India's caste system. Dalits are discriminated against, denied access to land, forced to work in degrading conditions, and routinely abused at the hands of the police and of higher-caste groups that enjoy the state's protection. In what has been called India's "hidden apartheid," entire villages in many Indian states remain completely segregated by caste. National legislation and constitutional protections serve only to mask the social realities of discrimination and violence faced by those living below the "pollution line."

Despite the fact that "untouchability" was abolished under India's constitution in 1950, the practice of "untouchability"—the imposition of social disabilities on persons by reason of their birth in certain castes— remains very much a part of rural India. "Untouchables" may not cross the line dividing their part of the village from that occupied by higher castes. They may not use the same wells, visit the same temples, drink from the same cups in tea stalls, or lay claim to land that is legally theirs.

Dalit children are frequently made to sit in the back of classrooms, and communities as a whole are made to perform degrading rituals in the name of caste. Most Dalits continue to live in extreme poverty, without land or opportunities for better employment or education. With the exception of a minority who have benefited from India's policy of quotas in education and government jobs, Dalits are relegated to the most menial of tasks, as manual scavengers, removers of human waste and dead animals, leather workers, street sweepers, and cobblers. Dalit children make up the majority of those sold into bondage to pay off debts to upper-caste creditors.

Dalit men, women, and children numbering in the tens of millions work as agricultural laborers for a few kilograms of rice or Rs. 15 to Rs. 35 (US$0.38 to $0.88) a day. Their upper-caste employers frequently use caste as a cover for exploitative economic arrangements: social sanction of their status as lesser beings allows their impoverishment to continue. Dalit women face the triple burden of caste, class, and gender. Dalit girls have been forced to become prostitutes for upper-caste patrons and village priests. Sexual abuse and other forms of violence against women are used by landlords and the police to inflict political "lessons" and crush dissent within the community.

According to a Tamil Nadu state government official, the raping of Dalit women exposes the hypocrisy of the caste system as "no one practices untouchability when it comes to sex." Like other Indian women whose relatives are sought by the police, Dalit women have also been arrested and tortured in custody as a means of punishing their male relatives who are hiding from the authorities.

The plight of India's "untouchables" elicits only sporadic attention within the country. Public outrage over large-scale incidents of violence or particularly egregious examples of discrimination fades quickly, and the state is under little pressure to undertake more meaningful reforms. Laws granting Dalits special consideration for government jobs and education reach only a small percentage of those they are meant to benefit. Laws designed to ensure that Dalits enjoy equal rights and protection have seldom been enforced.

Instead, police refuse to register complaints about violations of the law and rarely prosecute those responsible for abuses that range from murder and rape to exploitative labor practices and forced displacement from Dalit lands and homes.

Political mobilization that has resulted in the emergence of powerful interest groups and political parties among middle- and low-caste groups throughout India since the mid-1980s has largely bypassed Dalits. Dalits are courted by all political parties but generally forgotten once elections are over. The expanding power base of low-caste political parties, the election of low-caste chief ministers to state governments, and even the appointment of a Dalit as president of India in July 1997 all signal the increasing prominence of Dalits in the political landscape but cumulatively have yet to yield any significant benefit for the majority of Dalits. Laws on land reform and protection for Dalits remain unimplemented in most Indian states.

Lacking access to mainstream political organizations and increasingly frustrated with the pace of reforms, Dalits have begun to resist subjugation and discrimination in two ways: peaceful protest and armed struggle. Particularly since the early 1990s, Dalit organizations have sought to mobilize Dalits to protest peacefully against the human rights violations suffered by their community. These movements have quickly grown in membership and visibility and have provoked a backlash from the higher-caste groups most threatened—both economically and politically—by Dalit assertiveness. Police, many of whom belong to these higher-caste groups or who enjoy their patronage, have arrested Dalit activists, including social workers and lawyers, for activity that is legal and on charges that show the police's political motivation.

Dalit activists are jailed under preventive detention statutes to prevent them from holding meetings and protest rallies, or charged as "terrorists" and "threats to national security." Court cases drag on for years, costing impoverished people precious money and time. Dalits who dare to challenge the social order have been subject to abuses by their higher-caste neighbors. Dalit villages are collectively penalized for individual "transgressions" through social boycotts, including loss of employment and access to water, grazing lands, and ration shops. For most Dalits in rural India who earn less than a subsistence living as agricultural laborers, a social boycott may mean destitution and starvation.

In some states, notably Bihar, guerrilla organizations advocating the use of violence to achieve land redistribution have attracted Dalit support. Such groups, known as "Naxalites," have carried out attacks on higher-caste groups, killing landlords, village officials and their families and seizing property. Such attacks on civilians constitute gross violations of international humanitarian law. Naxalite groups have also engaged in direct combat with police forces.

In response, police have targeted Dalit villagers believed to be sympathetic to Naxalites and have conducted raids in search of the guerrillas and their weapons. While there is no question that the Naxalites pose a serious security threat and that the police are obliged to counter that threat, the behavior of the police indicates that the purpose of the raids is often to terrorize Dalits as a group, whether or not they are members of Naxalite organizations. During the raids, the police have routinely beaten villagers, sexually assaulted women, and wantonly destroyed property.

Higher-caste landlords in Bihar have organized private militias to counter the Naxalite threat. These militias, or *senas*, also target Dalit villagers believed to be sympathetic to Naxalites. Senas are believed responsible for the murders of many hundreds of Dalits in Bihar since 1969. One of the most prominent militias, the Ranvir Sena, has been responsible for the massacre of more than 400 Dalit villagers in Bihar between 1995 and 1999. In one of the largest of such massacres, on the night of December 1, 1997, the Ranvir Sena shot dead sixteen children, twenty-seven women, and eighteen men in the village of Laxmanpur-Bathe, Jehanabad district Bihar. Five teenage girls were raped and mutilated before being shot in the chest.

The senas, which claim many politicians as members, operate with impunity. In some cases, police have accompanied them on raids and have stood by as they killed villagers and burned down their homes. On April 10, 1997, in the village of Ekwari, located in the Bhojpur district of Bihar, police stationed in the area to protect lower-caste villagers instead pried open the doors of their residences as members of the sena entered and killed eight residents. In other cases, police raids have followed attacks by the senas. Sena leaders are rarely prosecuted for such killings, and the villagers are rarely or inadequately compensated for their losses. Even in cases where police are not hostile to Dalits, they are generally not accessible to call upon: most police camps are located in the upper-caste section of the village and Dalits are simply unable to approach them for protection.

In the southern districts of Tamil Nadu, clashes between Pallars (a community of Dalits) and Thevars (a marginally higher-caste non-Dalit community) have plagued rural areas since 1995. New wealth among the Pallars, who have sent male family members to work in Gulf states and elsewhere abroad, has triggered a backlash from the Thevars as the Pallars have increasingly been able to buy and farm their own lands or look elsewhere for employment. At the same time, a growing Dalit political movement has provided the Pallars with a platform for resisting the still-prevalent norms of "untouchability."

While some Dalits have joined militant groups in Tamil Nadu, such groups have generally engaged in public protests and other political activities rather than armed resistance. The Thevars have responded by assaulting, raping, and murdering Dalits to preserve the status quo. Local police, drawn predominantly from the Thevar community, have conducted raids on Dalit villages, ostensibly to search for militant activists.

During the raids they have assaulted residents, particularly women, and detained Dalits under preventive detention laws. With the tolerance or connivance of local officials, police have also forcibly displaced thousands of Dalit villagers. During one such raid, Guruswamy Guruammal, a pregnant, twenty-six-year-old Dalit agricultural laborer, was stripped, brutally beaten, and dragged through the streets naked before being thrown in jail. Excessive use of force by the police is not limited to rural areas. Police abuse against the urban poor, slum dwellers, Dalits, and other minorities has included arbitrary detention, torture, extrajudicial executions and forced evictions. Although the acute social discrimination characteristic of rural areas is less pronounced in cities, Dalits in urban areas, who make up the majority of bonded laborers and street cleaners, do not escape it altogether.

Many live in segregated colonies which have been targets of police raids. For example, in July 1997 police opened fire without warning on a crowd of Dalits protesting the desecration of a statue of Dalit cultural and political hero Dr. B. R. Ambedkar. The firing killed ten and injured twenty-six. Dalits throughout the country also suffer in many instances from de facto disenfranchisement. During elections, those unpersuaded by typical electioneering are routinely threatened and beaten by political party strongmen in order to compel them to vote for certain candidates. Already under the thumb of local landlords and police officials, Dalit villagers who do not comply have been murdered, beaten, and harassed.

Police and upper-caste militias, operating at the behest of powerful political leaders in the state, have also punished Dalit voters. In February 1998, police raided a Dalit village in Tamil Nadu that had boycotted the national parliamentary elections. Women were kicked and beaten, their clothing was torn, and police forced sticks and iron pipes into their mouths. Kerosene was poured into stored food grains and grocery items and police reportedly urinated in cooking vessels. In Bihar, political candidates ensure their majority vote with the help of senas, whose members kill if necessary. The Ranvir Sena was responsible for killing more than fifty people during Bihar's 1995 state election campaign. The sena was again used to intimidate voters in Ara district, Bihar, during the February 1998 national parliamentary elections.

Dalits who have contested political office in village councils and municipalities through seats that have been constitutionally "reserved" for them have been threatened with physical abuse and even death in order to get them to withdraw from the campaign. In the village of Melavalavu, Madurai district Tamil Nadu, following the election of a Dalit to the village council presidency, members of a higher-caste group murdered six Dalits in June 1997, including the elected council president, whom they beheaded.

According to the eyewitnesses, the leader of the attack instructed the Thevars (caste Hindus) to kill all the Pariahs (Dalits). They pulled all six out of the bus and stabbed them on the road. Five Thevars joined together, put Murugesan [the Dalit president] on the ground outside the bus, and chopped off his head, then threw it in a well half a kilometer away. Some grabbed his hands, others grabbed his head, and one cut his head. They deliberately took the head and poured the blood on other dead bodies.

As of February 1999, the accused—who had been voted out of their once-secure elected positions—had not been prosecuted. Those arrested were out on bail, while the person identified as the ringleader of the attack was still at large. The Scheduled Castes and Scheduled Tribes (Prevention of Atrocities) Act, enacted in 1989, provides a means to address many of the problems Dalits face in India.

The act is designed to prevent abuses and punish those responsible, establish special courts for the trial of such offenses, and provide for victim relief and rehabilitation. A look at the offenses made punishable by the act provides a glimpse into the retaliatory or customarily degrading treatment Dalits may receive. The offenses include forcing members of a scheduled caste or scheduled tribe to drink or eat any inedible or obnoxious substance; dumping excreta, waste matter, carcasses or any other obnoxious substance in their premises or neighborhood; forcibly removing their clothes and parading them naked or with painted face or body; interfering with their rights to land; compelling a member of a scheduled caste or scheduled tribe into forms of forced or bonded labor; corrupting or fouling the water of any spring, reservoir or any other source ordinarily used by scheduled castes or scheduled tribes; denying right of passage to a place of public resort; and using a position of dominance to exploit a scheduled caste or scheduled tribe woman sexually.

The potential of the law to bring about social change has been hampered by police corruption and caste bias, with the result that many allegations are not entered in police books. Ignorance of procedures and a lack of knowledge of the act have also affected its implementation. Even when cases are registered, the absence of special courts to try them can delay prosecutions for up to three to four years. Some state governments dominated by higher castes have even attempted to repeal the legislation altogether.

Between 1994 and 1996, a total of 98,349 cases were registered with the police nationwide as crimes and atrocities against scheduled castes. Of these, 38,483 were registered under the Atrocities Act for the sorts of offenses enumerated above. A further 1,660 were for murder, 2,814 for rape, and 13,671 for hurt. Given that Dalits are both reluctant and unable to report crimes against themselves, the actual number of abuses is presumably much higher.

The National Commission for Scheduled Castes and Scheduled Tribes has reported that these cases typically fall into one of three categories: cases relating to the practice of "untouchability" and attempts to defy the social order; cases relating to land disputes and demands for minimum wages; and cases of atrocities by police and forest officials. Although this focuses primarily on abuse against Dalit communities that have begun to assert themselves economically or organize themselves politically, it also examines the weakest sectors of the population: those with no political representation, living in the poorest of conditions, and made to perform the most degrading of tasks with little or no remuneration. To eke out a subsistence living, Dalits throughout the country, numbering in the tens of millions, are driven to bonded labor, manual scavenging, and forced prostitution under conditions that violate national law and their basic human rights.

An estimated forty million people in India, among them fifteen million children, are bonded laborers, working in slave-like conditions in order to pay off a debt. A majority of them are Dalits. According to government statistics, an estimated one million Dalits are manual scavengers who clear feces from public and private latrines and dispose of dead animals; unofficial estimates are much higher. An activist working with scavengers in the state of Andhra Pradesh claimed, "In one toilet there can be as many as 400 seats which all have to be manually cleaned. This is the lowest occupation in the world, and it is done by the community that occupies the lowest status in the caste system."

In India's southern states, thousands of girls are forced into prostitution before reaching the age of puberty. Devadasis, literally meaning "female servant of god," usually belong to the Dalit community. Once dedicated, the girl is unable to marry, forced to become a prostitute for upper-caste community members, and eventually auctioned off to an urban brothel.

For those at the bottom of its hierarchy, caste is a determinative factor for the attainment of social, political, civil, and economic rights. Most of the conflicts take place within very narrow segments of the caste hierarchy, between the poor and the not-so-poor, the landless laborer and the small landowner. The differences lie in the considerable amount of leverage that the higher-caste Hindus or non-Dalits are able to wield over local police, district administrations, and even the state government. Investigations by India's National Commission for Scheduled Castes and Scheduled Tribes, the National Human Rights Commission, the National Police Commission, and numerous local nongovernmental organizations all concur that impunity is rampant.

With the exception of a few transfers and suspensions, no action has been taken against police officers involved in violent raids or summary executions, or against those accused of colluding with private actors to carry out attacks on Dalit communities. Moreover, in many instances, repeated calls for protection by threatened Dalit communities have been ignored by police and district officials.

The "National Agenda for Governance," the election manifesto for the Bharatiya Janata Party (BJP), which came to power in the February 1998 elections, outlines a program of action for the "upliftment" of scheduled castes and scheduled tribes. It promises to take steps to establish "a civilised, humane and just civil order... which does not discriminate on the grounds of caste, religion, class, colour, race or sex"; ensures the "economic and educational development of the minorities"; safeguards the interests of scheduled castes, scheduled tribes and backward classes by "appropriate legal, executive and societal efforts and by large scale education and empowerment"; provides "legal protection to existing percentages of reservation in educational institutions at the State level"; and removes "the last vestiges of untouchability." However, to date, the Indian government has done little to fulfill its promises to Dalits.

A national campaign to highlight abuses against Dalits spearheaded by human rights groups in eight states began to focus national and international attention to the issue in 1998.

Actions to be Taken

In upholding constitutional guarantees of equality, freedom, justice and human dignity, the government of India should demonstrate its commitment to the eradication of caste violence and caste-based discrimination by implementing the following recommendations at the earliest possible date. In particular, the government should implement measures designed to ensure that states abolish the practice of "untouchability," in compliance with Article 17 of the constitution; commit to taking steps to prevent further violence and prosecute both state and private actors responsible for caste-motivated attacks on Dalit communities; enforce the Scheduled Castes and Scheduled Tribes (Prevention of Atrocities) Act, 1989 and other relevant legislation; and educate state agents and the Indian population on the rights and constitutional freedoms of all citizens.

Immediately and without fail, the government should disband the Ranvir Sena, prosecute and punish state and private actors responsible for a large number of abuses, and place a high priority on the protection of Dalit women. Naxalite groups have also committed egregious abuses, including murders of landlords and their family members.

Recommendations to the Government of India

The Indian government should fully implement the provisions of the Scheduled Castes and Scheduled Tribes (Prevention of Atrocities) Act, 1989 and the Scheduled Castes and Scheduled Tribes (Prevention of Atrocities) Rules, 1995. In particular it should:

— Ensure that states constitute and oversee state- and district-level vigilance and monitoring committees, as required by Rules 16 and 17 of the Scheduled Castes and Scheduled Tribes (Prevention of Atrocities) Rules, 1995, for the purpose of properly implementing the Scheduled Castes and Scheduled Tribes (Prevention of Atrocities) Act, 1989. This effort should ensure that a sufficient number of investigators (including appropriate representation of Dalit men and women) are included in the committees to guarantee full implementation of the act. Given the number of potential cases, the government should enlist lawyers, social workers, medical personnel, teachers, civil servants, and others involved in Dalit issues as investigators. Nongovernmental organization (NGO) representatives should also be consulted in the recruitment of investigators. Committees should submit their reports to district collectors to pursue prosecution. In turn, collectors should report on actions taken during committee meetings. Reports published by the committee should be made public, and in-depth training should be provided to district officials charged with enforcing the act.

— Ensure that states establish special courts in every revenue district and appoint special public prosecutors to try cases arising under the Atrocities Act.

— Ensure strict implementation of the Atrocities Act, as regards victims of violent abuse and other "atrocities." Each police station should have a scheduled caste/ scheduled tribe atrocities cell to handle investigations of abuses and alleged violations of the Atrocities Act. Each revenue district should also have a special deputy superintendent of police charged with investigating atrocities under the act. In keeping with the Atrocities Rules, police who refuse to register cases under the act should be punished accordingly. For full implementation of the act, these cells should be statutorily empowered to receive and address complaints of violations under the act and complaints of official misconduct. They should also be able to file "first information reports" (FIRs), the first step in prosecution of a criminal charge, when abuses are committed against Dalits. The cells should work closely with the vigilance and monitoring committees established under the Atrocities Rules to ensure full enforcement.

— Ensure immediate and full compensation by the district administration to victims of atrocities as per the Atrocities

Rules. The value of property destroyed and crops damaged should be included in the compensation schedule. The committees appointed by the government under the rules to estimate loss should include NGOs in addition to government officials. In accordance with Rule 11, the district administration should also ensure that victims' trial expenses are paid.

— Provide training to district officials charged with enforcing the Atrocities Act and ensure that a copy of the act (translated into the local language) and accompanying rules are easily available and prominently posted in all local level police stations and available in all courts trying cases under the act.

— Statutorily empower the National Commission for Scheduled Castes and Scheduled Tribes to oversee implementation of the Atrocities Act in all states. Strengthen the capacity of the National Commission for Scheduled Castes and Scheduled Tribes to operate legal cells and open branch offices in all states with enough financial resources and powers to initiate prosecution of cases. As recommended by the commission, amend Article 338 of the constitution to empower the commission to issue directions for corrective action and implement its findings.

— Strengthen the capacity of the National Human Rights Commission and the National Commission for Women to operate branch offices in all states with enough financial resources and powers to initiate prosecution of cases. Amend the Protection of Human Rights Act, 1993 so that national and state human rights commissions are not automatically exempted from inquiring into matters already pending before a state commission or any other commission duly constituted under any law.

— Establish a civilian review board or civilian ombudsman committee comprising judges and lawyers to monitor police stations and ensure that Supreme Court guidelines on treatment of persons in custody, as established in *D. K. Basu v. State of West Bengal*, are strictly enforced. NGO input should also be solicited. Ensure that complaints against law enforcement personnel are promptly and thoroughly investigated by adequately trained investigatory staff. The agency should have the power to subpoena documents, summon witnesses, and enter the premises of police stations, lock-ups, and detention centers to conduct thorough investigations.

— Implement the recommendations made by the National Police Commission in 1980, specifically those that call for a mandatory judicial inquiry in cases of alleged rape, death, or grievous injury of people in police custody and the establishment of investigative bodies whose members should include civilians as well as police and judicial authorities.

— Ensure that each police station has adequate female police personnel, consistent with recommendations made by the National Commission for Scheduled Castes and Scheduled Tribes. Female police should record complaints submitted by women. Each police station should also have adequate scheduled caste and scheduled tribe personnel and enough financial resources to carry out investigations.

— Ensure strict implementation of the bonded labor-related provisions of the Atrocities Act. As Dalits constitute the majority of bonded laborers, the government should ensure that states and districts establish and oversee bonded labor vigilance committees, as required by the Bonded Labour (System) Abolition Act, 1976. The government should ensure that a sufficient number of investigators can be included in the committee to guarantee implementation of the act. Lawyers, social workers, teachers, civil servants, and others with ties to bonded laborers and their families should be enlisted as investigators. Nongovernmental organization representatives should be consulted in the recruitment of investigators. The government should provide in-depth training to district officials charged with enforcing the Bonded Labour (System) Abolition Act, 1976, as directed by the Supreme Court in *Neeraja Chaudhary v. State of Madhya Pradesh*, 1984.

— Ensure appropriate implementation of the Employment of Manual Scavengers and Construction of Dry Latrines (Prohibition) Act, 1993, including prosecution of officials responsible for the perpetuation of the practice and non-rehabilitation of affected scavenger communities, the majority of which are Dalits. The government should ensure that states and districts constitute and oversee vigilance and monitoring committees with adequate representation of NGOs, women, and members of the scavenger communities. State governments should also train district officials charged with enforcing the act.

— Implement measures designed to ensure that states are in compliance with Article 45 of the constitution, which mandates free and compulsory education for all children up to the age of fourteen. Primary education is the first step in breaking the cycle of discrimination and caste-based employment.

— Incorporate education on relevant legislation for Dalits and women into school curricula.

— Launch a nationwide public awareness campaign regarding the legal prohibition of "untouchability," "atrocities" and other forms of discrimination and violence against Dalits. This campaign should explain in simple terms what actions are legally prohibited, what recourse is available to Dalits and their families, and what the procedures are for filing an FIR. It should also include a program of public service announcements in all states aimed at sensitizing the population on Dalit issues and creating awareness of Dalit rights.

— Make available to the public government studies on issues affecting Dalits. Specifically, the government should release the white paper on reservations and the white paper on land reform. The first outlines the extent to which constitutional reservations have been implemented at the state and central level since independence. In particular, attention should be given to implementation of reservations in all ministries, in the secretariats of the prime minister and president, and in the police and judiciary. The second outlines the extent to which tenancy acts and acts that establish ceilings on single landowners' holdings have been implemented in all states.

— Ensure that adequate financial resources are allocated to the proper functioning of the newly constituted government bodies under the seventy-third and seventy-fourth amendments to the Indian constitution. These amendments provide that in every *panchayat* (village council) and every municipality, seats shall be reserved for scheduled-caste and scheduled-tribe members in proportion to their representation in the population. Among the seats reserved for the scheduled castes and scheduled tribes, not less than one-third shall be reserved for women belonging to those castes or tribes. The government should work with intergovernmental and nongovernmental organizations to provide appropriate training to elected members of rural and urban bodies, including gender and caste sensitivity training. Women should take part in legal literacy workshops, and all those appointed to reserved panchayat positions should be provided legal protection to ensure that they are able to perform their duties.

The Indian government should provide full cooperation to relevant United Nations bodies in the implementation of the following recommendations:

— Invite the Working Group on Arbitrary Detention, and the Special Rapporteurs on Torture, on Extrajudicial, Summary and Arbitrary Executions, and on Violence against Women to visit India. The government should encourage them to include in their investigations allegations of illegal detention, abuse, and deaths of Dalits in police custody, of fake encounter killings, and of violence against Dalit women, including abuse by the police and by private upper-caste militias.

— Implement the recommendations of the 49th session of the Committee on the Elimination of Racial Discrimination (CERD). In particular, the government should implement the recommendation that "special measures be taken by the authorities to prevent acts of discrimination towards persons belonging to the scheduled castes and tribes, and in the case where such acts have been committed, to conduct thorough investigations, to punish those found responsible and provide just and adequate reparation to the victims." As per committee recommendations, the committee's findings should be available to the public in local languages.

— Promptly submit the Indian government's next periodic report on compliance with the International Convention on the Elimination of All Forms of Discrimination to CERD, as this has been overdue since January 4, 1998. As requested by CERD, the report should include "detailed information on the legislative aspects and the concrete implementation of the Directive Principles of the State Policy of the Constitution," as well as information on the powers and functions of the National Commission for Scheduled Castes and Scheduled Tribes.

— Promptly submit the Indian government's initial report on compliance with the Convention on the Elimination of All Forms of Discrimination against Women to the

Committee on the Elimination of Discrimination against Women, as this has been overdue since August 8, 1994.

— Ratify the United Nations Convention against Torture and Other Forms of Cruel, Inhuman, or Degrading Treatment or Punishment, 1984.

In addition to recommendations outlined for the government of India, state governments should implement the following recommendations at the earliest possible date:

— Ensure full implementation of the Scheduled Castes and Scheduled Tribes (Prevention of Atrocities) Act, 1989, including the appointment of special courts, special prosecutors, and vigilance and monitoring committees. Provide training in proper procedures under the act to judges and prosecutors charged with trying atrocities cases.

— Ensure ratification and implementation of the Bonded Labour (System) Abolition Act, 1976 and ratify and implement the Employment of Manual Scavengers and Construction of Dry Latrines (Prohibition) Act, 1993.

— Implement measures designed to ensure that states are in compliance with Article 46 of the constitution, which directs states to promote with special care the educational and economic interests of the scheduled castes and scheduled tribes and to protect them from social injustice and all forms of economic exploitation.

— Study and publicize the extent to which land and wage reforms have been implemented in the state. In particular, state governments should determine industry compliance with minimum and living wage standards, particularly those industries that employ a majority of Dalits, as well as the status of land reforms, land ceiling laws, and distribution of surplus land. The study should also review proof of ownership in land records, the extent of encroachment on scheduled caste/scheduled tribe lands. NGO participation should be ensured in the investigations.

— Take immediate steps to prevent further violence, social boycotts, and other forms of discrimination against Dalits and to investigate and punish those responsible for attacks and acts of discrimination in affected districts. Any officials or members of the police who fail to respond to repeated calls for protection from villagers, or fail to prosecute acts of violence or discrimination should also be prosecuted.

— Take decisive steps to ensure police agents use deadly force only as a last resort to protect life. Police agents should act in accordance with guidelines established in relevant state police manuals that meet international standards on use of force. The United Nations Basic Principles on the Use of Force or Firearms by Law Enforcement Officials emphasize that the use of force and firearms should be in consonance with respect for human rights and that deadly force should not be used against persons unless "strictly unavoidable in order to protect life."

— Take decisive steps to ensure that police do not conduct raids on villages or engage in arbitrary and unlawful destruction and seizure of property in response to caste clashes. Police involved in such activities should be promptly investigated by an independent judicial body and prosecuted accordingly.

— Ensure that investigations of complaints of violence against women include women investigators. Amend the Criminal Procedure Code so that rape victims are not restricted to approaching government hospitals for medical examinations and can instead be examined by any registered practitioner for the purposes of gathering evidence.

— Establish independent monitoring agencies to review cases of Dalits and Dalit activists detained under detention laws. All cases found to be without merit, or in violation of proper detention procedures, should be withdrawn.

— Compile and release state-level statistics on the number of atrocities committed against Dalits, the number of cases registered under the Atrocities Act, and the extent to which reservations have been implemented in the state. States should ensure that all NGOs and citizens have access to this information.

— Investigate the process of recruitment of police officers in the state to ensure that requirements of reservations for scheduled castes and scheduled tribes are met and that monetary bribes are not part of the police and judicial recruitment process. Prosecute and punish those found to have engaged in bribes or extortion while registering cases or conducting raids.

— Ensure speedy review and publication of findings by commissions of inquiry appointed by the state to investigate abuses against Dalits.

Naxalites and other armed opposition groups are at all times obliged to respect minimum standards of humane behavior. These standards require that civilians and other protected persons be treated humanely, with specific prohibitions on murder, torture, or cruel, humiliating or degrading treatment. Groups engaging in armed struggle should look to the provisions of Common Article 3 of the Geneva Conventions for additional guidance on the legal foundations of these basic principles. Additionally, the state government of Bihar should:

— Appoint an independent judicial body to investigate and punish those responsible for attacks in affected districts, including any officials or members of the police who failed to respond to repeated calls for protection for villagers or to prosecute previous acts of violence.

— Make special efforts to investigate and prosecute those responsible for attacks on women during the Laxmanpur-Bathe massacre of December 1997, and other massacres.

— Investigate the role of the police in conducting raids on villages in the aftermath of massacres and in illegally destroying or seizing property. Police responsible for such abuses should be prosecuted and punished accordingly. Dalits who have lost property during such raids should be compensated.

— Disband the Ranvir Sena, an upper-caste private militia which has been implicated in the massacre of hundreds of Dalits since 1994.

— Provide full security to villagers against further private militia attacks. Relocate village-based police pickets away from upper-caste areas to areas more accessible and secure for lower-caste communities.

— Ensure that in all districts affected by caste clashes (particularly in Jehanabad, Patna, and Bhojpur) at least one senior officer is a member of the Dalit community.

The state government of Maharashtra should:

— Prosecute officers found guilty of killing and injuring hundreds of Dalits in Bombay's Ramabai colony on July 11, 1997 when members of the Special Reserve Forces fired indiscriminately into a crowd of Dalits protesting the desecration of a statue of Dr. B. R. Ambedkar.

— Prosecute and punish those officials held responsible by the Gundewar commission for the Ramabai killings.

The state government of Tamil Nadu should:

— Use an independent judicial body to promptly investigate and prosecute police involved in raids on villages during the southern district clashes from July 1995 to December 1998. Dalits who lost property during such raids should be compensated.

— Ensure that in all southern districts affected by caste clashes at least one senior officer is a member of the Dalit community.

Recommendations to International Agencies

— Agencies should establish consultative mechanisms to seek Dalit NGO input in project design and evaluation.

— The World Health Organization should investigate and publicize the adverse health consequences arising from the practice of manual scavenging and promote measures to eliminate exposure of Dalits to hazardous work conditions.

— U.N. agencies that have programs for women in India, including WHO, UNDP, UNICEF, and UNIFEM, should use these programs to focus attention on the human rights implications of violence against Dalit women, including the role of official forces in perpetuating that violence.

— UNIFEM, in conjunction with the Indian government and NGOs, should expand its efforts in providing legal training to rural women elected as panchayat members.

Recommendations to the World Bank and other international lending institutions operational in India should:

— Ensure that anti-discrimination measures are built into World Bank and Asian Development Bank-funded projects in areas where the problems of caste violence and caste discrimination are severe. As part of its commitment to good governance, the World Bank, as well as other international lending institutions, should establish ongoing dialogue with Dalit NGOs at all stages of the decision-making process—before a loan is released, while the project is being implemented, and in the course of any post-project evaluation.

— Prior to approval of projects, and in consultation with NGOs, investigate the effect of proposed policies and programs on caste violence, caste discrimination, and discrimination against Dalit women, and explore ways in which programs could help alleviate violence and discrimination.

3

Caste and Inequality

There are many distinctive features of the programme in India, and in order to appreciate the features and understand how the programme has been faring in the last several decades, it is necessary to know something about the structure of society and the problems which the programme seeks to address. Each one of these topics — caste, inequality and affirmative action — is large and complex. It is true that caste has given rise to a massive programme of affirmative action in India, but there are also programmes of affirmative action which have been devised in other contexts where caste does not exist. So caste has to be understood to some extent on its own terms.

Certainly, the caste system is changing. Some say that affirmative action is essential, it is necessary in order to eliminate, or at least to reduce, the inequalities that have been inherited from the past. Others say that affirmative action in fact reinforces the sense of separate identity between members of different castes. Now caste, of course, is closely related to inequality but inequality is not all there is to caste.

There are many other aspects of caste which need to be considered at least briefly. And inequality is not simply a matter of caste. There are other aspects of inequality in Indian society which are extremely important. In the 1950's and 1960's, after the country became independent, there were sharp disagreements between Marxists and liberal theorists as to whether, in fact, caste was the real basis of inequality in Indian society. Some would say that it was, while others would say that the real basis of inequality was the ownership, control and use of land. For the latter, it was the agrarian social structure which provided the real basis of inequality in Indian society. In other words, there are aspects of caste which can be discussed independently of the issue of inequality, and there are aspects of inequality which can be discussed independently of caste.

Caste and inequality and to present the programme of affirmative action in the context of understanding of the inequalities of caste that continue to exist. Many students of Indian society have argued that caste was the country's fundamental social institution. If there was anything which gave Indian society its distinctive features, it was the caste system and caste was the basis of Hindu society over a very long period. It was very much tied up with Hindu attitudes towards ritual purity and pollution, to Hindu conceptions of hierarchy as the basic order of society, and in that sense they would say that caste is the fundamental institution of Hinduism, that it represents the social morphology, so to say, of Hindu society. Hinduism is a religion whose social aspect is expressed in the division of the population into castes and subcastes of many different kinds.

Caste has existed in India, particularly among the Hindus, over a very long period of time. It has long been a subject of discussion, and not simply among contemporary or modern social theorists. Caste was extensively discussed in the classical literature of Hinduism which tried to explain and even to justify the system. So there has been an elaborate discussion over a long period of time of the logic of caste, so to say. If you look at medieval European history, you will find elaborate discussions of the logic of the feudal system and the "estates". But India has a much greater continuity over time in the discussion of caste. So it was in that sense the definitive institution of Hindu society.

Caste was not confined to the Hindus and this is something which must be kept in mind. Divisions of a kind which are very similar to the divisions of caste among the Hindus have existed also among the Muslims in India and on the subcontinent over a very long period of time. When the British administrators began to construct a social map of India, they used their 10-year censuses as occasions for writing about the division of the population into its basic groups and communities. These census reports which start from the end of the nineteenth century provide very interesting information on the divisions and subdivisions of Indian society.

The census of 1921, which, of course, was of undivided India, had a special report on caste among the Muslim population. The detailed discussion of what the census commissioner described as caste among the Muslims generated a strong reaction from the Muslim intelligentsia who argued that caste was antithetical to the principle of Islam. How could one talk about caste among Muslims in India? But in the course of time, most students of Indian society and of the subcontinent have come to accept that caste-like divisions exist not only among the Muslims but also among Christians and other religious communities. They also exist in incipient form among the tribal communities in India.

The division of the population into a large number of groups which were ranked in some kind of a hierarchy was found throughout India and it was not confined to the Hindus. But of course, it was only among the Hindus that you found not simply the practice but also the theory of caste.

Over a period of 2000 years, the Hindus had developed a model of society in which the hierarchical division of the population was regarded as constitutive of their society and indeed of human society as such. It is distinctive of caste among the Hindus that you have not only the practice of caste, not only the division of society into innumerable groups, but you also have a theory which seeks to describe, explain and justify these divisions. When one uses the term "caste" in

English, one is actually translating two distinct terms in the classical as well as the modern languages of India.

The first term is *varna* and the second is *jati*. Varna and *jati* have both been described as caste. They are not unrelated to each other but they are not the same, and it is very important to understand the distinction between the two in order to understand the social logic of caste. The scheme of varnas has been elaborated in India among the Hindus for at least 2000 years. It has no counterpart among the other religious communities, and that is extremely important. The theory of varna lays down the logic of the system just as many medieval texts laid down the logic of the system of estates in medieval Europe. According to these classical texts and also according to later accounts, there were four and only four varnas - Brahman, Kshatriya, Vaisya, and Sudra. These are the four varnas and they are ranked in the order shown.

The distinctive feature of the system of varnas is that it was believed to be invariant, to be present throughout the country, throughout the length of the subcontinent. It was the same order, Brahman, Kshatriya, Vaisya, and Sudra which was believed to prevail throughout the country. Further, it was not only invariant, it was also believed to be permanent. The same order of the social world divided into Brahman, Kshatriya, Vaisya, Sudra remained unchanged over the centuries.

When we look at the history of modern India, we realize that the traditional order of varnas may not change, but it becomes obsolete. Fewer areas of life tend to be governed by varna than was the case in the past. And one can see this obsolescence of the social order of varnas in the course of the last 50 years. Discussions of caste in the regional languages in India make less and less use of the category of varnas. If one talks to modern Indians, if one looks at the newspapers, the discussion of caste is no longer in the language of varnas as was the case until the middle of the nineteenth century. Today the discussion of caste is in the language of jati which is the other aspect of caste.

Now, what are jatis? we said that there are four and only four varnas - Brahman, Kshatriya, Vaisya, Sudra - but the jatis are innumerable. A village in South India in the early 1960's. In that one single village, there were as many as 35 or 36 distinct jatis. If you take the region as a whole, you might find the population divided and subdivided and sub-subdivided into a couple of hundred different jatis. So, they are numerous and they are ranked, but the order of ranking is not as tidy or as rigid as the order of ranking of the varnas. Not only that, the jatis are not the same in all parts of the country. They vary from one part of India to another. Each region has its own distinctive complement of jatis, and, whereas the varnas are believed to have been unchanging and immutable, we know that new jatis were being created and old jatis were dying out all the time. So, it is a much more flexible and dynamic system than the system of varnas.

Today, when one talks about caste in India, one is really talking about jatis rather than varnas. What does this mean in sociological terms? It simply means that when one talked about varnas, one talked about the hierarchy that not only existed in fact, but also had a certain legitimacy in the normative order of society. Whereas, when one talks about jatis, one is talking about divisions of a kind which do not enjoy the legitimacy that the system had in the past. If we may use an analogy from other societies, we would say that the system of varnas corresponded to the medieval system of estates. "The rich man in his castle, the poor man at his gate, God made them high and lowly and ordered their estate." That is a Church of England hymn, as a matter of fact. It is a system whose legitimacy is accepted and taken for granted. In contrast, the jatis operate rather like the ethnic groups in the United States do.

The differences must also be noted: the varna order had far greater stability and continuity over time than the system of estates in medieval Europe did, and the system of jatis in contemporary India is far more elaborate than the system of ethnic groups in the United States. There is a ranking of jatis but there is a difference between groups which are ranked in terms of de facto criteria and the social hierarchy whose basic principles are accepted generally, if not universally, in society. If one looks at the traditional order of Hindu society and of Indian society in general, we would say that it was a hierarchical social order in the sense that inequalities not only existed, but that they were accepted as right, proper and desirable.

All this was considered to be part of the natural scheme of things, not just inequalities between the varnas but also between the jatis, because the varna system provided a kind of framework, a benchmark for ranking the different jatis. It was considered right, proper and desirable that they should be ranked in this way. This applied not just to the ranking of varnas and jatis, but also to the ranking of men and women. That was the traditional order, it was the most complete and the most elaborate hierarchical social order known to human history.

And the legitimacy of ranking was taken for granted by and large. It was questioned from time to time, but over a long historical period the legitimacy of this ranking of jatis and varnas was taken for granted in the classical, legal and religious literature of Hinduism.

Today, the Constitution of India provides a blueprint for an egalitarian society. The Constitution is not based on the premise of hierarchy, but on the premise of equality. But of course, you do not just erase or cancel out age-old inequalities simply by adopting new principles in a Constitution. So what else has to be done in order to reduce the inequalities of the past? This is what affirmative action or positive discrimination addresses itself to. The object is to reduce the level of inequality in a society which has had a hierarchical order over a very long period of time.

Affirmative action or positive discrimination was not the only major programme adopted when the country became independent and created a Constitution based on the premise of equality. For example, there was a massive programme of agrarian reform which was also designed to give greater thrust to the pursuit of equality. We would say that these were the two main programmes - agrarian reform and affirmative action - designed to improve the conditions of what came to be known as the backward classes in Indian society.

We have often been asked outside India about the insensitivity of Indians in using a term like this - the backward classes. It shows a certain kind of insensitivity and we have often been asked if we feel embarrassed to use this phrase when talking about a section of our own society. Well, yes and no. The term 'backward' has become a fighting word in India today so it is not necessarily something that one wants to sweep under the carpet. It has become a fighting word although it was not always a fighting word and this question of terminology, in fact, bedevilled the administrators of India even before independence.

One major component of the backward classes consists of those who are called Dalits today, or the Untouchables ,or the Harijans as Mahatma Gandhi called them. J. H. Hutton, a distinguished anthropologist who was also the commissioner for the 1931 census, wrote that this section of the Indian population had come to be called the 'depressed classes', which was an odious phrase to use in to reference to a whole section of society. He was very unhappy with the term and favoured 'exterior castes' in its place. Finally, the Government of India in 1935, that is before independence, settled for 'scheduled castes'.

Successive governments in independent India have used positive discrimination as an instrument for furthering specific political ends. So, what is tantalizing about positive discrimination in India is that it is not just a question of furthering social justice, it is also a question of maintaining a certain balance of power between different groups in society. This did not start with independence and the adoption of a new Constitution. In fact it started at least 30 years before the new Constitution was adopted. So, what is this programme of positive discrimination which has such a long history in India? We will now very briefly indicate the basic features of positive discrimination before we invite questions.

The first relates to the beneficiaries of positive discrimination -that is to say, those groups for whose benefit the programme of positive discrimination has been constructed and elaborated over the last 80 years. So one must get some idea of the interested beneficiaries of positive discrimination. They are not a single homogeneous block; in fact, they are very diverse and one must keep this diversity in mind in order to evaluate the success and the failure of positive discrimination.

One might take the view that positive discrimination is justified in the case of some of these groups, but not in the case of others. Secondly, one has to distinguish between the different kinds of programme that come under the broad policy of positive discrimination; here, one might say that positive discrimination is justified in certain areas of public life but not in others. At least, one must have some appreciation of the wide range of the beneficiaries of positive discrimination as well as a sense of the variety of policies which come under the umbrella of positive discrimination.

Let us first say something about the intended beneficiaries of positive discrimination, who are broadly known as the backward classes. Who are the backward classes? They are not a single homogeneous block, and this must always be kept in mind. And what must also be kept in mind is that the backward classes are not really classes in the ordinary sociological sense of the term. They are really groups of communities and not classes. These groups of communities fall into three broad divisions: firstly, there are the scheduled tribes, secondly, there are the scheduled castes and thirdly, there are the other backward classes (OBCs).

There are three divisions among the backward classes. The smallest group consists of the scheduled tribes. In a very rough way, they can be compared to the native American population of the United States but the analogy is deceptive beyond a certain point. They are the tribal population of Indian society and they are the smallest division of the backward classes. However, although they only comprise a little over 8.5 per cent of the population, that means over 85 million people. That is not a very small population by the standards of European countries or by the standards of countries anywhere in the world.

The scheduled tribes are very diverse, and this is directly relevant to the discussion, because the critics of positive discrimination point out that in India, it benefits not the most disadvantaged members of the backward classes but the least disadvantaged among them. The scheduled tribes are divided into more than 400 distinct tribes varying enormously in size, occupation, economic condition, habitat and many other things. Their general characteristic so far has been their physical isolation in the hill and forest areas either on the frontiers of the country or in the interior. But their isolation is no longer as conspicuous as it was till the middle of the nineteenth century.

So today it is often very difficult to decide whether a community is a tribe or a caste. The British were very keen to distinguish the tribes from the castes, but they frequently confused them. The scheduled tribes constitute the smallest section of the backward classes. The next consists of what are known as the scheduled castes. Whereas the scheduled tribes have been isolated in hill and forest areas, the scheduled castes have been segregated. They have been very much a part of the economy of land and grain on which Indian society was based. But they were segregated and were not allowed access to many civic amenities. They were denied access to education and the other advantages through which one could achieve success in economic and social life. They comprise over 16 per cent of the population, so around 165 million persons. But they are also highly divided.

First of all, they are regionally divided. India is a country of many regions, each with its own distinctive language, and the scheduled castes are divided by language just like the rest of the population, although they come at the bottom of the hierarchy. This means that there is a distinction between the scheduled castes of Tamil Nadu who speak Tamil like the non-scheduled caste population of Tamil Nadu and the scheduled castes of Bengal who speak Bengali. Even if we confine our attention to the scheduled castes of one particular region, there also we will find a considerable amount of differentiation as well as ranking.

The ranking of castes did not stop at the boundaries of untouchability, it went right down. So the scheduled castes or the so-called untouchables were themselves also ranked. It is this that makes the problem of the scheduled castes quite different from the problem of the blacks in the United States. It is this that makes the problem of administering a policy of positive discrimination so much more difficult and so much more complex in the Indian case because the benefits of the programme tend to be gathered not by the weakest among the scheduled castes but by the strongest among them. There are analogies to this of course in the affirmative action programme in the United States. But in India the problem is far more complex.

Finally, there are what are called the "other backward classes". The Constitution of India was drawn up at a time when the country had been partitioned on the basis of religion so the mood was against further divisiveness. Therefore, in the Constitution of 1950, special provisions were only made for the scheduled castes and the scheduled tribes. But it did not stop there because one of the directive principles of state policy said that some measures may also be adopted for the benefit of other backward classes without specifying what these measures should be and who the other backward classes were.

So commissions were set up and as a result we have today a third section of the backward classes consisting once again of numerous castes and communities, which are even more diverse in their economic and social standing than the scheduled castes or the scheduled tribes and which are known as the other backward classes. They comprise anything between 25 to 50 per cent of the population.

One can give exact figures for the scheduled tribes and the scheduled castes, but not for the other backward classes. What the British did was to enumerate all castes and communities throughout the country. At the time of independence it was felt that the benefit of this was outweighed by the divisive implications of enumerating caste in the census. So the enumeration of castes was discontinued in the censuses from 1951 onwards with the exception of the scheduled castes and the scheduled tribes, who have been enumerated separately. So these are the three broad divisions, very different in their social standing. Some of the other backward classes are and have been politically dominant in their areas although their social and ritual standing in the traditional hierarchy was not very high. Whereas the scheduled caste and scheduled tribes, one would agree on the whole, have been severely disadvantaged and deprived, this is not true, or not true to the same extent, of the other backward classes.

These groups are the intended beneficiaries of positive discrimination. What are the benefits? There are three main kinds of benefit and we will just enumerate them and then stop. The first is what may be described as political reservation. This means that a certain number of seats in Parliament and in the state legislatures are reserved for members of the scheduled castes and the scheduled tribes, roughly in proportion to their strength in the population. Political reservation in Parliament and in the state legislatures is only for the benefit of the scheduled castes and the scheduled tribes, not for the other backward classes.

Political reservations are written into the Constitution of India and the provisions reveal the ambivalence of the makers of the Constitution as well as of policy makers in contemporary India. The constitutional provisions for political reservations for the scheduled castes and scheduled tribes are mandatory. That is, the Constitution says that 'seats' shall be reserved in Parliament for such and such. However, when the provisions were made mandatory in 1950, it was decided that this would apply only for ten years, so they would last for a single decade. But since then the Constitution has had to be amended every ten years to keep on extending political reservations for the scheduled castes and the scheduled tribes.

The second kind of reservation which is even more contentious than the first is known as job reservation. Job reservations apply mainly to government appointments at union and state level and also to organizations which are substantially funded by the government. The provisions for job reservation apply not only to the scheduled castes and the scheduled tribes but also to the other backward classes. Over the years there has been an extension of job reservations for the benefit of the other backward classes. This has now become the most contentious issue, whether the wholesale extension of job reservations for the other backward classes accords with the spirit of the Constitution or not. For job reservations, unlike political reservations, the provisions are not mandatory; they are enabling provisions. The Constitution says that the state may take such measures as are necessary for the special benefit of the other backward classes.

Finally, there are what may be called reservations in education. These, again, are matters of contention, for reservation exists not only in general arts and science courses but also in medical and engineering schools. In India, reservation in law schools somehow has not been a subject of such bitter contention. But reservation in medical and engineering schools is very controversial.

Once again, when assessing the merits of this, one must ask whether provisions that are justified for the scheduled castes and scheduled tribes on a limited scale should be extended on such a large scale. What is the problem with extending these reservations on such a very large scale? The logic of reservations or of positive discrimination is that special opportunities should be created for some over and above the general provisions for equality of opportunity for all. Now, if you create special opportunities for some, then it does eat into the provision of equal opportunities for all.

The question is one of balance and, once again, this question came up at the time of the making of the Constitution of India. And the man who piloted it through the constituent assembly was himself from an untouchable caste: Dr. Ambedkar, a formidable lawyer. In putting these proposals forward to the constituent assembly, Ambedkar argued that there are several conflicting aims which have to be reconciled. First, there is the aim of providing equal opportunity for all, irrespective of caste, creed and community. That is very important. The second aim is to create special opportunities for those sections of society which have been severely deprived and disadvantaged. But he went on to add that these special opportunities should not be so extensive as to 'eat up' the general provision of equality of opportunity for all. Those were the words he used.

Now many people feel that the extension of reservations to the other backward classes on such a large scale has carried the policy of reservations so far that in many ways it threatens the more general principle of equality of opportunity irrespective of caste, creed and community which is also inscribed into the Constitution of India. So this is the framework within which the problem of positive discrimination or affirmative action in India has to be assessed.

4

Racism and Public Policy

One sixth of India's population are Dalits. These 160 million people are divided into numerous communities with distinct customs and histories, but they are bound together by a common history of grinding oppression. Dalit literally translates to broken people, with broken often glossed as oppressed. Since the 1970s, radical Dalits have claimed the word for their communities and their liberation. Dominant castes used to call them untouchables. Gandhian liberals call them Harijans and the Indian Republic calls them Scheduled Castes.

Most Dalits are poor folk who work in the fields, factories, streets, shops, and public buildings-wherever labor is in demand. Unlike people of color in the U.S. or blacks in South Africa, Dalits are not physically distinguishable from other Indians. In some regions, occupation, surname, or dress can sometimes identify them, but Dalits are usually hard to pick out. The experience of Dalits shows that apartheid-like conditions can be imposed upon people who are marked by history, not appearance.

India's powerful independence movement produced perhaps the world's most extensive system of affirmative action for oppressed peoples like the Dalits. And, since the 1970s, Dalits have organized to use these assets to overturn the caste system, organize for power, and fight for their rights. Yet Dalits still face an uphill struggle against starkly unequal conditions. When national level discussions for the WCAR began in India last year, the problem of caste immediately stirred controversy.

The Hindi-Right dominated government was chary to raise the issue of caste on the world stage, particularly at this juncture when it revels in the US-sponsored praises for being the world's largest democracy. The government seeks to avoid anything that makes India look bad on the world stage. Apart from these international political reasons, the Hindu-Right government has a commitment to the perpetuation of caste discrimination. Not only are its ranks filled with representatives of the dominant castes, but its public policy platforms frequently privilege the rights of those dominant castes who hold wealth over the rest of society.

Furthermore, allied organizations of the Hindu-Right have even convened religious conclaves given to the topic of a formal revival of strict Brahmanical social organizations, such as varnashramadharma or the four-fold division of varnas. On 7 February 2001, the External Affairs Minister Jaswant Singh noted that we must ensure that the Conference does not lose sight of its focus on racism. In other words, the Hindu-Right would then be able to preserve itself not only as an anti-racist nationalist force, but that it could occlude the several discriminations and prejudices that structure the Indian polity.

Dalit rights activists have, naturally, been eager to raise the question of caste discrimination on the international stage, particularly since this government has been the first to block discussion of caste in international forums. Martin Macwan, national head of the National Campaign for Dalit Human Rights, reminds us that in earlier international forums, notably the Committee on Elimination of Discrimination Against Women, the Government of India had successfully taken up the issue of caste-based discrimination. Why is it insisting that caste is an 'internal' matter? The idea that caste is an 'internal' matter is specious, mainly because 'caste' as we know it today is decidedly fostered by a combination of Indian social relations, European-driven colonialism, and global capitalism. These three factors produce what we know as caste today, since the practice cannot claim to be an ahistorical reflection of what one reads in Sanskrit texts.

Caste, then, is not 'internal', but a form of social discrimination that is in conversation with similar forms elsewhere. It is in this spirit that most Dalit rights activists want to hold the international discussion. It should be said, however, that there are some that want to reduce caste to a form of race, and therefore make a strong connection between the anti-racist work and the anti-caste work.

Afrocentrics and Dalitocentrics are particularly notable here, especially with the claim that Dalits are 'negritos' and that they suffer oppression at the hands of their 'Aryan' oppressors, just as black folk around the world are held down by white folk. That the evidence for race as biology has been discredited does not seem to bother the indigenistas, many of whom deploy old racist texts to make their claims.

One of the dangers of US imperialist hegemony is that the global anti-imperialist agenda may also end up being set in US anti-imperialist terms. That is, the anti-racist program for organizations and activists from across the global might replicate the terms of the US movement. Race, then, as a central category for the struggle may be self-evident in the US context, but it may not be as useful in other settings.

The enthusiasm for epidermal determinism occurs despite the Dalitcentric editor V. T. Rajshekar's early warning that in India, it is no longer easy to distinguish a touchable from an Untouchable, especially for foreigners. Whether it was ever possible to tell caste by skin color is a question for debate, but certainly to make such judgements now is rather impossible.

No discussion on caste can be conducted without a discussion of the fight against discrimination in South Asia.

Then, offer an analysis of the fight against caste in contemporary India, as well as a few suggestions for the international engagement in this struggle.

Dalits as Citizens

In 1947, the Indian national movement ejected British colonialism and inaugurated a period of national construction. These were heady days, as anti-colonial movements from Indonesia to Ghana took power of States to make freedom something tangible for the masses. India was no exception.

The first Indian Prime Minister Jawaharlal Nehru was impatient to rework the oppressive present, so the State in the 1950s took a few bold steps toward the emancipation of the Dalits. Ambedkar is known, in many Dalit circles, as the architect of the Indian Constitution. Recruited by Nehru, and well-known for his outspoken views on the need for a wide sense of democracy, Ambedkar pushed through many enlightened articles into the Constitution, and, as India's first Law Minister, he was instrumental in creating a very progressive legal regime to ensure protections for Dalits as well as mechanisms for their emancipation. If there was no political movement of Dalits to back-up Ambedkar, the judiciary provided that cover.

When the government's protections of freedom for Dalits was challenged in the Courts, a Supreme Court justice argued that 'advantages secured due to historical reasons cannot be considered a fundamental right guaranteed by the Constitution'. When Martin Luther King, Jr., traveled to India in 1959 he was stunned by the State's monetary and legal commitment to Dalit emancipation. When Nehru was asked if this discriminated against other jatis, he replied that 'well it may be, but this is our way of atoning for the centuries of injustices we have inflicted upon these people'.

While Article 14 of the 1950 Indian Constitution guaranteed equality before the Law, the Courts refused to interpret it to mean absolute and unequivocal equality. In order to produce equality, the courts developed a framework to prevent the notion of equality from suppressing active governmental intervention on behalf of certain groups. In order to produce social and economic equality, the Courts allowed the State to intervene on behalf of oppressed and exploited groups, to use equality as the means to freedom.

The Courts identified women and backward classes as the two major groups towards whom the State was enjoined to act in a compensatory manner. In 1964, Justice Subba Rao argued the logic of compensation forthrightly: centuries of calculated oppression and habitual submission reduced a considerable section of our community to a life of serfdom. It would be well nigh impossible to raise their standards if the doctrine of equal opportunity was strictly enforced in their case. They would not have any chance if they were made to enter the open field competition without adventitious aids till such time they could stand on their own legs.

The institutions that the Indian State created were a means to the politicization of 'equality' in order to produce a future moral, free community. Rather than bear the full implications of this courageous policy, the Indian administration settled for the 'reservations' policy that enabled a few Dalits to join what was once called the 'Harijan elite'. The actual benefits from the policy of compensation were not evenly distributed among the Dalits because certain caste groups benefited more than others and only a few individuals and their families were able to capitalize on State policy.

The vast mass of the Dalits remained outside the purview of the reservations packages. The Balmikis, for instance, were only able to take advantage of the reservations scheme as a collectivity in their monopoly over one particular occupation in the municipalities: Class IV employment, typically with the sanitation departments. Most of the reservations are in low-skilled, low-paying jobs that do little to move Dalits up the economic ladder. Since compensatory discrimination is restricted to government jobs, the much larger private sector remains free to discriminate against Dalits. Reservations, in this manner, are a far cry from the enlightened State policy envisaged by the Indian Judiciary.

By the mid-1960s, the limited compensation schemes began to suffer from the economic and political crisis that followed the Sino-Indian war of 1962, the Indo-Pakistan war of 1965 and the monsoon failures of 1965 and 1967. A serious crisis of political hegemony followed from the late 1960s, which developed into the ruling clique taking extraordinary powers into its own hands through centralization, whose most notable instance was the promulgation of the Emergency in 1975.

Among Dalits, serious doubts were being raised about the commitment and ability of the State to provide the conditions of equality. In 1969, L. Elayaperumal's report on Dalits for the Department of Social Welfare pointed out that 'to utter dismay the Committee found that untouchability was still being practiced in virulent form all over India'. In the Lok Sabha on 19 August 1970, the Minister of State for Home announced that between 1967 and 1969, 1117 Dalits had been reported murdered. Of these, 63 cases were in Maharashtra, 332 in Uttar Pradesh and 76 in Punjab.

The 'Harijan Atrocity' of the 1970s was not part of an ancient story of the caste system, but must be imbedded in the social relations of the caste struggle that intensified after Dalits felt emboldened by their constitutional protections. When Chief Minister Kapoori Thakur's regime in Bihar opened space for Dalit advancement, the dominant castes, the Kurmis, massacred some of Pipra village's Chamars in 1980. Pipra was in line with a host of such massacres whose aetiology may be in the revanchist attempt by dominant castes to hold onto power that seemed to be on the wane.

In response to the failure of India to resolve the contradictions of political democracy, young Dalits in the late 1960s took inspiration from world-wide student movements, from the Black Panther movement in the United States and from the resurgence of militant left-wing activity within India to escalate their own struggle for freedom. On 29 April 1968, Shyam Sunder launched the Bheem Sena in Gulbanga to militarily confront caste Hindu atrocities against Dalits. In June 1972, the Dalit Panthers emerged as the major political formation of this new militancy. In a manifesto penned by one faction of the movement, the Panthers declared themselves in favor of 'a complete revolution' as opposed to 'partial change'.

After independence, they argued, the 'government did not do anything to eradicate [untouchability] except passing some laws against it'. This was, for the Panthers, insufficient. In their 18 point program, they called for land redistribution, an increase in wages, free education, and censorship of offensive literature, and an end to economic corruption and most radically, all means of production must belong to the Dalits. Calling for people's democracy, the Panthers argued against the contradictions of the liberal state and put forward the slogan, in struggle we will become free. The Panthers' alert us to the manner in which the Indian State attempted to resolve the contradictions of 'equality'.

The Untouchability Offences Act of 1955 and the workings of the Commission of Scheduled Castes understood untouchability to mean the social and cultural oppression of the Dalits by caste Hindus and by Muslims. To compensate for the lack of access to public buildings and lack of expression were the central tasks set by the state in its anti-untouchability campaign.

Most of the recorded complaints by Dalits to the Commission were along these lines. By the late 1970s, however, most complaints to the Commission concerned issues such as land rights, housing and education. Harassment continued to be an important issue, but it was not the major issue. From the perspective of the Panthers, untouchability had to be seen both as status and class inequality, for that is the peculiarity of Dalithood.

The Panther intervention dramatized the structural critique of untouchability and it alerts us to see caste not only as a political-cultural-ritual system, but also as the form of socio-economic exploitation. Colonialism recast caste in such a way as to provide for the various economic and political needs of a system ravenous for the wealth generated in India. In his thoughtful study of the ideology of Lucknow Chamars, Khare makes a remarkable statement: 'from the Untouchable's position all the powerful waves of social reform, radicalism, and revolt must finally crash within the same old Manu-ordained parameters.

No doubt the Dharmashastras continue to influence the doings and thinkings of caste Hindus, but the experience and structures of contemporary untouchability can hardly be interpreted on the basis of a text written sometime in the first two centuries B. C. E. To interpret the quotidian experience of untouchability we must investigate both the political-cultural and the socio-economic dimensions as well as locate the conditions of today's untouchability in the modern structures whose roots are found in colonial times.

The Panthers were unable to craft wide enough solidarities to make a mark on the national political scene; further, infighting amongst the leaders and the cadres on the status of whom to ally with ended any hope of building a political opposition to the State's limited policy towards untouchability. In recent years, the most effective, but largely opportunistic, Dalit political bloc to emerge on the national scene has been the Bahujan Samaj Party (BSP).

The BSP has its roots in the All-India Backward SC, ST and Minority Communities Employees Federation (BAMCEF) founded in December 1978 by Kanshi Ram to organize the elite among the Dalits to fight for social change. Since the government put restrictions on its employees from doing political work, Ram formed the Dalit Shoshit Samaj Sangharsh Samiti (DS-4) in December 1981, which, in April 1984, formed an electoral wing, the BSP. In 1987, Ram told the media that the Dalits nurse a feeling that the government in spite of its best efforts has not been able to remove poverty. This is truly unfortunate.

The bureaucracy, which we inherited from the British, is caste ridden and officers have yet to rise above caste. How they work half-heartedly towards implementing the government's programmes for the backward communities. The BSP is not the only organization to lay claim to the Social Democratic tradition of Dr. Ambedkar. They are joined in their commitment to Dalit politics by the historic Dalit parties, the Scheduled Castes Federation and the Republican Party of India and by various socialistic parties which draw from Rammanohar Lohia and from Jayaprakash Narayan. What these parties share is a commitment to protecting the Dalits from the harshness of capitalism: as Barbara Joshi put it.

Equality has increasingly taken on tones of equality of political power needed by the Scheduled Castes to fend for themselves. Political power could generate more paved streets in Scheduled Caste neighborhoods, more education and jobs for the neighborhood's young men, as well as protection from what the businessmen saw as the discriminatory harassment of government bureaucrats and the encroachment of higher caste business competitors. The brief alliance between the BSP and militant Hinduism in 1995 demonstrated the impoverishment of the defensive agenda which has been cultivated by the social democratic parties which draw inspiration from Dr. Ambedkar.

The contradictions of equality reappeared on the national political agenda in the 1980s through the second Backward Classes Commission that the government appointed on 1 January 1979 under the chairmanship of B. P. Mandal. The Janata Government responded to the grassroots mobilizations which characterized the 1970s in India by putting forth certain limited reforms of which the Mandal Commission was exemplary. The Commission offered its report on 31 December 1980. On the issue of equality, the Commission was remarkable: In fact, what we call merit in an elitist society is an amalgam of native endowments and environmental privileges. The conscience of a civilized society and the dictates of social justice demand that 'merit' and 'equality' are not turned into a fetish and the element of privilege is duly recognized and discounted when 'unequals' are made to run the same race.On the face of it the principle of equality appears very just and fair, but it has a serious catch. It is a well-known dictum of social justice that there is equality only amongst equals. To treat unequals as equals is to perpetuate inequality.

The Mandal Commission warned Indian society in 1980 of the very contradictions identified by Ambedkar in 1949: the contradiction between the principle of equality before the Law and social and economic inequality. Unwilling to grapple with the contradictions at the foundation of Indian society, the unrest over Mandalization after 1990 revealed the reluctance of many Indians to even consider the project of producing equality. The attacks on the 'protections' to 'minorities' and to the 'public sector' have made the struggle for freedom hard and yet imperative.

The State is pledged to interpret untouchability as harassment and the anti-untouchability movement as a struggle for civil rights; once the question of structural disenfranchisement is put on the table and once the struggle is for human rights, the dominant classes and castes enjoin the state to undercut those political gestures. 'Mandal' has prevented the dialogue about equality from proceeding in a productive manner: the privileged has used it as a means to mock the project of compensation, the State has used it as a means to roll-back on the project and the Dalits and the Left have once again been put in the defensive position of praising policies which do not truly get at the heart of exploitation. For the Balmikis, compensation has meant that a few of the community succeed and that they are allowed to control the sanitation departments in municipalities; there is little to defend in the system from their point of view.

Democracy works in that the Dalits now have the possibility to effect change; that they have not been able to effectively gain power is a mark of the strength of the dominant classes and castes in India. Dalits still fight forms of apartheid. The State failed the Dalits because it did not truly dismantle the 'advantages secured for historical reasons' such as land relations and the control over capital. Attempts by the state to extend favor to Dalits, draw an enormous resistance from the dominant jatis.

Among Dalits, as a result, their rate of literacy is barely 22%, only 16% of Dalits live in cities, about 50% are agricultural laborers, and only 4% work in the industrial workforce. The extent of poverty, because of these factors, is about 50% (as against 30% for the population as a whole). Of those who work in the fields, 71% are marginal farmers who must sell their labor at low rates to dominant jatis.

The poverty of Dalits is matched by their lack of political power. Since the 1970s, militant Dalit groups emerged to fight landlords and to use the franchise. The exertions of the Dalits have, by all accounts, increased anti-Dalit violence. In this cauldron of struggle, many Dalit organizations emerged, such as the Dalit Panthers, the Republican Party of India, and the Bahujan Samaj Party. Over the years, these groups have floundered on the rocks of either opportunism or of extreme nationalism.

In recent years, liberal Dalit groups have made linkages with non-governmental organizations to create such platforms as the National Campaign on Dalit Human Rights. Their exertions, Smita Narula of HRW says, drew the attention of the Human Rights Watch to the atrocities against Dalits. The National Campaign has produced a series of 'Black Papers' with a stark subhead 'Broken Promises and Dalits Betrayed'.

Part of the problem is the lack of focus on land relations, and this is what differeniates the fight for anti-racist justice in the advanced industrial North with the relatively rural South. The compensatory discrimination scheme created by the

Indian government concentrates on public jobs, but this occludes the fact that only 16% of the total Dalit population live in urban India. Most of the rest are marginal farmers, sharecroppers or landless laborers. For these Dalits land ownership is the cornerstone of liberation.

The recent reportage of celebrated journalist P. Sainath confirms the centrality of land, as do news reports of anti-Dalit violence in rural Bihar and Haryana. Indeed, the failure to underscore the importance of the land question serves to undermine the centrality of the Left to Dalit liberation. For most Dalits, wealth is land. This is not the view of the so-called Dalit parties, such as the BSP: when Dalit landless workers forcibly occupied the land of the ex-Raja of Benares in Uttar Pradesh, the BSP Chief Minister Mayavati sent in the police to arrest them. Her actions once more subordinated the Dalits to poverty.

The centrality of land to the Left, on the other hand, is made clear by the 20 December 1998 All India Democratic Women's Association Convention in support of Dalit women's rights against untouchability and oppression. The first demand of the convention reads as follows: 'Land reforms - land distribution, joint pattas, special priority to Dalits and in particular to Dalit female headed households. Return of land to Dalits which are in illegal occupation and arrest of the guilty. Access to all community land and use for fuel and fodder collection'.

Meanwhile, on the ground, change is afoot, processes of emancipation can be gleaned in the fight to gain local political power. In 1996, the Dalits of Melavalavu (Tamil Nadu) won control of the local governmental body. As they tried to take office, local goons killed six of the leaders. Of the six, the man elected to lead the body was beheaded, a 'brutal reminder'. Brinda Karat of the Communist Party of India (Marxist) notes, that, for the non-Dalits, Dalits are meant to serve, not rule. Karat points to the data from West Bengal where the Left has been in power since 1977.

Only there, she says, the Dalits have benefited from land reforms and from the devolution of political power. West Bengal has only 3.58% of the cultivatable land in the Indian Republic and yet, it has contributed over 20% of the total surplus land that falls under the land ceiling laws. Of the 4.8 million acres distributed in the country as a whole, West Bengal contributed 920,000 acres. Further, of the 2 million landless cultivators who received land, 56% came from socially oppressed communities. Apart from land reform, the Left Front-initiated Operation Barga in 1978 which registered 1.4 million tenant farmers and provided them with legal instruments to stave off eviction and to struggle for shares of the harvest. These land reforms are the backbone of Dalit self-respect and dignity in the state. In 1949, Ambedkar told the political leaders of India that their hesitant approach to land reform did not bode well for democracy. How long shall we continue to deny equality in our social and economic life? If we continue to deny it for long, we will do so only by putting out political democracy in peril.

Caste, as constructed in colonial times and lived in the contemporary moment, is not identical to race, even though both emerge simultaneously as methods to exert imperial control and to justify white supremacy. Where caste and race share much is in the way in which these forces of social oppression are related to the economic domain: both are about the denial of the means of production to certain peoples. Nevertheless, the agenda for social justice is not identical, since the social context of the fights are separate: where the human rights agenda of civic justice may be more important in one context, the fight for land rights may be central in the other. To collapse the contexts of social justice in the service of internationalism and solidarity is to harm all our struggles. The Left and liberal Dalit groups have taken it upon themselves to be the guardians of political democracy by fighting for social and economic democracy. One hopes that their struggles will make India truly the world's largest democracy in the fullest sense of the word.

5

Cast Clashes

Caste clashes in the southern state of Tamil Nadu have predominantly involved two communities: the Thevars (a backward caste) and the Pallars (or Dalits). As has been the case in other states, Dalits in Tamil Nadu have long suffered from exploitative economic relationships and have frequently been the victims of violence. However, changes since the early 1990s have altered the economic relationship between the Thevars and the Pallars and have changed the contours of the conflict. Having benefited from the state's policy of reservations in education and from the income provided by relatives working abroad, the Pallars have become much less dependent on Thevar employment and have begun to assert themselves in the political arena. The Thevars have responded to this threat to their hegemony with violence. Dalits, too, have begun to fight back.

Caste clashes in the state's southern districts between July 1995 and December 1998. Unlike the conflict in the eastern state of Bihar, the violence is often spontaneous and not the result of organized armed movements. Much as in the state of Bihar, however, the police have colluded with the caste Hindus to preserve the status quo and keep Dalits from peacefully claiming their rights. The police, many of whom are Thevars themselves, have conducted raids on Dalit villages ostensibly to search for Dalit militants. During these raids, police have assaulted villagers and detained many under preventive detention laws. Women in particular have been targeted.

According to the Indian government's 1996-1997 annual report for the Ministry of Human Affairs, caste-related incidents in 1996 in the southern state of Tamil Nadu increased by 34 percent over previous years. Out of 282 reported incidents, took place between scheduled castes and other backward communities. The main caste groups involved were the Thevars, Naidars, and Vanniyas (all backward castes) and the Adi Dravidas and Pallars (both scheduled castes or Dalits).

The number of incidents between Pallars and Thevars increased again dramatically at the height of caste clashes in the southern districts of Tamil Nadu from April 1997 to December 1998. The nexus between Thevars, the police, and district officials in the affected areas was repeatedly reflected in violent search and raid operations in Dalit villages, in the forced displacement of thousands of Dalit villagers, often with the aid of district officials, and in the disproportionate number of Dalits arrested under preventive detention statutes during the clashes. Abuses against Dalits continued following a police raid on the Dalits of Gundupatti village in February 1998 and violent clashes between Dalits and Thevars from October to December 1998. According to the state government, at least 251 people died in caste violence between August 1995 and October 1998.

Clashes in the southern districts of Tamil Nadu have largely been attributed to increased Pallar economic and political autonomy and the backlash against it. Since the mid-1990s, the Pallars have begun to support a new political leadership, unaligned to mainstream political parties, and promoted by two movements: the Dalit Panthers of India (DPI) Tamil Nadu, and the Devendra Kula Vellalar Federation (DKVF) led by Dr. K. Krishnaswamy, a member of the Tamil Nadu legislative assembly. In 1998 the DKVF became a political party and named itself Puthiya Tamalingam.

These political movements have provided an organized platform for growing resistance to the still prevalent norms of "untouchability" in the state. Dalits have demanded equal treatment in temple festivals, have refused to carry out ritually demeaning tasks, have demanded access to public water sources, and have claimed an equal share of public goods and village properties. Thevars have responded by "clinging more resolutely to their caste status as a way of affirming their superiority." Government statistics from 1995 revealed that Thevars were the perpetrators in 91 percent of cases involving the coercive enforcement of "untouchability" practices.

Context of Clashes

Between July 1995 and June 1996, clashes between Thevars and Pallars resulted in large-scale destruction of property, loss of life on both sides, and the arrest of many Dalit youths under preventive detention laws like the Tamil Nadu Goondas Act and the National Security Act, 1980. In most cases, the usually spontaneous clashes originated over issues of land, the holding of protests and rallies, the use of village resources, or any Dalit attempt to defy the caste-based order. Typically, both sides were armed with stones or agricultural tools.

The cycle of violence began anew in late April 1997 when the government announced the creation of a new transport corporation in Virudhunagar district in the name of a Pallar community member (the Veeran Sundaralingam Transport Corporation, VSTC). Thevars opposed the proposal and, according to press reports, some were heard to remark, "How do you expect us to travel in a bus named after a Dalit? It is a personal affront to our manhood." On May 1, 1997, VSTC was inaugurated; Thevars threw stones at the buses and refused to ride them.

On May 2, Dalit leader Dr. Krishnaswamy was arrested and accused of sparking violence with his "inflammatory speeches." Spontaneous protests erupted as news of his arrest spread through the region. Protesters staged several road blocks and, for the three days that Dr. Krishnaswamy remained in jail, "police resorted to firing, lathi-charges and bursting tear gas shells to control agitating Dalits." Two Dalits were killed by police bullets. On May 7 three Thevars were killed by the police at Sivakasi in Virudhunagar district while protesting the arrest of two Thevar youths.

In protest against police action on Thevars at Sivakasi, Thevars in Mansapuram village attempted to introduce coconut shells at tea stalls for Dalits to keep them from sharing tea tumblers used by caste Hindus. When Dalits resisted, Thevars torched and looted Dalit houses in Amachiyarpatti village. In Rengappanaikkanpatti Thevars vowed to make Dalits "dig pits for the burial of bodies of dominant castes." The entire Dalit population of the village was later forcibly driven out, as Thevars set fire to their homes and fields.

In the months following the renaming of the transport corporation and Dr. Krishnaswamy's arrest, the districts of Theni, Madurai, Virudhunagar, Tirunelveli, and Tuticorin witnessed periodic eruptions of violence and the forced displacement of thousands of Dalits from their homes. Police and district officials treated the situation as a law and order problem, and under the guise of seeking out Dalit militant activists, conducted search and raid operations exclusively on Dalit villages. They arrested and assaulted hundreds of men and women as they looted their homes and destroyed material possessions. Women were the primary victims.

A June 1997 fact-finding mission by the People's Union for Civil Liberties (PUCL), the country's largest civil rights organization, concluded that in caste clashes in Madurai district, "Dalits were the worst affected in terms of property loss and physical injuries sustained, like hand and leg fractures, due to violent attack[s] on them"; that police had filed many false cases against Dalits; and that "increased political consciousness amongst the Dalits... regarding their fundamental social, political and economic rights expressed in terms of demands for social equality [and] equitable distribution of resources" played a major role in the attacks against them.

Links between Thevars and State Agents

The Thevars numerically outnumber other backward castes in the region. The Thevar Peravai (Thevar Front), the most active and organized of Thevar organizations, was until early 1998 led by retired Director General of Police (DGP) Pon Paramaguru. His successor, Dr. N. Sethuraman, was also the general secretary of Moovendar Munnetra Kazhagam, a political party launched by the All India Thevar Peravai in 1998.

During his tenure as DGP from 1972 to 1975, Paramaguru recruited many Thevars into the police force. J. Jayalalitha, leader of the All India Anna Dravida Munnetra Kazhagam party (AIADMK), was considered a "strong Thevar community supporter" during her five-year tenure as chief minister of the state from 1991 to May 1996. Her support included extending influential political and police positions to members of the Thevar community—allowing them to further consolidate their power base. N. Sasikala, Jayalalitha's aide and confidante and a Thevar community member, was also accused of "astutely promoting her caste." Lawyers, human rights activists and the local press have noted that, as a result, a majority of the police force in the southern districts now "hails from [the Thevar] caste and, often, have been unable to overcome their caste affiliations."

According to Dr. Krishnaswamy, though "atrocities against Dalits were institutionalised during the previous AIADMK regime," a 1996 shift in political power to the DMK party, led by M. Karunanidhi, did not result in a "change in the behaviour of the police." Inspector General Vijay Kumar, former security officer under Jayalalitha's administration, was accused by human rights activists of using the police force to engineer attacks on Dalit villages during the 1997 clashes.

Activists have also charged that the district collector of Virudhanagar district, Rajagopal, a Brahmin native of Thevar-dominated Enjar village, supported the Thevar community during the 1997 clashes: "He committed all sorts of atrocities against Dalits, including lathi-charge and unnecessary shootings." Rajagopal was also accused of forcing Dalits to abandon their houses.

In June 1997 the state government responded to police excesses during the clashes by transferring large numbers of officers out of "sensitive" districts, without meting out any additional punishment. Chief Minister Karunanidhi ordered the transfers after noting "some disturbing trends in the functioning of the lower levels of police during the disturbances, particularly in the southern districts."

Economic Context

In recent years the economic relationship between Thevars and Pallars (Dalits) has shifted notably. Like most Dalits in rural India, the Pallars traditionally were employed as agricultural laborers (on Thevar lands) and were paid less than minimum wage. In the early 1990s, Pallars began to enjoy minimal upward economic mobility, which reduced their dependency on Thevars. Pallars became able to own and farm their own lands or look elsewhere for employment.

A researcher at the Madras Institute of Development Studies attributes increased Pallar prosperity to two factors: The first is the policy of reservations, which has been more effectively implemented in this state, more than other states. Reservations in education frees Dalits from land-based occupation. The relationship between the landlord and the laborer has given way to urban-based occupations. The second reason is that many Dalits have been recruited by Gulf countries. They send their proceeds home, and their families are able to acquire land through this process. So feudal dependency has lessened.

Marginal landowners themselves, Thevars have dealt with this new economic threat through caste mobilization: The main backward classes in the state, the Thevars, are opposed to the Dalits. They themselves are not an advanced community. They are landlords but not in a big sense. They are not advanced in education, but still they employed Dalits as laborers. Because of the move away from production sectors, Thevars now can only assert their power through caste pride. So it takes on paper dominance. Before, caste was deployed through land.

The Dalit communities, for their part, have realized the political potential of their somewhat better economic status by becoming more organized in their demands. This has affected state-wide patterns of violence and reactions by state agents. For the first time, the Pallars have begun to resist their traditional mistreatment: politically, by contesting elections, and physically, by responding to violence with violence.

Some Dalit activists have argued that their people's armed response is necessary for self-preservation and economic survival. As Murugeswari, the first Dalit female president of the Kandamanur village council, Tamil Nadu, has stated:

> While both parties have indulged in violence, there is an essential difference. Dalits are fighting for their rights and Thevars are fighting to retain their hegemony. It would be cruel to equate the fight for livelihood to the arson [sic] to retain power on the basis of birth.

Thevars argue that the Dalits are merely self-interested and provoke the clashes themselves. Thevar leader Dr. N. Sethuraman claimed that the violence was being instigated by militant Dalit activists: the clashes, he asserted, ensured the survival of Dalit organizations and their ability to attract funds from foreign donors. Dalit-oriented NGOs are promoting hatred between the two communities. Foreign Christian organizations fund these Dalit organizations. Their intention is not to eradicate hatred but to perpetuate hatred so that their organization can survive. They induce violence, take photos and get money. They want the clash to continue so they can survive. It is a very negative attitude. Doubt whether their intentions are really Christian.

Dr. N. Sethuraman led the Thevar procession through Desikapuram village minutes before the police surrounded the Dalit colony and conducted a violent search and raid operation. According to Sethuraman, the practice of "untouchability" has been virtually eradicated in the state. But according to several human rights groups, government reports, as of February 1998 "untouchability" was still practiced in various forms in most villages where Dalits were minorities. These forms include separate tea tumblers at tea shops and prohibitions on entering places of public worship or wearing shoes in the presence of upper castes.

Sethuraman also claimed that "Thevar minorities are being chased out of their lands and homes," a practice that he termed "reverse untouchability." He went on to add that "the same has not happened to Dalits in a single village." But in several southern district villages Dalits had been pushed out of their homes by Thevars and, months later, were unable to return. In several villages social and economic boycotts against Dalits are still in effect and others where murders and large-scale displacement of Dalits had taken place.

In September 1996, the village of Melavalavu, in Madurai district, was declared a reserved constituency under Article 243D of the Indian constitution. The declaration signaled that the Melavalavu panchayat (village council), which covers eight villages with approximately 1,000 Dalit families, would have seats reserved for scheduled-caste candidates. In June 1997, a group murder of elected Dalits by neighbouring Thevars signaled that constitutionally mandated shifts in legal power to scheduled castes would not be tolerated by caste Hindus displaced from their once secure elected positions.

Several observers have attributed the violence in the village and the resulting tensions to a shift in power relations brought on by the government's mandate of reservation of panchayat seats for Dalits. Dr. George Mathew of the New Delhi Institute of Social Sciences visited the area along with two other researchers soon after the murders. He published his conclusions in an article in The Hindu:

> The murders of the Dalit leaders of Melavalavu Panchayat were clearly because "untouchability" was still ingrained in the social system. The economic conditions in the village were abysmal, but the power was concentrated in the hands of a privileged few. These people had hitherto enjoyed a hold over the common properties such as fish ponds, temple lands and forest produce and did not want to relinquish these privileges to the Panchayat Raj system run by the downtrodden... [T]he violence was basically a result of a shift in the power equations from the haves to the have nots.

The article also noted that the leasing of the twenty-five fish ponds alone would fetch an income of Rs. 500,000 to Rs. 1,000,000 annually (US$12,500 to $25,000). The new panchayati raj system put control of such common properties in the hands of the panchayat—that is, in Dalit hands—since the 1997 elections. In a separate article, Mathew referred to the killings as a serious attack on the institution of panchayati raj, which has the potential of changing the powerful rural groups. The new panchayats are perceived by the traditional powerful groups as a threat. Melavalavu and similar villages are paying a price for not holding the panchayat elections regularly and strengthening the foundations of democracy.

The case of Melavalavu provides an example of the interaction of social forces, efforts at reform, violent reaction, and impunity. The announcement of reservations in Melavalavu in 1996 led to a threat of "economic sanctions" by the majority caste Hindu community should any Dalit file for the position of panchayat president. The sanction would effectively leave Dalits without employment or access to economic and social services in villages in that area. As reported in the Bombay-based daily, Times of India, "They were warned that they would lose their jobs as farmhands and not be allowed to graze cattle or draw water from wells located on 'patta' [unutilized] land held by the dominant castes."

The elections, scheduled for October 1996, were subsequently canceled, as all three Dalit nominees withdrew their candidacy for fear of sanctions against the entire scheduled-caste electorate. When polling finally did take place in February 1997, the election was suspended after several incidents of booth capturing. A thirty-five-year-old Dalit named Murugesan won the presidency in the third round of polling, which took place under heavy police protection and was boycotted by the dominant castes. He was, however, unable to perform his tasks as president: neighboring Thevars physically prevented him from entering his office space at the panchayat building.

According to several village residents violence against Dalit voters are increasing during the elections:

> With police protection the election was held, but at the end of the day upper-caste people entered into the booth and threatened and stabbed one boy and beat both men and women and took away the ballot boxes and threw them into the well. Then again they declared elections after one week. In that one we elected Murugesan. There was heavy police protection. Still the Amblakars [Thevars] boycotted the elections. Then Murugesan was not able to go to the office. Only during the swearing-in ceremony did he go to the office because he had a police escort.

On the day of the attack, June 30, 1997, Murugesan was returning from a visit to the collector's office to inquire about compensation for houses burned in an earlier incident. Kumar, an eyewitness who barely survived the attack himself, boarded the bus and sat next to Murugesan. According to him

> "The assault was led by a Thevar named Ramar. Ramar and Alagarsamy, the formerpanchayat president, gave explicit instructions to their gang of Thevars to "kill all the Pariahs [Dalits]."

> "There were nearly forty of them. They were all Thevars. They stabbed Murugesan on the right side of his belly. It was a very long knife. From outside the bus Ramar instructed the Thevars to kill all the Pariahs. Among twelve, six were murdered on the spot. They pulled all six out of the bus and stabbed them on the road with bill hooks more than two feet long."

When the attackers noticed his presence, Kumar was chased into the fields and cut with a bill hook on the back of his neck, his right underarm, and his finger but ultimately managed to escape by fleeing into the plantation fields of a Dalit village. Family members of the six murder victims received Rs. 150,000 (US$3,750) in compensation from the state government under the Scheduled Castes and Scheduled Tribes (Prevention of Atrocities) Act, 1989. A total of twelve persons were arrested within a month of the incident. However, eyewitnesses have claimed that the ringleaders were not among them. Those arrested were charged under sections 341, 307, and 302 of the Indian Penal Code for wrongful restraint, attempted murder, and murder, respectively, and under Section 3(1)(10) of the Atrocities Act, the act's least serious offense, for name-calling or insulting a Dalit person in a public place.

Kumar claimed that the police had an eyewitness and victim sign papers saying that one of the accused, named Sedhu, was innocent. According to a witness, a forty-five-year-old agricultural laborer, who told us the following:

> The police told me to sign papers saying who the real culprit was, so I signed it. I signed a plain piece of paper. Mellur DSP Subramanium came here in a jeep and called for me and asked me why I put my signature on a white paper. "Someone got Rs. 50,000 [US$1,250] for it," he said, "did you get your share?" I said I got nothing from him. "You must have gotten Rs. 25,000 [US$625] at least," he said. I don't know what happened with the paper.

A two-member team from the State Human Rights Commission visited the village in early August, five weeks after the killings. Hundreds of women testified to incidents of theft, the burning of Dalit houses, and stone-throwing at night. They also complained of their inability to go to work in the fields, of a lack of police protection, and that most of the men had fled the village out of fear. Karupaia, Murugesan's older brother, organized a march on August 8, 1997 to protest the lack of action on the part of the police. Participants estimated the number of marchers at 3,000, both men and women. They named the principal culprits as Ramar, Alagarsami, Poniah, Baskarar, Andichami, Markandan, Duraipandian, Chandran, Selvam, Alagu, Vadivelu, Karanthamalai, Ranganathan, Chakarmurti, Chockanathar, Sedhu, Rajendran, and Jothi.

When one of such march approached the taluk [village block] office, the superintendent of police (SP) and other officials were there. A "country bomb" fell in to the march and exploded. Everyone scattered. Tirumavalavan, the leader of the Dalit Panthers of India who led the procession, was the intended target. Tirumavalavan proceeded to inform the SP that the people who threw the bomb had descended from a near-by building. Many pointed them out, but the police refused to arrest them. The marchers then started throwing stones.

The SP ordered a lathi-charge on the procession, and many of the protesters were severely injured. The police arrested a total of thirty-six protesters and charged them under the Indian Explosives Act and under Indian Penal Code sections 147, 148, 323 and 436 for rioting, rioting with a deadly weapon, voluntarily causing hurt, and mischief by explosive substance. They also arrested a member of DPI and held him responsible for setting off the bomb. Tirumavalavan expressed outrage at the police's failure to arrest "the main accused Ramar in the Melavalavu incident," while simultaneously "nabbing a DPI member and holding him responsible for the blast."

On August 9, 1997, the thirty-six people arrested were sent to Madurai jail. They were held for forty-five days. Released on bail, they were required to check in twice a day at the Trichitown police station, over 125 kilometers from the village. According to Karupaia, the arrests were retaliatory: The police put false cases against us because we organized a procession. They wanted to teach us a lesson. The Section 436 charge [mischief by explosive substance] is still pending. One shop was burned but we did not do it. One hundred Thevars came behind us in the procession and set fire to a shop on the main road.

A forty-year-old resident of Melavalavu who was arrested during the lathi-charge said that:

> I was in jail for forty-five days. My son was also arrested. After the arrest the police said that we looted the shops and set fire to them, but we never did any of those things. In the jail it is a routine practice to ask what cases you came in for, and then they give you blows with their lathis. It is an "admission beat." I was injured in the head and taken to the jail hospital. I was beaten two times with the lathi.

The leader of DPI and Dr. Krishnaswamy have both charged that the "National Security Act as well as the [Tamil Nadu] Goondas Act were being grossly misused against the Dalits by the state government" and that several Dalits had been kept in preventive custody for many days. In the months following the murders, concerned groups demanding appropriate action by the police organized several protests and marches. On July 10, 1997, members of the Social Action Movement, a grassroots NGO, demonstrated in front of the Madurai collectorate's office in order to highlight the plight of the villagers in the aftermath of the murders. On July 23, 1997, DPI marched to demand the release of all Dalits arrested under the National Security Act in connection with the murders.

By the end of September 1997, more than forty people had been charged in the Melavalavu murders case, while eleven had been formally accused but remained at large. On November 24, 1997, DPI members marched again to urge the government to arrest those absconding in the murders and to demand a Central Bureau of Investigation (CBI) inquiry into the case. Members of the Thevar Peravai, who organized a protest on October 28, 1997, also demanded a CBI inquiry. The then-vice president, Dr. N. Sethuraman, claimed that innocent people had been arrested. According to Dr. Sethuraman, now president of Thevar Peravai claimed it had no basis in caste conflict.

This is not a fight between Dalits and Thevars. There's a lot of proof. It was a personal quarrel between the milk society president, a forward-caste member, and Murugesan, the Dalit president. But they have sorted it out now, and the new president can now perform his duties without any problem. The chief minister says that is a quarrel between Thevars and Dalits, but it is not.

The new Dalit panchayat president was again unable to perform his duties, and Thevars—in a concerted campaign to punish Dalits—had ceased to employ Dalits as laborers on their lands. The Thevars also encouraged others to refrain from awarding farm work to Dalits. Many Dalit students were also afraid to go to school for fear of further reprisal. The Dalit panchayat president, Raja, claimed that the threats from Thevars had continued and that the police protection he received was inconsistent and insufficient to ward off another attack. Five Dalit women, elected members of the panchayat, had also been unable to perform their duties. If the elected Dalit women go there, the upper caste would do some harm. If the womeninsist on going into the office, they will hit them.

The February 1998 national parliamentary elections brought a new wave of violence to the village: Thevars allegedly beat Dalit women in poll booths when the women went to cast their vote. As of July 1998, Raja had still not received funds normally allocated to panchayat presidents for village development—leading human rights activists to believe that the local administration had yet to legitimize his presidency. As of February 1999, the forty people arrested for the murders were out on bail, and no one had been prosecuted.

Ramar, the person identified by eyewitnesses as the ringleader of the attack, was still at large.

Displacement of Dalit Villagers

In villages where Dalits constitute a minority, caste clashes have led to large-scale displacements of Dalit communities. The displacement often follows an attack by neighboring caste Hindu villagers in which Dalits are assaulted and their houses are burned. In some cases, beyond ignoring repeated calls for protection, police have directly aided in the displacement. Dalit fields are then taken over by the majority caste Hindu communities while displaced villagers languish in makeshift homes on government property for months. Aside from distributing nominal amounts in compensation or promising construction of new houses, the local administration does little to ensure that the Dalits are able to return to their homes and fields, or to prosecute those responsible for the attacks. Two examples of displacement are described below.

The village of Mangapuram, part of Rajapalayam in Virudhunagar district, once housed 3,000 Thevar and 250 Pallar (Dalit) families. On March 7, 1996, upon returning from a conference organized by Dr. Krishnaswamy, several Pallars were assaulted by Thevars in this village. Following the attack, 150 Pallar houses were set on fire; a Pallar resident of the village was thrown into the fire and burned alive. Soon after the incident the Pallars rebuilt their houses and continued to reside in the village. Tensions in the village increased in May 1997 with the renaming of the transport corporation. Escalating tensions led the Pallars to request police protection in early May 1997. Several police officers were deployed in the area as a result. On May 12, 1997, in renewed violence, Pallars destroyed several Thevar houses; ten were promptly arrested. Thevars retaliated on May 15 by throwing petrol bombs into the Pallar residential area.

On June 9, 1997, Pallar villagers asked the district collector to provide them with adequate protection against future Thevar attacks. The collector was unsympathetic. On June 10, the deputy superintendent of police, a Thevar, attempted to force Pallars out of the village. On the same day, hundreds of Thevar villagers attacked the Pallars and set their houses on fire. As most of their houses had burned to the ground, the Pallars took refuge in nearby villages.

The displaced Pallar families had taken shelter in area just over three acres in size, literally adjacent to Mangapuram village, housed more than 350 people in 200 poorly constructed huts. An adjoining area housed over 200 people in seventy huts. Families with over four members, many with small children, were made to live in huts approximately thirty-five square feet in size.

The small spheres of public space were used for cattle and makeshift latrines. Most families were left without a source of income, and there was little word from the government about returning them to their village. No action was taken against the Thevars responsible for the attacks or against police officials complicit in allowing the displacement to occur. Many villagers still bore scars, which they attributed to lathi attacks by police officers who took part in the displacement.

Before 1997 the village of Rengappanaikkanpatti, situated in Virudhunagar district, was a minority-Pallar, majority-Thevar village. The Thevars comprised nearly 400 families. Among the thirty Pallar families who lived there at the time, many owned agricultural lands and brick houses, a clear indication of their relative prosperity and reportedly a motivation for the attack. On June 13, 1996, when Dr. Krishnaswamy visited the village, Thevars threw stones at his vehicle and five days later disconnected street lights and threw bombs into the Pallar settlement. When the incident was reported to the sub-inspector of the Rajakularaman police station, he refused to register the complaint.

On May 12, 1997, the Thevars of Rengappanaikkanpatti, together with Thevars from a nearby village, set fire to Pallar houses. The fire also destroyed farm lands, coconut groves, and motor pumps. After the attack, which lasted four hours, Pallars took refuge in the neighboring village of Sholapuram and asked the government to provide them with housing facilities.

Dharmalingam, the seventy-five-year-old head of the family, stated:

> Nearly twenty houses were burned down. We were an easy target because we were a minority in the village. Only three houses were spared. Our house is still there; it's very strong. They stole the motor pump set and motor oil from the garden... We cannot go back to our house, they will beat us. We have our own field, four acres in all. But we won't go to the house. We had six rooms, a kitchen and a common room.

Valliamai, Dharmalingam's sixty-five-year-old wife, lamented, "We had such a big house but see our fate now. One of my grandsons is handicapped. The government had to give him a new wheelchair; even that they damaged." Although the government gave the family Rs. 10,000 (US$250) in compensation, the amount covered very little of what they had lost. Dharmalingam registered a complaint with the police, but they did not take any action.

The sub-inspector of the police station, a member of the Thevar community and the same officer who refused to register earlier complaints by Pallars against Thevars, instead filed a case against Dharmalingam, charging him with setting fire to the houses himself in order to bring false charges against others. Dharmalingam was held at the police station for four days. His nineteen-year-old grandson, Dharmaraj, believed that the Thevars were threatened by the prosperity of their Dalit neighbors and were trying to take Pallar lands for themselves:

> Thevars had no lands. All thirty Dalit families had lands. In all houses one or two people from Dalit houses went to government postings [jobs]. They were jealous... We live on fertile lands. We had government postings so they were jealous. Most of us did not use reservations. We got it on our own merit.

Displaced Pallar families have also been unable to cultivate the lands they left behind. As Dharmaraj explained, "After the rainy season we put paddy [rice] on the fields; but they are damaging our fields and don't let us go there. We put paddy again, but again they damaged it. They scold us whenever we go. They let loose their own cattle in the field. There is no police protection at all." Despite the numerous attacks on Pallars in this area, the police have continually failed to heed calls for protection. If there were police protection, Dharmalingam argued, they would be able to go back to their house and their land. Instead, he said: "Whenever the police come to the village, they go to the Thevar area. The Thevars gave them chicken and other good meals. The sub-inspector belongs to the Thevar community, and most others also belong to that community."

Police Raids in the Southern Districts

In the aftermath of clashes in the southern districts, and under the guise of seeking out firearms and militant activists, police forces numbering in the hundreds conducted raids in Dalit villages. The pattern of the raids consisted of arbitrary arrests and assaults on Dalit men and women and often included looting and destruction of property. In some cases, police removed their badge numbers so villagers would not be able to identify and file cases against them.

Since 1980 the Dalits of Kodiyankulum village, in Tuticorin district, have benefited from the flow of funds from family members employed in Dubai, Kuwait, and the United States. On August 31, 1995, a 600-member police force attacked the all-Dalit village in the presence of the superintendent of police and the district collector and destroyed property worth hundreds of thousands of rupees. In what appeared to be a premeditated attack, police destroyed consumer durables such as televisions, fans, tape-recorders, sewing machines, bicycles, agricultural implements, tractors and lorries, and also demolished food grain storages. They made a bonfire of clothes and burned the passports and testimonials of educated Dalit youth. The village post office was targeted, and police allegedly poisoned the only village well. A village elder claimed that "all through the operation, the policemen were showering abuse on us and made derogatory references to our caste, which only showed their deep-rooted prejudice." District collector Paneerselvam, accused of leading the raid, was subsequently transferred to Madras. The stated purpose of the raid was to capture Dalits allegedly involved in the murder of three Thevars in a nearby village two days earlier. Many suspect that it was the "relative affluence of the Dalits that attracted the attention of the uniformed men. The idea, it appears, was to destroy their economic base, because the police feel the Kodiyankulum Dalits provide moral and material support to the miscreants in surrounding areas."

Similar raids have taken place during the southern district clashes. Punduthai, a forty-five-year-old Pallar widow of Thevar-dominated Vanaltaiparam village, was stripped of all her valuables. At the time of the caste riots, "They entered the house and took all house things, dresses and everything. We kept quiet. We didn't say anything. If we said something we would get beaten or they would set fire to the house." Since the riots, Punduthai and her two children have relocated to a Pallar-dominant village. Two other clash-related raids are described below.

On February 26, 1998, in the village of Gundupatti, Dindigul district, some one hundred policemen and thirty policewomen, along with four truckloads of unidentified men thought to be affiliated with the ruling Dravida Munnetra Kazhagam (DMK) party, attacked Dalits and bonded laborers residing in two villages in Kookal Panchayat, a remote area of the Kodaikanal hills. Attackers reportedly looted and destroyed property and assaulted residents, including women, children and elderly persons. Kerosene was poured into stored food grains and grocery items. The attackers, including police personnel, reportedly urinated in cooking vessels.

According to a local human rights organization, women were kicked and beaten, their clothing was torn, and police forced sticks and iron pipes into their mouths. The police attack, whose victims were predominantly women, was apparently in retaliation for a decision made by residents of the Kookal Panchayat to boycott the national parliamentary elections.

After conducting its own investigation into the incident, the National Commission for Women, a government agency, issued an enquiry report on the Gundupatti case. The report concluded that the police "took sides with a political faction," that the criminal force used against women was unwarranted, and that the actions of the police "ha[d] not advanced beyond the colonial concept of power and the subjects." The police had a field day breaking open houses, pulling out people, beating them up and even violating their modesty, using criminal force on women and girls, pulling out their mangla sutras [marriage necklaces], abusing them with filthy language.

They allegedly dragged women and arrested sixteen of them along with nine men. One woman's baby was thrown while they were starting off with their truck. The whole village made many entreaties to the police and then alone the child was allowed to be taken by the mother. In this state of terror and panic, one of the young pregnant women had a miscarriage on the road itself. The twenty-five men and women were then beaten in the police station and sent to jail after being taken before a magistrate. They remained in prison for nearly a month.

The People's Watch activist who initially brought this case to the attention of the National Commission for Women was later charged with dacoity. In early September 1998 the One Man Commission of Enquiry appointed by the government of Tamil Nadu submitted its report on police excess to the state's chief minister.

The same pattern of destruction was apparent during a raid on Desikapuram village in Virudhunagar district in June

1997. The arrest of Dalit leader Dr. Krishnaswamy on May 2, 1997 led to a staged roadblock by the village population, composed entirely of Pallars. On May 22 protesters were confronted by some 1,000 police officers, many of whom then proceeded to enter the village and search the houses. According to a People's Watch report, "The police had entered the village in the name of 'search,' damaged the houses and looted the jewels, money, watches and whatever they could pick up." The next morning, some officers entered the village and demanded a total of Rs. 15,000 (US$375) from residents. On June 22, Thevar Peravai leader Dr. Sethuraman led a procession of eighteen cars, nineteen vans and several trucks through the affected areas.

Two jeeps followed by a busload of police were also part of the procession. When the procession passed through Desikapuram, both sides started throwing stones at one another. The fighting escalated as Thevars began throwing sickles and setting fire to haystacks while Pallars damaged the Thevar vans with stones. Around 3:00 p.m. the police raided the village. Many villagers, including a total of nineteen women, were arrested during the raid: fifteen women were held for fifteen days and four for twenty-nine.

Many of the men and women suffered fractured arms and legs as a result of the attack. The police entered the village and the villagers' homes in avery cruel manner. According to Muniamal, a forty-year-old agricultural laborer and mother of four : "They made a circle and surrounded the entire village. There were nearly a thousand or more. They entered the village. We locked our doors. They broke down the doors of my neighbor's house, where I was at the time. Nearly ten police entered my house. They broke the trunk that contained all our valuables. They took all the dresses and threw them out. My daughter's gold earrings, anklets of silver, my husband's watch, a chain and a ring, and a total of four pounds of gold. "

The police then arrested Muniamal in her house and demanded that she leave her four-year-old son behind. She refused, so they took her son as well. "They used vulgar words, caste names like podivadi and pallachi [caste name for prostitute] Using a lathi they hit me on my thigh, shoulder, and on my back. I had big bruises." Muniamal spent the night at the Rajapalayam North police station. She was given only ointment for her wounds, and not permitted to see a doctor.

The next morning both men and women were taken by bus to the Rajapalayam government hospital. Although the men were treated for fractures, the women did not receive any treatment. The women were then taken to the Siviputur magistrate court, and the men were taken to Madurai central jail. They were charged collectively under the Tamil Nadu Public Properties (Prevention of) Destruction Act, 1992, and under Indian Penal Code sections 147 (rioting), 148 (rioting with a deadly weapon), 324 (causing hurt with dangerous weapons), and 307 (attempted murder). The public property charge was allegedly for setting fire to a Thevar van earlier in the day.

All people behind the [Thevar] procession came into the village. They damaged the houses, set fire, and looted the properties. The police were also there. Then at 11:00 a.m. they left. Then around 3:00 p.m. the police alone came... They surrounded the village and entered into the houses. They damaged the radios, fans, televisions, and took gold chains and other valuables. Munusu was also beaten and arrested by the police.

According to Dr. N. Sethuraman, leader of the Thevar procession, Desikapuram is a center for militant activity. These Dalit islands are used for anti-social activities like manufacturing bombs and militant training for unemployed youngsters. They hide culprits so the police cannot enter. If police want to enter they have to do it in the thousands. The police are not practicing tactical methods. They are brutal but not clever. The police's behavior during the raids was not indicative of a systematic search for armed activists. Rather, the attacks and assaults were characterized by large-scale destruction of property, leading many NGOs and government officials to believe that attacks by the Thevar-dominated police were motivated by personal caste affiliations.

Violence Against Dalit Women

As Dalit men migrate to cities in search of jobs, women are left to work as agricultural laborers in rural areas. Women "bear the brunt of attacks because they are stuck in these feudal arrangements." As a result of escalating caste clashes, attacks on Dalit women, by state and private actors, have also escalated.

Violence by Private Actors

On January 25, 1998, the Dalit colony of Veludavur village in Villapuram district was attacked by members of seven caste Hindu villages. The attack was allegedly perpetrated by the Vanniya caste and instigated by the Naidars (both backward castes). Tensions began with a government auction of common properties in the village, such as ponds and tamarind trees; the Dalits were demanding their right to participate. The same evening, Vanniyas entered and destroyed 400 Dalit huts.

Many of the young Dalit men were in Andhra Pradesh at the time, cultivating sugarcane. Only women, children and the elderly were left in the village, and the women were particularly targeted. A social worker in the village claimed that there were "sexual attempts on many women, but they don't want to talk about it. Many are unmarried or their husbands are away. They fear the consequences if these things are revealed." Over 700 families were displaced as a result of the attack. They took shelter in neighboring villages.

Burnad Fatima of the Tamil Nadu Women's Forum (TNWF) explained the number of cases TNWF had come across in which women were targets of caste clashes: Any time any caste riots take place, there is immediate action against women and immediate raping. During last year's riots, a forty-year-old woman was gang raped. A seventy-year-old was dragged out of her house and stripped. In Anchipet a handicapped girl was thrown from her wheelchair which was then damaged. Innocent women are butchered, raped, and killed even though they are not directly responsible for any of the riots.

TNWF and People's Watch members went on to describe another attack during the southern district clashes, and the lack of press attention to such cases:

> In Nammakal [district] a girl was gang raped, murdered, and then butchered. She belonged to the scavengers community. The men belonged to the weaving community. They cut off her hand and leg and shaved her head. They then cut her head and put a stick into her private parts and then hung her head with the stick. Why are they driven to this extent? Because for them Dalits are nothing. They give more respect to their animals... The papers are censored, they don't name the community, and they don't report the figures.

Of instances of rape by landlords, other upper castes, and the police, a representative of the Rural Center for Women's Development in Tirunelveli district said like this: "the police, "always support the landlords... [W]omen never say anything because they are afraid and need employment. Also society would blame them. Even their husband would separate from them. In the village, the Thevars entered the house and had sexual intercourse with the Dalit women. In November 1997 a twenty-two-year-old Dalit woman spoke up against the debt bondage of her husband and his family (Thevars are the dominant moneylenders and Dalits their primary borrowers). As a result she was brutally beaten and sexually abused by a Vanniya landlord: Her husband and father-in-law did not go to work for two days. The landlord came and asked why. He threatened and insulted her, and she said, "We are not living here under your mercy." The landlord went wild. He started beating her, he tore her blouse to pieces, touched her breast, hit her in the vagina and rolled her on the ground. There was no one to stop him.

Due to disinterest, ignorance of proper procedure, or their own caste biases, the police failed to register or properly investigate many cases of attacks against women during the clashes. Only with pressure from organized women's and human rights groups has the issue been placed before national commissions. The recommendations of these commissions, however, are not binding under statutory law.

Police torture of Women/Custodial Violence

In addition to attacks by members of the upper castes, women are attacked by the police, security forces, and private militias or armies hired by Thevars. V. Shankar, director for the Adi Dravida Tribal Welfare Department, of the state government of Tamil Nadu, explained: We found that women are put in front in both communities and act as a buffer. This has resulted in police action against women. They are taken far away from their homes. Unless they were directly involved in violence, they should not be arrested. In some cases we felt that the arrests could have been avoided.

H. Hanumanthappa, then-chairman of the National Commission for Scheduled Castes and Scheduled Tribes, added: "Once the police start raiding, the menfolk run away. Then they [police] make women the victims. The procedure they adopt is to take the child or wife so that the men come back. They feel that they are the masters of the situation. It has resulted in mass rapes."

The police practice of taking family members as hostages in order to force their relatives to turn themselves in is a common occurrence in Tamil Nadu and other parts of the country. Specific incidents of hostage-taking and custodial violence against women are described below.

Guruswamy Guruammal, a twenty-six-year-old agricultural laborer, suffered a miscarriage as a result of brutal beatings during a police raid on December 2, 1997. She is a resident of Chilaumbotti village of the southern district of Theni andearns Rs. 20 a day (US$0.50). The raid had preceded a planned visited by Dr. Krishanaswamy; posters had been distributed to announce his arrival. On December 2, one such poster was burned by Thevars in the district which led to a Pallar protest and road block. Police raided the village in response to the protests and assaulted many Dalits with their lathis. The police lathi-charged the villagers. Superintendent of Police Rajesh Das called me a pallachi, which is a caste name for prostitute. He then opened his pant zip. Sub-Inspector Arivanandam, who is from same community as me, was also there.

The police, numbering in the hundreds, returned early the next morning and again lathi-charged the village. They broke all the doors and arrested all the men in the village. Arivanandam and Rajesh Das said, "Where is Guruammal's house?" My husband hid under the cot. My mother was with me at the time. I was in my night clothes. The police started calling me a prostitute. I replied, "Your wife is a prostitute." They beat me. I was four months pregnant at the time. He pulled me naked on the road for one hundred feet. I got injuries on my legs. There were two elderly witnesses, a woman and my grandfather. The police also beat the woman when she asked them to stop dragging me. She is sixty years old; her hand was fractured. There were two men police and two lady police. They brought me to the police van and took me to the office of the Theni superintendent of police. Fifty-three men had been arrested. One of them took off his lungi [wrap-around cloth] and gave it to me to cover myself. He was only wearing shorts after that. Guruammal begged the police at the station to help her. She explained that she was pregnant and in need of medical attention. In response, they called her names and mocked her for making such bold statements the day before. Eventually, Guruammal was transferred to the Trichi jail hospital, where she remained for twenty-five days. After ten days, she had a miscarriage. As a result of being dragged and beaten by the police fists and guns, Guruammal was still visibly scarred on her neck, arms, legs, and abdomen.

She claimed that the police told her to testify that the raid on her village was in search of the illicit brewing of arrack (illicit liquor): They said if you accept the fact that the raid was for arrack, then you will be released. They said, "If you don't say arrack, we will file charges against you." So these are the cases that were filed against me and the fifty-three men. Although Guruammal was attacked as punishment for speaking up against the police, many other women are punished for alleged crimes committed by their male relatives.

Activists from People's Watch and the Tamil Nadu Women's Forum explained the tactics employed by the police: The police enter houses and attack the women even though they should never search when the women are alone. The police are arresting women if either the husband or son is absconding. They take them into custody and rape them. Three years ago, in a slum nearby, a forty-three-year-old woman lost her husband. Her son was involved in a murder case. She was arrested along with her daughter and daughter-in-law. They were taken to the police station where the police raped the mother in front of the other women. They then brought her home and burned her in her hut.

The activists also described a new tactic employed by the police of removing women's clothes and beating them from their knees to their shoulders, "because they know that women will not show others these parts." At a Madras conference on women's rights, held on April 28 and 29, 1995, dozens of Dalit and tribal women publicly came forward to testify about their experiences of custodial rape at the hands of Tamil Nadu police. The conference was sponsored by the Tamil Nadu Women's Forum and Asia Pacific Forum for Women, Law and Development.

In many of the statements, women claimed that the police were searching for their male relatives when they first came upon them. Pursuant to Section 160 of the Criminal Procedure

Code, police conducting investigations are prohibited from questioning female witnesses at any place other than their residence. Women are often unaware of these laws, and their ignorance is exploited by the police.

In the village of Muthaandikuppam, South Arcot district, a husband filed a complaint against his wife, Vasantha, after a misunderstanding between the couple. On the night of March 21, 1994, Vasantha was forced to spend the night in the police station under the pretext that there were no women police available to escort her home. She was "gang raped by four constables and a sub-inspector of the same police station and [then] murdered. They attempted to dispose [of] the body but could not succeed. They spread a rumour that Vasantha committed suicide by hanging from the fan at the police rest room in the police station." Community members, civil liberties groups, and political parties demanded appropriate, severe sanctions against the perpetrators. The Tamil Nadu government responded by temporarily suspending the constables involved.

On February 21, 1995, twenty-year-old Poonkothai witnessed the rape and murder of her forty-eight-year-old mother by police who were searching for her brother. The incident took place around 7:00 a.m. when police arrived at Poonkothai's house looking for her brother Murthy: "They blamed my mother [for] hiding the whereabouts of my brother, who is suspected in a murder of a person found dead_ near his house." Despite her mother's repeated denials, the police took both of them, along with Poonkothai's one-and-a-half-year-old daughter, to the Vannarapettai police station.

> We were beaten up severely and were tortured with abusive words and brutal attacks... One of the senior personnel ordered the others to use the "Punjab method" to elicit facts from my mother. They stripped my mother in front of me and took her inside. I repeatedly heard my mother groaning and pleading them not to torture her. With tears she was telling me that four men gang raped her and tortured her by inserting the lathi in the vagina and beat[ing] her in her private parts.

The police later brought her mother home, stuffed a piece of cloth in her mouth, poured petrol over her, and set her on fire. They left the scene soon thereafter. A neighbour intervened and took the mother to the hospital, where she later died. When Poonkothai's husband approached the police station to file a case, the police registered the death as a suicide. After many NGO protests, the police filed a First Information Report (FIR). Poonkothai's two neighbors, whose sons were also police suspects, and her two sisters-in-law were also taken into custody for several days and similarly tortured. One sister-in-law had just delivered a child. A report produced by the women's conference stated: "The drama usually played by police is just this. They come in search of the offenders and finding them absconding, whisk away the womenfolk to the police station and outrage theirmodesty." The conference also concluded that atrocities committed on women by the police were increasing.

Renewed Clashes

From October to December 1998, violent confrontations in the districts of Ramanathapuram, Pudukkottai, Perambalur, and Cuddalore signaled that caste clashes had not only continued but had spread to once-peaceful districts. In Ramanathapuram district, Thevars responded to a state-wide Dalit conference by organizing a rally on October 4, 1998. That afternoon, streams of lorries carrying Thevar youths were seen heading toward Ramanathapuram. On the way, several vehicles stopped at roadside villages and Thevars entered Dalit and Muslim hamlets throwing petrol bombs and ransacking houses. Two women were killed. Thevar youths claimed that they were provoked, allegedly by Dalits placing barriers on the road. As news of the attacks spread, Dalits retaliated. Despite all the violence, Koottamaippu—the Thevar coalition sponsoring the rally—was allowed to hold it. Among its demands: the repeal of the Scheduled Castes and Scheduled Tribes (Prevention of Atrocities) Act, 1989.

Dalits and journalists throughout the affected areas have blamed the police and district administration for their failure to effectively respond to increasing tensions in the district arising from publicity for the conference. According to Frontline, a bi-monthly news magazine, "The police presence was minimal and vehicles were not being checked for weapons. This was in contrast to the intensive searches carried out by the police when Puthiya Tamalingam [a Dalit organization] held its rally on September 11."

The situation remained volatile in the district for days afterwards. Police were given shoot-on-sight orders for arsonists, while a large contingent of the striking police force was rushed in. Both sides also alleged harassment and torture by the police conducting raids under the pretext of searching for criminals and weapons. According to People's Watch, the death toll on both sides reached fifteen.

On October 7, 1998, three days after the incident, state Governor Fathima Beevi called for an overhauling of the police system to prevent "police excess." The director general of the Bureau of Police Research and Development urged implementation of the National Police Commission recommendations, while the chairperson of the State Human Rights Commission recommended that police personnel should be made to undergo human rights awareness training every six months. None of these recommendations had been implemented as of February 1999.

Just over a month after the violence in Ramanathapuram, caste tensions erupted in Thirunallur village in nearby Pudukkottai district. On November 19, 1998, three Dalit youths were stripped, tied to a tree, and beaten through the night. According to a press report, their "heads were tonsured, and they were also made to roll around the village temple in the presence of a large gathering which included their kith and kin. The next morning they were asked to leave the village." The attack was part of a judgment handed down by twelve members of the all-caste Hindu local village council: the young men were being punished for marrying non-Dalit Hindu girls. Tensions remained high in the village for weeks following the beatings. Not until a month later were the culprits charged and the victims given part of their compensation, under the Scheduled Castes and Scheduled Tribes (Prevention of Atrocities) Act, 1989.

On December 1, 1998, in a massive operation reminiscent of the 1995 police raid on Kodiyankulum village, 300 armed policemen entered the Dalit colony at Ogalur village in Perambalur district. Under the pretext of rounding up "anti-social elements," police reportedly entered over 1,000 homes and, using lathis and iron rods, attacked the residents. After causing extensive damage to their homes and property, police arrested sixty-nine Dalits. Among them were thirty-four women, some with babies in their arms and a few who were pregnant.

The attack was a dispute between the Dalits and the caste Hindus over a piece of temple land and the attempted sexual assault of a Dalit woman by a caste Hindu man in the village; the man accompanied the police during their attack. As of January 1999, the Dalit laborers were still unable to work in the caste Hindu fields and their children were unable to go to school. Another incident, reported by the news magazine Frontline, took place on December 16, 1998. In Puliyur village, Cuddalore district, a mob of caste Hindus (Vanniyas) numbering about 300 raided a Dalit settlement and attacked its residents with sticks and iron rods.

Approximately 500 houses were ransacked and thirteen Dalits seriously injured. The day before the attack, a Dalit funeral procession was stopped as it passed a Vanniya house. "In the melee that followed, the caste-Hindu resident was reportedly assaulted by a Dalit, who, it is said, had been slapped a day earlier for smoking in the presence of the caste-Hindu resident." In this case, smoking was a luxury to which the Dalits were not entitled in the presence of a caste Hindu.

Government-Appointed Commissions

State governments in India share a common history of appointing judicial commissions of inquiry to quell public outcries against police excesses during large-scale communal and caste clashes. Although these commissions do serve a political function, their findings, if and when released to the public, are frequently in favor of the state. The Tamil Nadu experience is no exception to this rule.

As of December 1998 the state was one of five to have established a state human rights commission (SHRC). The commission's investigations into human rights abuses by the police and caste Hindus are, however, blocked if the state first appoints its own judicial commission of inquiry. Like the National Human Rights Commission, state human rights commissions are denied jurisdiction over an investigation if the matter is pending before "any commission duly constituted under any law for the time-being [sic] in force."

The state government of Tamil Nadu has exploited this provision by appointing its own commissions of inquiry before state human rights commission investigations get underway. States have little control over the investigations of statutory (human rights) commissions. Conversely, government-appointed commissions almost invariably find in favor of the state and the police. Those findings that go against the state are rarely implemented or made public.

A Tamil Nadu government official explained that judicial commissions' findings "do not become public unless the government tables it with the legislature; findings that are against the state are often not tabled... By appointing its own commissions, the state government does not permit the State Human Rights Commission to do the investigation. It literally ties its hands." The appointment of judicial commissions has become almost routine following caste clashes.

The Justice Mohan Commission, for example, was appointed by the state government in July 1997 to look into recurring caste clashes and suggest measures to prevent them, but only "after the state government knew that the State Human Rights Commission was on the job." The Justice Mohan Commission submitted its report in September 1998. In October 1998, Chief Minister Karunanidhi announced that not all the recommendations could be accepted.

In another large-scale clash in Coimbatore in November 1997, Muslims shops and houses were burned down by Hindus, reportedly with support from the police. Before the SHRC could take up the investigation, the state appointed the Justice Gokulakrishnan Commission, and "[a]gain their hands were tied." During the southern district clashes of April to December 1997, police opened fire in two villages and attacked Dalit women in a third. Three commissions headed by three district judges were immediately appointed. The director of People's Watch contends that "it has been the history of Dalit people that every commission of inquiry has gone against their interests." Another activist added that "the retired judges who are appointed always toe the line of the government."

Given proper resources, state human rights commissions stand to play an important role in the protection of human rights. Because their investigations enjoy greater independence from the state than judicial commission investigations, the statutes under which they are formed need to be amended to ensure that judicial commissions cannot be appointed as a means of undermining their powers. Moreover, the mandates of human rights commissions themselves need to be strengthened to ensure that their recommendations are binding and their findings are made public.

Discrimination and Explotative Forms of Labour

Allocation of labor on the basis of caste is one of the fundamental tenets of the caste system. Within the caste system, Dalits have been assigned tasks and occupations that are deemed ritually polluting for other caste communities.

The dalit agricultural laborers who work for a few kilograms of rice or Rs. 15 to Rs. 35 (US$0.38 to $0.88) a day. A sub-group of Dalits is condemned to labor even more exploitative. An estimated forty million people in India, among them fifteen million children, are bonded laborers. A majority of them are Dalits. According to government statistics, an estimated one million Dalits are manual scavengers who clean public latrines and dispose of dead animals; unofficial estimates are much higher. In India's southern states, thousands of Dalit girls are forced into prostitution before reaching the age of puberty.

Bondage is passed on from one generation to another. Scavenging and prostitution are hereditary occupations of "untouchable" castes. Dalits face discrimination when seeking other forms of employment and are largely unable to escape their designated occupation even when the practice itself has been abolished by law. In violation of their basic human rights, they are physically abused and threatened with economic and social ostracism from the community for refusing to carry out various caste-based tasks.

Bonded Labor

"Bonded labor" refers to work in slave-like conditions in order to pay off a debt. Due to the high interest rates charged and the abysmally low wages paid, the debts are seldom settled. Bonded laborers are frequently low-caste, illiterate, and extremely poor, while the creditors/employers are usually higher-caste, literate, comparatively wealthy, and relatively more powerful members of the community. The Bonded Labour System (Abolition) Act, 1976 abolishes all agreements and obligations arising out of the bonded labor system. It aims to release all laborers from bondage, cancel any outstanding debt, prohibit the creation of new bondage agreements, and order the economic rehabilitation offreed bonded laborers by the state. It also punishes attempts to compel persons into bondage with a maximum of three years in prison and a

Rs. 2,000 (US$50) fine. However, the extent to which bonded laborers have been identified, released, and rehabilitated in the country is negligible.

Most agricultural laborers are paid between Rs. 15 and Rs. 25 (US$0.38 to $0.63), or two to three kilograms of rice, per day, well below the minimum wage prescribed in their state. Women were consistently paid less than men. Many laborers owed debts to their employers or other moneylenders. Under the Bonded Labour System (Abolition) Act, 1976, payment of less than minimum wage for the purposes of working off a debt amounts to bondage. The act's definition of the "bonded labour system" includes "any system of forced, or partly forced labour under which a debtor enters, or has, or is presumed to have, entered, into an agreement with the creditor to the effect that (v) by reason of his birth in any particular caste or community, he would (1) render, by himself or through any member of his family, or any person dependent on him, labour or service to the creditor, or for the benefit of the creditor, for a specified period or for an unspecified period, either without wages or for nominal wages....

Nominal wages are defined as wages which are less than:

(a) the minimum wages fixed by the Government, in relation to the same or similar labour, under any law for the time being in force; and

(b) where no such minimum wage has been fixed in relation to any form of labour, the wages that are normally paid, for the same or similar labour to the labourers working in the same locality.

Caste and Employment Discrimination

In traditional Indian society, the fourfold varna theory describes a broad functional division of labor. Though the caste system has not prevented occupational mobility for caste Hindus, many "untouchable" communities have been forced to continue their occupations as leather workers, disposers of dead animals, or manual scavengers, and to perform other tasks deemed too ritually polluting for upper castes.

The constitutional abolition of "untouchability" meant that caste Hindus could no longer force Dalits to perform any "polluting" occupation. Yet sweeping, scavenging, and leatherwork are still the monopoly of the scheduled castes, whose members are threatened with physical abuse and social boycotts for refusing to perform demeaning tasks. Migration and the anonymity of the urban environment have in some cases resulted in upward occupational mobility among Dalits, but the majority continue to perform their traditional functions. A lack of training and education, as well as discrimination in seeking other forms of employment, have kept these traditions and their hereditary nature alive.

Manual Scavenging

Manual scavenging is a caste-based occupation. Dalit manual scavengers exist under different caste names throughout the country, such as the Bhangis in Gujarat, the Pakhis in Andhra Pradesh, and the Sikkaliars in Tamil Nadu. Members of these communities are invariably placed at the very bottom of the caste hierarchy, and even the hierarchy of Dalit sub-castes. Using little more than a broom, a tin plate, and a basket, they are made to clear feces from public and private latrines and carry them to dumping grounds and disposal sites. Though long outlawed, the practice of manual scavenging continues in most states.

Those working for urban municipalities are paid Rs. 30 - 40 a day (less than US$1), and those working privately are paid Rs. 5 (US$0.13) a month for each house they clean. Even those working for municipalities rarely get paid and are offered little health benefits for a job that entails many health hazards. In cities scavengers are actually lowered into filthy gutters in order to unclog them; they are fully immersed in human waste without any protective gear. In Bombay, children made to dive into manholes have died from carbon monoxide poisoning.

In many communities, in exchange for leftover food, scavengers are also expected to remove dead animal carcasses and deliver messages of death to the relatives of their upper-caste neighbors. Their refusal to do so can result in physical abuse and ostracism from the community.

A social worker in the Dhandhuka taluk of Ahmedabad district, Gujarat, explained the relevance of caste to this work: Bhangis are the section of Dalits that do this work. The funds come from the government. In villages, the cleaners and who they clean for are always divided by caste... At all levels, villages and municipalities, Bhangis are the workers and they always work for upper castes.

In a 1997 report, the National Commission for Safai Karamcharis claimed that manual scavengers are "totally cut off from the mainstream of progress" and are "still subjected to the worst kind of oppression and indignities. What is more pathetic is the fact that manual scavenging is still largely a hereditary occupation. Safai karamcharis are no doubt the most oppressed and disadvantaged section of the population." The commission is a statutory body set up pursuant to the National Commission for Safai Karamcharis Act, 1993. Safai karamcharis are defined as those persons engaged in, or employed for, manually carrying human excreta or any sanitation work.

Martin Macwan is founder-director of Navsarjan, an NGO that has led the campaign to abolish manual scavenging in the western state of Gujarat. When Navsarjan had attempted to rehabilitate scavengers it was difficult to find alternative employment for them, and even more difficult to convince scavengers that they were able to take on, or were "worthy of performing," different occupations.

Members of the Bhangi community in Gujarat are paid by state municipalities to clean the gutters, streets, and community dry latrines. The Bhangis lives in a residential area called Bhangivas separate from the Dharbars, Rajputs, and Vanniyas who constitute the caste Hindus in the area. The

Bhangis were primarily employed as manual scavengers. They were also responsible for removing dead cats and dogs and were given Rs. 5 (US$0.13) or small amounts of food for doing so.

Most looked considerably older than their stated age. In addition to the above mentioned diseases of the poor, manual scavengers also tend to suffer from respiratory infections, gastrointestinal disorders, and trachoma, a chronic contagious bacterial conjunctivitis commonly resulting in blindness.

Several workers have vision problems and other diseases. Asixty-five-year-old Bachubhai Chaganbhai, who suffered from tuberculosis claimed that the illness was due to "working as a cleaner. I used to clean openlatrines. Because of this work I am sick. I stopped working five years ago and have been sick with TB ever since." Because Bachubhai was a "permanent" worker, he received Rs. 1,500 (US$37.50) pension per month. He used to earn Rs. 2,000 (US$50) a month, or approximately Rs. 65 (US$1.63) a day. Activist Martin Macwan explained that [b]eing permanent means that you have an appointment letter. You also get health benefits but not much; you get to visit government dispensaries, which are not in good shape. But the state government has to give grants to the state municipalities depending on the number of permanents that are employed, so the municipalities try to keep them as casual laborers instead. But the number of hours they work is usually the same.

Despite the similarity in work and hours spent, casual laborers are paid only Rs. 34 (US$0.85) a day while permanent laborers were paid Rs. 80 (US$2). Most casual laborers never achieve permanent status, even after years of employment. Leelaben, another scavenger, had been cleaning the latrines in Birla High School for over twenty years, "Still they have not made me permanent," she said. "I used to get paid Rs. 15 (US$0.38) a month, now I get paid Rs. 200 (US$5) a month."

The situation of private workers, mostly women working in upper-caste households, is even bleaker. In the Bhangivas residential area, in July 1998, there were a total of thirty private workers; the rest were employed by the municipality. Many private workers were paid only Rs. 3 (US$0.08) a day.

An activist in the southern state of Andhra Pradesh, who has been working for the rehabilitation of cleaning workers for the past fourteen years, described a similar pay scale in his state:

Private cleaners receive Rs. 5 to 10 a month for each house they clean [US$0.12 to $0.25]. They clean up to ten to fifteen houses a day, many of which have six or more family members. Those employed by urban municipalities are paid Rs. 2,000 to Rs. 2,500 [US$50 - $63] a month but are only paid once every four to six months. Some are permanent, and some are casual. There are no health benefits, no gloves, no masks, no utensils. The majority are women. A survey conducted by Safai Karmachari Andolan, an NGO movement for the elimination of manual scavenging, found over 1,650 scavengers in ten districts in Andhra Pradesh. Many were also engaged in underground sewage work. The survey also revealed that 98 percent of manual scavengers in the state belonged to scheduled castes.

A third category of cleaning workers are responsible for cleaning the railway systems. In Andhra Pradesh they are paid Rs. 300 (US$7.50) a month with very few benefits. In Gujarat, they are paid Rs. 12 (US$0.30) a day "for unlimited hours of work. They are told they can stop working when the train comes, but in India you never know when the train will come." An activist working with the Sikkaliar (Dalit) community of Tamil Nadu described the community's economic exploitation and the tasks that its members are forced to perform. His village had 200 Thevar families. Seventy Sikkaliar families lived in a separate government-built colony. Those who worked as scavengers and removed dead animals from the village received Rs. 150 (US$3.75) per month for their services.

Social discrimination against scavengers is rampant. Most scavengers live in segregated rural colonies and are unable to make use of common resources. According to an Andhra Pradesh activist: In one toilet there can be as many as 400 seats which all have to be manually cleaned. This is the lowest occupation in the world, and it is done by the community that occupies the lowest status in the castesystem. Even other scheduled-caste people won't touch the safai karamcharis. It is "untouchability" within the "untouchables," yet nobody questions it.

In many tea stalls there is a separate tea tumbler system in which scavengers are made to wash and handle their own tumblers so that glasses reserved for caste Hindus are not "polluted." When we are working, they ask us not to come near them. At tea canteens, they have separate tea tumblers and they make us clean them ourselves and make us put the dishes away ourselves. We cannot enter temples. We cannot use upper-caste water taps. We have to go one kilometer away to get water.

Despite their appalling work conditions, manual scavengers are unable to demand higher wages or sanitary instruments for use in the collection of human excreta: "When we ask for our rights from the government, the municipality officials threaten to fire us. So we don't say anything. This is what happens to people who demand their rights." According to Macwan, in Ranpur town, Ahmedabad district, women who arrived late for work were made to clean men's urinals as punishment, "even if the men were still inside." Another social worker active in Gujarat added that Bhangis were forced to deliver messages of death to upper-caste family relatives; "They will be boycotted and beaten so they cannot say no."

Apart from having to perform degrading tasks, the Sikkaliars are also subject to physical and sexual abuse as well as restrictions on their right to vote. Sikkaliars have to bury the Thevars' dead animals, and women have to collect waste. They only get meals for their work, even for burying animals. Sometimes Sikkaliars take the dead animal's meat and divide it among themselves. The Thevars harass women laborers, particularly young ladies. Once a girl attains puberty, she is harassed by Thevar men. If anyone opposes it, they will be severely punished. Sikkaliars depend on Thevars, and because there is no other support they often leave for other villages out of fear when fighting occurs. They are doing scavenger work as well as [agricultural] laborer work for which they are paid less than minimum wage. They clean the latrines, the bathrooms, the drains, and they do cremation work. If not they are severely punished by the Thevars. The children are not able to go to school.

The activist also described how Dalits are unable to freely exercise their constitutionally guaranteed right to vote. During the February 1998 elections, Sikkaliars were forced to vote according to the demands of the Thevar community or risk losing the little income they had: "Because Thevars are in the majority, they will come inside the voting booth and tell them who to vote for. If they don't act according to instructions, then they don't get employment, or they will be beaten."

Thevars treat Sikkaliars as slaves so they can utilize them as they wish. They exploit them sexually and make them dig graveyards for high-caste people's burials. They have to take the death message to Thevars. These are all unpaid services. Maybe they give them Rs. 10 [US$0.25] for the message. There are also very meager wages for grave digging. Still they have to do these things or they will be thrown out of the village.

The activist referred to the women in his village as "sexual slaves" and claimed that Thevar men frequently enter Dalit houses at night to rape the women: "Dalit people have anger against Thevar people in mind. Thevars use their women, but Dalits cannot do anything." According to R. Balakrishnan, director of the Tamil Nadu chapter of the National Commission for Scheduled Castes and Scheduled Tribes, the raping of Dalit women exposes the hypocrisy of the caste system: "No one practices untouchability when it comes to sex."

Rrelationship between scavenging and debt bondage

Given the insignificant amounts of remuneration and the need to engage several family members in work assigned to one, it comes as little surprise that many families borrow money from their upper-caste neighbors and consequently going into bondage. Their poverty is so acute that Macwan has even documenteda Bhangi practice of separating non-digested wheat from buffalo dung to make chappatis. One scavenger commented: There is no health care, no benefits from the government. We cannot live on what we get paid, but we have to. We also have to take loans from the upper caste. They charge 10 percent in interest per month. We have no clothes, no soap, no wages, and no payments on time.

Failure to Implement Protective Legislation

The Employment of Manual Scavengers and Construction of Dry Latrines (Prohibition) Act, 1993 punishes the employment of scavengers or the construction of dry (non-flush) latrines with imprisonment for up to one year and/or a fine as high as Rs. 2,000 (US$50). Offenders are also liable to prosecution under the Scheduled Castes and Scheduled Tribes (Prevention of Atrocities) Act, 1989. In 1992 the government launched a national scheme that called for the identification, training, and rehabilitation of safai karamcharis throughout the country.

According to the National Commission for Safai Karamcharis, the progress "has not been altogether satisfactory." As a result it has benefited only "a handful of safai karamcharis and their dependents. One of the reasons for unsatisfactory progress of the Scheme appears to be inadequate attention paid to it by the State Governments and concerned agencies." When confronted with the existence of manual scavenging and dry latrines within their jurisdiction, state governments often deny their existence altogether or claim that a lack of water supply prevents states from constructing flush latrines. This despite the fact thata sum of Rs. 4,640,000,000 (US$116 million) was allocated to the scheme under the government's Eighth Five Year Plan. Activists claim that the resources, including government funds, exist for construction and for the rehabilitation of scavengers; what is lacking is the political will to do so. Members of the National Commission for Safai Karamcharis consider it imperative that the commission be "vested with similar powers and facilities as are available to the National Commission for Scheduled Castes and Scheduled Tribes." Currently the commission only has advisory powers and no authority to summon or monitor cases.

The Devadasi System: Ritualized Prostitution

The practice of devadasi, in which a girl, usually before reaching the age of puberty, is ceremoniously dedicated or married to a deity or to a temple, continues in several southern states including Andhra Pradesh and Karnataka. Literally meaning "female servant of god," devadasis usually belong to the Dalit community. Once dedicated, the girl is unable to marry, forced to become a prostitute for upper-caste community members, and eventually auctioned into an urban brothel. The age-old practice continues to legitimize the sexual violence and discrimination that have come to characterize the intersection between caste and gender. The patrons of the devadasis are generally from the higher castes because those from the devadasis own castes are too poor to afford to [pay] for the rituals. In many cases a patron kept many girls and the number of girls used to be a yard stick of the status of that man. This system of patronage has given way to [a system of] commercial prostitution in the populated big cities.

Activists involved in the Dalit women's movement explain that the nexus between caste and forced prostitution is quite strong and that the devadasi system is no exception. Most Indian girls and women in India's urban brothels come from lower-caste, tribal, or minority communities. Like other forms of violence against women, ritualized prostitution, activists believe, is a system "designed to kill whatever vestiges of self-respect the untouchable castes have in order to subjugate them and keep them underprivileged." By keeping Dalit women as prostitutes, and by tying prostitution to bondage in rural areas, upper-caste men reinforce their declaration of social and economic superiority over the lower castes.

According to the Ambedkar Centre for Justice and Peace, a Canada-based NGO:

> Thousands of untouchable female children (between 6 and 8 years) are forced to become maidens of God (Devadasis, Jogins, a Hindu religious practice in Andhra Pradesh, Karnataka State, Maharashtra, Orissa State, to mention only a few). They are taken from their families, never to see them again. They are later raped by the temple priest and finally auctioned secretly into prostitution and ultimately die from AIDS. It is estimated by NGOs that 5,000 to 15,000 girls are auctioned secretly every year.

According to the head of an NGO in Karnataka, in her state the girl is offered to the Goddess Yellamma in a village ceremony: Earlier it was for priests, but now it is for high-caste men. They used to live in the temples now anyone can use them including lorry drivers. Dreadlocked hair is taken as a sign from the Goddess Yellamma that the girl is meant to be a devadasi. In a festival, a marriage ceremony takes place between the girl and god. The eldest lady of the devadasi community ties the mangal sutra [marriage necklace]. In some ceremonies the girl wasparaded almost naked. The girl is then given some money but still works in the fields. She lives separately in the village and is used by all the men, including Dalit men.

In 1992 the Karnataka state government passed the Karnataka Devadasi (Prohibition of Dedication) Act and called for the rehabilitation of devadasi women. Like many laws aimed at protecting women and lower castes, the act suffers from a lack of enforcement. Moreover, the police themselves have been known to use devadasis. As the Karnataka activist explained, the law works to the disadvantage of women because it criminalizes their actions and not the actions of their patrons. Police will even go so far as to demand sex as a bribe: "They will threaten to file charges under the act if the woman says no." Their perceived status in society, as women who are supposed to serve men sexually, also makes it more difficult for devadasis to approach the police for help: "When a devadasi is raped, it is not considered rape. She can be had by any man at any time."

In reviewing India's third periodic report to the U.N. Human Rights Committee, submitted under Article 40 of the International Covenant on Civil and Political Rights (ICCPR) in July 1997, the Human Rights Committee regretted "the lack of national legislation to outlaw the practice of Devadasi, the regulation of which is left to the states," and added that "it appears that the practice continues and that not all states have effective legislation against it." The committee emphasized that the practice was incompatible with the ICCPR and recommended that "all necessary measures be taken urgently" toward its eradication.

Criminalisation of Social Activism

In violation of the right to equal protection before the law, as guaranteed by Article 14 of the constitution and Article 26 of the International Covenant on Civil and Political Rights, local police routinely abuse vaguely worded provisions of the Indian Penal Code, the Criminal Procedure Code, and various preventive detention statutes to thwart attempts by Dalits to demand their legal rights. The arbitrary detention of Dalits and treatment of Dalit men and women in custody are also clear violations of laws governing police conduct.

State agents have acted directly and forcefully against those attempting to claim their rights. Dalit activists throughout the country face charges as "terrorists," "threats to national security," and "habitual offenders." Many have to spend much of their income on lawyers' fees or anticipatory bail. Dalit activists are frequently charged under the National Security Act, 1980, the Indian Explosives Act, 1884, and even the Terrorism and Anti-Disruptive Activities Act (TADA). The most common charges under the Indian Penal Code include sections 147 and 148 on rioting and rioting with a deadly weapon; Section 341 for wrongful restraint; sections 323 and 324 for voluntarily causing hurt; sections 302 and 307 for murder and attempted murder; and Section 427 for mischief. Provisions of the Criminal Procedure Code are also used to detain Dalit activists and deter them from organizing Dalit community members.

Rights of the Accused

When an accused is arrested, he or she has the right to: be informed of the reasons for the arrest; see the warrant if arrested under a warrant; consult a lawyer of his or her choice; appear before the nearest magistrate within twenty-four hours; and be told whether he or she is entitled to be released on bail. Section 163 of the Criminal Procedure Code prohibits any officer from making any threat or promise for the purpose of obtaining a statement from a witness or an accused. Causing harm to obtain a confession or to obtain information regarding an offense is also punishable by up to ten years imprisonment under Section 330 of the Indian Penal Code. Police torture of an accused is a violation of the detainee's fundamental rights to life and liberty guaranteed under articles 20 and 21 of the constitution. Nevertheless, police torture persists. Several Supreme Court cases have also determined that victims of police torture are entitled to compensation.

6

Violence against Dalits

The eastern state of Bihar, with a population of eighty-six million people, is notorious for its poverty and lawlessness and for an ongoing conflict between Naxalites and private upper-caste militias set against the backdrop of acute social disparities. Since independence, Bihar has consistently ranked among the worst of India's larger states in urbanization, production, and income; it has the highest number of very large landholders and one of the largest landless populations among all Indian states. Agrarian issues have long dominated the state's political life as the feudal nature of landholding has remained largely unchanged despite legislation establishing ceilings on the maximum amount of land one individual can own.

Political leaders who depend on landed elites for support have had little interest in pursuing reforms. Wages for agricultural laborers are also among the lowest in the country. In many districts workers are not paid in money but instead often work a full day for as little as two kilograms of rice. Since the 1960s, social activists advocating on behalf of low-caste groups have attempted, through various forms of peaceful protest, to pressure the government to institute land reforms; at the same time, Naxalite groups have advocated armed resistance and have carried out targeted assassinations of landlords. In turn, higher-caste landholders have retaliated by forming private militias, known as senas (armies), to fight the

Naxalites and terrorize and kill low-caste villagers whom they believe to have provided support to the Naxalites, or who have organized to demand better wages and other reforms. Hundreds of Dalits have been killed in sena attacks since the early 1990s. The attacks frequently take place at night; in many cases, the victims, including women and children, have been shot in their beds while they were sleeping.

Members of the senas have also raped women and girls during the attacks. They have often claimed responsibility for the attacks and have even announced beforehand which villages they planned to target. However, because the senas enjoy the patronage of powerful elites, they operate with impunity.

Rather than addressing the security needs of landless laborers most affected by the violence or provide protection to villagers at risk, a series of inefficient and corrupt state governments since the early 1970s has only exacerbated the problem. In many instances, government officials—many of whom are alleged to have caste ties or other affiliations with the senas—have acted as agents of the private armies and have turned a blind eye to the killings. State security forces have helped train the senas, and in some cases, police have accompanied the militias during their attacks on Dalit villages.

Police have also conducted their own raids on Dalit villages in the aftermath of massacres carried out by upper-caste militias. The ostensible reason for police raids has been to capture suspected Naxalites, but the raids are frequently used to punish villagers suspected of sympathizing with the militant groups. Like the attacks by private militias, police raids have been characterized by violence, looting, and assaults on women.

The state's response to militant activity by Naxalite groups and by the senas is conspicuously uneven. Sena members have rarely been prosecuted for acts of violence. Police routinely detain and charge suspected Naxalite militants, however, and many are killed in so-called encounters with the police. This chapter traces the conflict in Bihar since the birth of the Ranvir Sena, an upper-caste militia formed in 1994.

Context of the Conflicts

Scheduled castes constitute close to 14 percent of the population in Bihar; most of the agricultural laborers belong to these castes. The four main upper castes in the region are the Brahmins, the Bhumihars, the Rajputs, and the Kayasthas. There are more than one hundred backward castes, the dominant of which are the Yadavs and the Kurmis. In 1996 and 1997 the state government was led by Laloo Prasad Yadav, president of the Rashtriya Janata Dal party and member of the Yadav backward caste; although his administration was dominated by upper castes. Laloo Prasad Yadav resigned in 1998; he was replaced as chief minister by his wife Rabri Devi.

The implementation of reservations in favor of the backward castes has improved their status throughout the state; the same has not held true of scheduled castes whose status continues to deteriorate. Central Bihar in particular has seen a consistent rise in abuses against scheduled castes since the early 1990s at the hands of upper castes and backward castes who employ them as laborers on their lands. Rapes and murders of Dalit women in particular have reportedly increased during this period. As one long-time observer of violence in the state has noted, "Disparities in socioeconomic hierarchy run alongside the caste hierarchy throughout Bihar although the degree of relationship may differ in some districts... Scheduled Castes invariably fall in the lowest category both socially and economically."

There is little organized official effort to bridge the class gap. Administrations that have governed the state since independence have not even succeeded in completing any land surveys. In the districts of central Bihar, money-lending, bonded labor, sexual assaults on ıural women, and abuse of the landless class by landowners have all contributed to violent clashes between various castes.

Successive Bihari governments have failed to implement land reforms and guaranties of minimum wages for agricultural laborers; as a result, disparities in wealth between landless Dalit laborers and their landed upper-caste and middle-caste counterparts have increased. The disparity and increasing economic exploitation have given rise to numerous militant leftist groups who have increased their membership, their political clout, and their weaponry since the 1970s.

The central Bhojpur district of Bihar has long been a stronghold of these so-called Naxalite groups that operate under various political banners. The increase in Naxalite activities has also ushered in a rise in the number of private upper-caste militias, including the Ranvir Sena, that have been responsible for killing hundreds of Dalit laborers between 1995 and 1998. In these areas of Bihar, a class struggle has escalated into an armed caste conflict.

The Naxalites

Following the Naxalbari uprising in West Bengal in 1968, various Marxist-Leninist factions began calling for a militant peasant struggle against upper-caste domination in Bihar. An armed struggle in the countryside against semi-feudal interests, combined with area-wide seizures of land, were the groups' primary tactics. Throughout their history, Naxalite groups have engaged in attacks on civilians and abuses that directly violate international humanitarian law.

Critical of the parliamentary tendencies of the Indian Communist movement, especially the Communist Party of India and Communist Party of India (Marxist), the Naxalites actively recruited Dalit and lower-caste peasants into their militant struggle. By 1998, Naxalite groups were operational in thirty-six out of fifty-four districts in Bihar.

The Naxalite groups are dominated by the Maoist Communist Centre (MCC), the Communist Party of India (Marxist-Leninist) Party Unity, and the Communist Party of India (Marxist-Leninist) (CPI(M-L)) Liberation. In 1977 CPI (M-L) Liberation moved away from an emphasis on "annihilation of individual class enemies" to an attempt at organizing mass peasant movements through Kisan Sabha (peasants' organizations).

In 1982 the group decided to enter parliamentary politics under the banner of the Indian People's Front (IPF). Though IPF won one parliamentary seat in 1989, and sent seven members in 1989 and six members in 1995 to the Bihar state assembly, its overall electoral success has since declined.

While CPI(M-L) Liberation has pursued a parliamentary path, Party Unity and the Maoist Communist Centre have spearheaded a militant grassroots movement, that, in turn, has been targeted by Ranvir Sena attacks. Both the MCC and Party Unity are banned underground movements. The MCC was responsible for the killing of at least fifty-four upper-caste Rajput community members in Dalelchak Baghaura in May 1987.

The incident was the worst massacre in the state until the Ranvir Sena killing of sixty-one Dalits in Laxmanpur-Bathe on December 1, 1997. MCC was also responsible for slitting the throats of forty-four upper-caste farmers in Bara village on February 12, 1992. Thirty-six died on the spot, and one died in the hospital. The killings were reportedly in retaliation for the murders of ten MCC supporters by the Savarna Liberation Front, an upper-caste Bhumihar militia, two months earlier. MCC has also targeted police officers, who find themselves ill-equipped to respond. According to press reports, 295 people were killed in Naxalite violence in 1995, 436 in 1996, and 424 in 1997. Not all clashes involve police: many of these deaths were attributed to interfactional fighting between Party Unity and MCC.

On August 11, 1998, CPI(M-L) Party Unity merged with CPI (M-L) People's War, popularly known as the People's War Group (PWG). The merger was the culmination of five years of negotiations between the two underground movements. The unified party retained the name CPI(M-L) People's War. Ever since its founding in 1980, PWG has attempted to unify all Marxist-Leninist groups under its umbrella. Strongest in the southern and central states, its merger with Party Unity gave it a foothold in the north.

Like MCC and Party Unity, PWG has advocated the use of violence against the upper castes in organizing Dalits to achieve land reform. Firearms used by Naxalites are often looted or bought from corrupt police. As is typical of guerrilla organizations, Naxalites recruit members from villages where they operate and draw on the support of the local population. It does not follow, however, that all villagers in a Naxalite stronghold are members of the organization, though they may have relatives or neighbors who do belong.

Caste Militias

Starting in the late 1960s, various upper-caste senas began to emerge in Bihar with the reported aim of containing Naxalite groups and protecting land belonging to upper castes. A look at their history reveals their political patronage. In 1969 the upper-caste Rajputs formed a militia named the Kuer Sena. In 1979 the Kunwar Sena of Rajputs was formed; it disintegrated in 1986. The Sunlight Sena, also dominated by Rajputs, came into being in 1988. One of its founders was a former governor of the state of Tamil Nadu.

The Brahmarshi Sena, which represented Bhumihars before the creation of the Ranvir Sena, was launched at a conference in Patna, Bihar's capital, in 1981. The Samajwadi Krantikari Sena, formed of Rajputs, was founded by a member of the state legislative assembly. The Bhumihar-dominated Savarna Liberation Front came into existence in 1990. Also known as the Diamond Sena, the militia was responsible for many massacres.

On September 27, 1991, the sena beheaded seven Dalit and tribal laborers in Sawanbigha village in Jehanabad district. Soon thereafter, strong men hired by landlords of Teendiha village in Gaya district beheaded nine laborers for their refusal to work as farm-hands for paltry wages. Like the upper castes, backward-caste landlords have cultivated private militias for protection. The Bhoomi Sena was formed by backward-caste Kurmis. Its founder was a former state minister and Janata Dal (People's Party) leader. The Lorik Sena was formed by the Yadav landlords of Jehanabad district, while the Kisan Sangh is a militia of middle-caste landlords.

Ranvir Sena

The Ranvir Sena was founded by upper-caste Bhumihars in Belaur village, Bhojpur district, in 1994. It first made international headlines in July 1996 with its attack on Bathani Tola in Bhojpur district, Bihar, which left nineteen Dalits and Muslims, mostly women and children, dead. Sixty members of the sena reportedly descended on the village and set twelve houses on fire. Using lathis, swords, and firearms, the attackers continued the onslaught for two and a half hours.

The attack was reportedly in retaliation for the earlier killing of nine Bhumihars in Nadhi village, also in Bhojpur district, by the CPI(M-L). The conflict began when CPI(M-L) began organizing the agricultural laborers to demand the statutory daily minimum wage of Rs. 30.75 (US$0.77). Landowners were only willing to pay Rs. 20 (US$0.50). CPI(M-L) members convinced laborers to refuse employment at that wage and called for an economic blockade against landowners.

The attack on Bathani Tola, press reports claim, was an effort to weaken the resolve of CPI(M-L) cadres organizing in the village and to prevent a labor boycott on hundreds of acres of land. None of the Ranvir Sena leaders were ever arrested for the Bathani Tola massacre. Since its inception, the Ranvir Sena has been implicated in killings, rapes and lootings in the villages of Belaur, Ekwari, Chandi, Nanaur, Narhi, Sarathau, Haibaspur, Laxmanpur-Bathe, Shankarbigha, and Narayanpur.

On April 22, 1996, the sena gunned down five members of a marriage party in Nanaur village. The victims were believed to be CPI(M-L) supporters. In 1997 the sena killed three Dalits in Jehanabad district for raising their voice against the rape of a Dalit girl by upper-caste youths. Sena membership is divided by districts and that all districts has a commander and at least 500 landowners "ready to take uparms." Although Patna is the center, the sena is also present in Jehanabad, Aurangabad, Bhojpur, Rotas, Gaya, Bahuwan, and Baxar districts. As of 1998 sena members established a presence in Bhagalpur and Muzafarrpur. Bhojpur, Patna and Jehanabad, also Naxalite-affected areas, have been centers of violence in the last several years.

Upper- and lower-caste villagers in Ekwari claimed that Singh was on the CPI(M-L) hit-list. Another member of the sena, Arvind Singh, claimed that the CPI(M-L) had resolved to kill one rich landlord in each village: "They kill us and take our crops. To protect ourselves we started the Ranvir Sena." According to members of Bihar Dalit Vikas Samiti (Bihar Dalit Development Organization, BDVS), a grassroots group active in the region for over ten years, the Ranvir Sena even has a program of life insurance: "Their families get paid Rs. 100,000 (US$2,500) if they get killed in a massacre, in the line of duty." Reportedly, the Ranvir Sena has sophisticated arms, including semi-automatics bought with money raised through donation drives.

Confrontations over Land

Dissatisfied with the pace of reforms, or the lack thereof, the underground armed movement of CPI(M-L) first launched a "land grab" movement in the early 1970s. Under the protection of CPI(M-L), sharecroppers began harvesting crops on upper-caste land in Bihar's central districts as Naxalite cadres burned grain storages and imposed economic blockades on hundreds of acres of land that landlords were forcibly kept from cultivating. Blockades were often accompanied by labor strikes. The Ranvir Sena, and other senas before it, emerged to curb the movement and to quash its economic blockade.

Wages in these areas have ranged from two kilograms of rice to Rs. 25 a day (US$0.63). Women have consistently been paid less. The Minimum Wages Act, legislated as early as 1948, and revised many times thereafter, now prescribes a daily wage of Rs. 32 (US$0.80), but Dalit demands for minimum wages have resulted in a violent backlash from landlords and their caste-based armies. According to government figures for 1995 and 1996, 84.9 percent of landowners in the state are marginal farmers owning less than five hectares each. With landholding ranging between five and twenty bighas (3.1 to 12.4 acres), even the slightest increase in wages paid to laborers would eat into the farmers' minimal profits.

A representative from the People's Union for Democratic Rights (PUDR), a well-respected national human rights organization that has previously documented abuses by security forces, was a member of a fact-finding team that visited Bihar to investigate police raids on Dalit villages in the aftermath of massacres in 1997. He explained the relevance of land to the conflict:

> There are many fallow lands in these districts: at least thirty to forty acres in each village. With the Ranvir Sena in place, the land comes under the cultivation of landowners. Other villages have [Dalit] cooperatives, villages where the CPI(M-L) is stronger. The money from the cooperatives goes to lawyers who are fighting cases filed by the police against them [Dalits]. Their major aim is revolution... Even marginal upper-caste farmers employ Dalits to push the wages down. The agricultural laborers are largely Dalits, so the upper castes are united in this

> way... Dalits don't live in the same settlements. The Mushahars, who are the lowest of the Dalits in these areas, are always segregated. They are also the poorest and the strength of these movements. They are the ones targeted in police raids and massacres when they are unorganized and unprotected by CPI(M-L). Their belongings are small, so it is easy to destroy their livelihood and take them to a stage of destitution.

Between April 1995 and July 11, 1996, the date of the Bathani Tola massacre, forty-six people were killed on both sides in battles between the Ranvir Sena and CPI(M-L) in Bhojpur district. According to press reports, over 400 people, many of them civilians, were killed in conflict between the two organizations in 1997. Although the number of fatalities on both sides is high, the state's treatment of the two camps differs significantly.

The raping of women is a common tactic employed by members of the Ranvir Sena and other caste militias to spread terror in lower-caste communities. In 1992 over one hundred Dalit women in the Gaya district of Bihar were reportedly raped by the Savarna Liberation Front. Pregnant women and children have also been killed. When members of the People's Union for Democratic Rights asked the Ranvir Sena why they were killing children, they replied, "Because they will grow up to become Naxalites. We kill women because they will give birth to Naxalites." The sena has also been known to loot many of the houses they raid.

Ranvir Sena Massacres

In the districts of central Bihar, over 300 people were killed between 1995 and October 1997 in large-scale massacres committed by the Ranvir Sena. Three massacres since October 1997 have increased number of deaths to over 400. Human rights activists add that many have also been killed in smaller confrontations. Extrajudicial executions of Naxalites, coupled with evidence of police collusion with the Ranvir Sena, as documented below, have led to charges that the sena is being backed by the state administration and non-left political parties to check the growing Naxalite movement. Soon after a January 1999 sena massacre in Shankarbigha village, Jehanabad district, a senior police official was quoted as saying, "The administration would be happy if they kill the real extremists among the Naxalites, but they are killing soft targets like women and children and attacking villages of Dalits and weaker sections, which are unprotected."

Like other senas before it, the Ranvir Sena enjoys considerable political patronage. The sena is said to be dominated by politicians from various parties, including Congress, the Janata Dal, and the Bharatiya Janata Party (BJP), which in 1998 led India's coalition central government. In turn, the BJP has enjoyed Bhumihar support in local elections, as described below. Notorious Ranvir Senaleader Bharmeshwar Singh is also a known BJP activist. While Bihar's former Chief Minister Laloo Prasad Yadav, a member of a powerful backward caste, has accused the BJP of backing the sena, he himself has been blamed for only going after Naxalites, despite vows to disarm caste armies. Moreover, state agents at the village and district level are dominated by upper-caste members who often operate as "functionaries of mainstream political parties [and] are either active with or sympathize with the Ranbir Sena."

According to press reports, in districts across central Bihar, and particularly in Bhojpur district, the police force has traditionally been dominated by Bhumihars and Rajputs. Since the implementation of the Mandal reservations, the OBCs too have been represented, but these are primarily Yadavs and Kurmis who also happen to be the new landowners in the districts. Caste as a factor in the police and administration is relevant in Bhojpur more than anywhere else in Bihar. The reported nexus between sena members and official paramilitary forces has also come under scrutiny:

> According to the officials, the Sena goons received arms training from some former CRPF (Central Reserve Police Force) personnel. Bhojpur [district]... has a tradition of sending its young to the Army and paramilitary forces. While on leave, the paramilitary personnel equip the Sena goons with the latest tactics, keeping them constantly ahead of the Naxalites.

The licensing of guns for sena members came under attack in a report by the People's Union for Democratic Rights:

> According to Home Ministry reports, the Ranbir Sena possesses 4,000 guns, both with and without licences. Until they actually fire their weapons, a group of Ranbir Sena members could be merely a group of landlords carrying legal arms. On the other hand, guns carried by labourers and poor peasants are likely to be unlicenced... The SSP [senior superintendent of police] gave an interesting explanation for not trying to withdraw licences from weapon-wielding members of the Ranbir Sena—that in the present state of agrarian conflict, the state could not protect all the bhumihars. Hence they had to be allowed to have guns for their own security and to safeguard their properties. When asked whether likewise the state was in a position to defend all dalits who did not possess weapons, he maintained a telling silence.

Bihar is also notorious for instances of "booth-capturing" at election time; the practice of forcibly entering voting booths and stealing or rigging ballots. Political candidates ensure their majority vote with the help of senas, whose members kill if necessary. This phenomenon has been covered widely by the press and by human rights groups. The Ranvir Sena was responsible for killing more than fifty people during Bihar's 1995 state election campaign. A 1998 article noted the use of senas in Ara district, Bihar, during the February 1998 national parliamentary elections: "It is a measure of the chicanery and double-standards of most Ara politicians that when the opportunity arises, they do not hesitate in using the sena, though their public posture against the private army is holier than thou."

The impunity with which Ranvir Sena leaders carry out their attacks—at election time and other times—provides further evidence of government support. The police record speaks for itself. None of the Ranvir Sena leaders have been prosecuted for the murder of nineteen Dalits and Muslims in Bathani Tola in 1996 and the murder of eleven in Haibaspur in 1997. In Ekwari village in April 1997, police pried open the doors of lower-caste homes and watched as sena members killed eight residents. No sena member was prosecuted.

The officers were subsequently suspended, then transferred, but they, too, escaped prosecution. A December 1997 massacre in Laxmanpur-Bathe left at least sixty-one Dalits dead. According to survivors in the village, the attackers identified by eyewitnesses were never arrested. Villagers also received threats of a future attack and felt unprotected despite the presence of a police camp in the village. In January and February 1999, the Ranvir Sena killed over thirty people within seventeen days in Shankarbigha and Narayanpur villages. Sena members had announced the attack in local papers two weeks ahead of time.

The state did nothing to stop them. According to an article in The Statesman, a Delhi-based daily, sena members were aided by the police in entering Narayanpur village. State intervention often comes to a halt after the distribution of paltry compensation packages and the posting of police camps in massacre-affected villages. In most villages police camps were located in the upper-caste areas, effectively inaccessible to Dalits and other lower-caste villagers.

Sena members who have been arrested have quickly been released on bail; none have been convicted. By contrast, some Naxalites who have been prosecuted have been awarded death sentences. Not only does the state treat the crimes of the two groups differently, but police and local officials openly tolerate the senas. On August 8, 1995, a little over two weeks after the killing of six Dalits in Sarathua village, the state government announced its decision to ban the Ranvir Sena. Sena members continued to hold meetings and conventions to openly outline their strategy and response to Naxalite attacks. Several leaders wanted by the police were present during one such meeting held on October 8, 1997, in Belaur village, Bhojpur district. The local administration was reportedly fully aware of the meeting and its participants but did nothing to disarm the group or arrest the wanted men.

Shankarbigha and Narayanpur

On the evening of January 25, 1999, at least twenty-two Dalit men, women and children were killed in the village of Shankarbigha, Jehanabad district, by members of the Ranvir Sena. The massacre was the fifth of its kind since July 1996 in which Dalit and lower-caste men, women and children were killed by the sena for their suspected allegiance to CPI(M-L) or MCC.

According to press reports, members of the Ranvir Sena entered eight thatched huts in the village during the night and fired indiscriminately on the occupants. Many of the victims, including several children, were shot in the head and stomach at point-blank range. Police suspected that the attacks were in retaliation for the killing of two sena activists the week before by MCC members. According to Jehanabad District Magistrate P. Amrit, the killers shouted Ranvir Sena slogans throughout the attacks. The village is only ten kilometers away from Laxmanpur-Bathe, the site of the December 1997 sena massacre. Ranvir Sena supporters told Times of India that the sena had planned to kill almost all the Dalits in the village, close to seventy people, but were unable to complete their task.

The police ignored early warnings that a massacre was likely. On January 8, 1999, a little over two weeks before the attack, Ranvir Sena leader Bharmeshwar Singh admitted in an interview to a local daily that the sena was planning an attack in Jehanabad district, "with renewed vigour [and] in a very calculat[ed] manner." Singh also admitted that the sena had already chosen its target and was simply waiting for the "right time" to strike. According the CPI(M-L) General Secretary Dipankar Bhattacharya, his group made a written submission to the local administration providing a list of villages deemed vulnerable to sena attacks. A list of "already-accused sena members" was also included.

The National Human Rights Commission, a statutory body set up pursuant to the Protection of Human Rights Act, 1993, has asked the state government to investigate the massacre and prevent a recurrence of such incidents. Twenty-four people were arrested in late January 1999 in connection to the massacre, all of whom belong to the Bhumihar caste. Activists are pessimistic, however, that any will be prosecuted.

A little over two weeks after the Shankarbigha massacre, on the night of February 10, 1999, the sena attacked neighboring Narayanpur village. Sena members killed twelve and injured seven. According to press reports, over one hundred heavily armed sena members descended on the village during the night and forced their way into homes, shooting at will. The attack, which began at 9:00 p.m., lasted for one hour. The police did not arrive until 8:00 a.m. the following morning. Bihar Governor Sunder Singh Bhandari stated that a "lack of vigil and alertness [had] led to a repeat of yet another strike by the Ranvir Sena."

In a press release issued soon after the incident, the Ranvir Sena claimed responsibility for both massacres. Shamsher Bahadur Singh, leader and spokesman for the sena, stated that sena members were forced to "take up arms to save the honour, dignity, and life and property of the innocent farmers." The killings were meant as retaliation for the deaths of farmers at the hands of Naxalites over the past thirty years.

On February 12, 1999, the Indian president dismissed the state government and imposed federal rule in Bihar, citing as the reason a breakdown of law and order and constitutional machinery. The following day, paramilitary forces numbering in the thousands were dispatched to the state. Two days later, on February 14, CPI(M-L) Liberation members reportedly gunned down seven people, including four upper-caste Bhumihars who were said to be Ranvir Sena supporters, at Usri Bazaar, Jehanabad district. The police alleged that the attack was in retaliation for the killings in Shankarbigha and Narayanpur. In early March 1999, the central government reversed its decision to impose president's rule. As of this writing, Bihar's state government, with Rabri Devi as the chief minister, had been reinstated. Sena leaders Bharmeshwar Singh and Shamsher Bahadur Singh had yet to be arrested.

Laxmanpur-Bathe

On the evening of December 1, 1997, armed sena activists crossed the Sone river into the village of Laxmanpur-Bathe where 180 families lived. They raided fourteen Dalit homes and killed a total of sixty-one people: sixteen children, twenty-seven women, and eighteen men. In some families, three generations were killed. Twenty people were also seriously injured. As most of the men fled the village when the attack began, women and children numbered high among the fatalities. During the attack, at least five girls around fifteen years of age were raped and mutilated before being shot in the chest by members of the Ranvir Sena. Most of the victims allegedly belonged to families of Party Unity supporters; the group had been demanding more equitable land distribution in the area.

The village of Laxmanpur-Bathe has no electricity and is virtually inaccessible by road. In crossing the Sone river to reach the village, sena members reportedly also killed five members of the Mallah (fisherman) community and murdered the three Mallah boatmen who had ferried them across the river on their way back. According to newspaper reports, the main reason for the attack was that the Bhumihars wanted to seize fifty acres of land that had been earmarked for distribution among the landless laborers of the village.

A group of peasants, reportedly affiliated with Naxalite activity, was ready to take up arms against them. Authorities apparently knew of the tensions but "had not cared to intervene in the land dispute and nip the trouble in the bud and instead allowed things to come to a head." Following widespread publicity about the massacre, Bihar Chief Minister Rabri Devi suspended the Jehanabad district superintendent of police and replaced several senior officers.

According to villagers who survived the attack, close to one hundred members of the Ranvir Sena arrived en masse and entered the front houses of the village: "Their strategy was to do everything simultaneously so that no one could be forewarned."

Local police had been aware of the possibility of violence long before the Bathe massacre. On November 25, 1997, sena leaders openly held a strategy meeting seven kilometers away from Bathe. Sena leader Shamsher Bahadur Singh had also been touring the area in the months before the massacre openly seeking donations from supporters. Police officers claimed to be aware of these meetings but dismissed them as routine—missing yet another opportunity to intervene and preempt a sena attack. One officer was quoted as saying, "It's like crying wolf. The Communist Party of India (M-L) keeps sending us complaint letters every week, we can't take action every time."

According to members of Bihar Dalit Vikas Samiti, a grassroots organization, the events that unfolded in Bathe were more complex than a random attack on a Dalit hamlet: CPI was organizing in Bathe because the residents were so poor and exploited, they couldn't even feed themselves after a full day's work. When they asked for more wages, they were beaten down even more. Some CPI(M-L) and Party Unity people had a split. A few people leftthem and gave information about party activities to landlords. The landlords contacted Ranvir Sena in Bhojpur, saying that they needed help controlling them. The Ranvir Sena came out at 4:00 p.m. They ate and drank liquor with the landlords and attacked at 9:00 p.m. They had a list of whom to attack but got drunk and killed anyone and everyone. The activists also claimed that the purpose of Bathe was "to teach others not to rebel or raise a voice.

Since the massacre, police protection in Bathe has remained grossly inadequate. The Bihar government announced soon after the Bathe killings that police would be deployed in the area to set up camp and maintain law and order. However, when parliamentary elections were later announced, the police force was directed to control election-related violence. Despite their dual assignment of controlling the Ranvir Sena and watching the polls, the police seemed more intent on conducting raids on Dalit villages in the name of controlling "extremism" and seeking out Naxalite cadres than on protecting Dalit villagers.

Police response to attacks is hindered by insufficient funding, infrastructure, and equipment for village-based police camps. These arguments fail, however, when one notes the frequency of police search and raid operations on remote Dalit villages. Tis officers had enough guns to provide security, and are able to communicate quickly with the area police station, he claimed that more men and more facilities were needed and that the roads to the village were in very poor condition. Road construction had begun soon after the massacre but came to a halt when "VIPs" stopped visiting the area.

On January 9, 1998, nine people suspected to be supporters of the Ranvir Sena were killed by CPI(M-L) activists in Chouram village, forty-five kilometers from Jehanabad. The killings were reportedly in retaliation for the Bathe massacre. The attackers opened fire indiscriminately on the victims as they were returning home from a funeral. Several Dalits in the Bathe area were subsequently taken into custody by the police. Bathe villagers claim that the sena members were actually killed by Marxist-Leninist party members who were not from their village. Despite the arrests immediately after the massacre, as of February 1999 none of the sena members responsible for the Bathe attack had been prosecuted.

Ekwari

On the morning of April 10, 1997, members of the Ranvir Sena gunned down eight residents of Ekwari village in Bhojpur district in an operation that lasted two hours. Police officers stationed nearby forced open the villagers' houses and then stood by and watched as the massacre took place. Seven of the eight killed belonged to the lower-caste Lohars, Chamars, Dhobis and Kahars. The village is known to many as the birthplace of CPI(M-L) in the 1970s.

An article in *The Telegraph*, a Calcutta-based daily, reported that the attackers raped two women before killing them: a fifteen-year-old girl and a woman who was eight months pregnant. A ten-year-old boy was shot in the head. The partisan role of the police could not have been clearer. While policemen pried open doors of houses, the Ranbir Sena activists followed them in and mowed the people down. Sunaina Devi, an eyewitness to the murder of her father-in-law and sister-in-law, said that when they refused to open their doors, the policemen broke them open and let the killers in... Sagar Mahato said he saw the police running away and watching from a distance.

The article also reported that the CPI(M-L) Politburo member and member of legislative assembly, Ram Naresh Ram, claimed that the murders were premeditated and that police were bribed by the landlords. A probable cause of the conflict, a villager added, was that many acres of land were lying fallow in the village due to a blockade imposed by the CPI(M-L).

A police camp had been established in upper-caste territory, an area inaccessible to Dalits who were afraid to cross the road dividing the two parts of the village. In the Ekwari village police camp there were two sub-inspectors, one sub-inspector BMP (Bihar Military Police), and seventeen constables, making a total of twenty officers. A second camp located near the village fields had nineteen officers. The sub-inspector claimed that the police presence was sufficient to maintain law and order in the village. At the time of the massacre, he was on assignment at the police station eight kilometers away.

There was a fight between CPI(M-L) and the Ranvir Sena. One Ranvir Sena member was killed. Eight CPI(M-L) were killed some days later. They were not members of CPI(M-L) but were killed based on caste. They have been fighting for years. People are killed on both sides. All have been arrested and charged. Thirty-six were named; approximately thirty were from the Ranvir Sena. All are in jail. There is only one absconder. He escaped from jail. When a CPI(M-L) dies, it's always the Ranvir Sena; when a Ranvir Sena dies it is always a CPI(M-L) who kills. We also caught the CPI(M-L) who killed the Ranvir Sena. We are here for now and most likely will stay for a while.

In the aftermath of the killings, seven police officers were suspended. Another police camp officer claimed that the suspensions were a political move. "Both sides are political, so whenever there are problems there is a lot of pressure on the state, the superintendent of police, the district magistrate. So in order to remove the pressure they suspend officers.

The same officers come back on duty in a different police station." When asked to describe the current situation, the sub-inspector responded that it was "peaceful and normal. There's been so much violence here that even one murder every few months is considered peaceful. Labor is an ongoing problem. It's a very old problem. Whenever killings take place, there is a strike. But now work is ongoing."

Residents of the Dalit and backward-caste hamlet agreed. They explained that work had started again, but "there was a lot of fear" and little protection. Although CPI(M-L) is active in the village, the lower-caste villagers claim that the "Ranvir Sena is more powerful. They have rifles, semi-automatics, and guns. We only have sticks." The head of the lower-caste section of the village was also apprehensive about the police and had little faith in the protection they provided.

Police are here for law and order. They see what's going on, but they are allied with the Ranvir Sena. They get money and food from the forward castes so they favor the forward castes. The police don't care about the poor. We don't go to the police, nor any other state agencies. We asked for help from the Bhumihars to keep the killings low. They said they cannot control them even though the Bhumihar population belongs to the Ranvir Sena. We have no protection.

According to the former deputy superintendent of police (DSP) for Bhojpur district, Bihar, the April 1997 attack was due to "police negligence": The police completely failed in giving protection. They went in one house, and the Ranvir Sena went into another. The guards did nothing to protect them. The Ranvir Sena killed everyone in the police's presence. By the time the station police came, the Ranvir Sena had run away.

The former DSP went on to describe the situation of women and children. There are 106 widows in Ekwari. At least fifty women have also been killed in the past several years. The Dalit men go to jail and get sentenced, while the Ranvir Sena has enough money to fight the case all the way to the Supreme Court. Dalit women are made homeless, and the children cannot go to school because the family needs the money to fight the cases against the men. The Ranvir Sena cares only about high numbers. They also rape the women. The police send innocent people to jail. No one can surrender for fear of so-called police encounters. They do not get justice from the police. That is the main factor.

Even the landlords of the village (members of the Ranvir Sena) complained that the police, under pressure to maintain "law and order" in their jurisdiction, have arrested indiscriminately on both sides. First the police were with us, now they have left us. Since 1995 the police have really bothered us. In April, people were killed here. They killed one farmer and destroyed all crops. Seven CPI(M-L) were killed by Ranvir Sena for retaliation. The police just take care of the dead bodies. They don't really help. In response to the April massacre, the police destroyed a landowner's house after arresting him. They also arrested thirty-nine people. All landowners were innocent. They were not part of the Ranvir Sena. The police were also involved in the Ranvir Sena massacre. Seven people were suspended. The police are not with anybody they are trying to scare people. They always capture the innocent, even when CPI(M-L) strike. As of February 1999, none of the sena members or police officers responsible for the killings in Ekwari had been prosecuted.

Haibaspur

On March 23, 1997, ten landless laborers were killed in Haibaspur village in Patna district, Bihar, apparently for aligning themselves with the CPI(M-L) Party Unity. Before leaving the village, the Ranvir Sena inscribed its organization's name in blood on the rim of a dry well. Party Unity forces retaliated within a month by killing six Ranvir Sena supporters on April 21, 1997. According to BDVS activists, alcohol and the rape of Dalit women by the Bhumihar men played a role in the attack on the village: The Dalits made alcohol, and Bhumihars drank it. When Bhumihars fought among themselves, they went to the Mushahars [Dalits], gave them drinks, and got them to take revenge on their enemies by taking their field crops and so on. But the Dalits were working for both sides so the Bhumihars killed them. They were double-crossing them. They only gave them liquor to get them to do the work. Bhumihars give them money to make the liquor, then give some liquor to the Dalits to get them to do the work. Whoever makes alcohol also pays a commission to the police. When the Bhumihars came and drank, they also raped the Mushahar women. Mushahar men did not like it so they protested and were killed. The people killed were mostly innocent, but these are the two reasons it happened.

According to an article in *The Hindu*, a Madras-based daily, although the police were informed immediately of the Haibaspur killings, they did not arrive on the scene until the following morning, after hearing that the chief minister was due to visit the site.

Bathani Tola

In response to the Ranvir Sena attack on the Dalit hamlet of Bathani Tola in July 1996, then-Home Minister Indrajit Gupta expressed dissatisfaction with police protection in the affected region. Even though four police camps had been posted in the area, Gupta charged that they were, "paralysed, impotent and did nothing." Residents of the village claimed that most of the main perpetrators were still roaming freely in their village, though the police claimed to have arrested all sixty men involved. A new police camp was soon set up near the site but was considered largely ineffective in checking threats from upper-caste landlords. "They are at the beck and call of the landlords. Their food comes from the landlords' houses. How can they render us justice?" one villager asked.

Despite signs of rising tensions in the area, police neglected to shift their picket (booth) to Bathani Tola. On July 26, 1996, the Bombay-based daily Indian Express reported that officials had received written notification of the possibility of an attack. In a letter dated July 4, 1996, to the district magistrate, the Bhojpur district committee of CPI(M-L) complained that the Ranvir Sena had "renewed its campaign of terror in the villages" and charged that the night before, "a gang of the Ranbir Sena [had] been engaged in indiscriminate firing."

The committee added that there was much tension and fear and urged the district magistrate to "take strong action immediately." CPI(M-L) had also sent requests for protection on June 26, June 29, and July 2. According to press reports, Superintendent of Police S. N. Pradhan dismissed the letters as "routine." The killings took place on July 11. During the attack itself, the police reportedly made no attempts to intervene despite being on duty a "stone's throw" away from the scene. Soon after the incident the chief minister suspended police officers stationed in camps near the tola, but failed to prosecute them.

Government Compensation Packages

Instead of prosecuting accused sena members or taking action against colluding police officials, official action in cases of caste-based killings in Bihar has generally come to a halt after a few officers have been temporarily suspended and surviving family members have received the preliminary disbursements of their compensation money. The promised relief package has often included food rations, temporary manual labor jobs, and when the victims were Dalit and poor, an offer to build pucca (solid) houses. Solid houses are essential for instilling a sense of security for villagers whose flimsy mud huts are easier targets for police and sena raids. The government, however, has seldom followed through with promised relief packages.

In Shankarbigha, the government promised monetary compensation, a government job, and pucca housing to the victims' dependents. Two and a half weeks later, in Narayanpur, the government promised Rs. 140,000 (US$3,500) to each of the victims' dependents. In Bathe, the Paswan family lost seven of its members. It received Rs. 100,000 for every family member killed from the Bihar and central government, for a total of Rs. 1,400,000 (US$35,000).

The family used the interest from the money to construct a new house. Even though the entire village remained vulnerable to future attacks, pucca houses were only provided to the families of those that were killed. According to BDVS Director Dr. Jose Kananaikal, "Over 2,000 people have visited in the two months following Bathe. But now nobody cares. The chief minister also said they would get land, but that never happened. They also promised a school and a road, but that didn't happen either."

When the chief minister arrived at the Haibaspur massacre site, he promised a compensation package to the families of the victims but failed to disarm the sena members responsible for the killings. The government announced Rs. 120,000 (US$3,000) as compensation for each victim. It also assured work and food rations for three months and promised pucca houses for the entire Dalit hamlet.

In February 1998, almost a year after the massacre, a civil rights fact-finding team reported that only Rs. 20,000 (US$500) had been paid, that no work or food rations had been provided, and that the houses had only been partially constructed. Moreover, police raids since the beginning of 1998 had destroyed the little construction that had taken place. Dalit residents were also unwilling to work in adjoining villages where they were earlier employed for fear of another orchestrated attack by their employers.

The State's Targeting of Naxalites

Although both the Naxalites and the private militias share the responsibility for increased violence and deaths in the state, the state's response to the Naxalites has been markedly different. Police have frequently operated as agents of the landed upper castes, conducting raids on Dalit villages and disguising killings as "encounters." According to a People's Union for Democratic Rights report, "The administration bans both the Ranveer Sena and the CPI(M-L) Party Unity but in effect treats them differently. [T]he judiciary is [also] influenced bythe social and political background of the people concerned." PUDR members also believe that the government is under pressure to show that the killings will be stopped, but its actions have focused primarily on Naxalite activities.

Many are arrested under Criminal Procedure Code Section 107 for preventive detention. The Supreme Court has stated that the detention cannot be more than twenty-four hours, but in many cases it takes fifteen to thirty days to get a lawyer; sympathetic lawyers are already overburdened. The charges are bailable but they have no property, no surety. So they remain in jail for long periods of time... They won't settle land disputes because land is in the hands of landlords. So they treat it as a law and order issue and arrest and raid instead.

The pattern of extrajudicial executions by security forces in disturbed areas and by police forces in Naxalite-affected areas has been documented by international human rights organizations and Indian civil liberties groups. The police routinely claim that the killings occur in so-called encounters. The People's Union for Civil Liberties, the largest civil rights organization in the country, has described the use of the term "encounter killing" as a unique contribution of the police in India to the vocabulary of human rights... it represents in most cases the taking into custody of an individual or a group, torture and subsequent murder. The death generally occurs as a result of the brutal torture or stage-managed extermination in an appropriate area. An official press release then elaborately outlines a confrontation, an encounter where the police claim to have fired in "self-defence."

Such tactics have long been used against suspected Naxalites. In the southern state of Andhra Pradesh, the Naxalite threat has been used to justify state violence against all forms of peasant resistance and against other critics of state policy. A pattern of systematic human rights violations that has formed part of the state government's counterinsurgency efforts. Since 1968, security forces have murdered hundreds of villagers, guerrilla group sympathizers, and suspected militants in the state.

On April 15, 1994, police reportedly killed eleven MCC members in an "encounter" in Gaya district, Bihar. According to a report by People's Union for Democratic Rights, since then, "there has been a significant rise in the number of people killed in this manner." On December 27, 1997, an "encounter" took place in Kodihara village, Patna district. At 5:30 a.m. that day, the police entered the village and caught hold of and beat people who were going out to work. There was a Naxalite squad in the village which noticed the arrival of the police and slipped away. The police fired at them but they escaped. Two of them hid in the fields nearby, but the police soon found them. The two of them handed over their weapons to the police and offered (to) surrender. But the police shot them dead in cold blood. This murder was seen by all the villagers assembled there. Villagers reported that after searching Kodihara, police moved on to Jhunauti. The raid on Jhunauti is described below.

Police have also repeatedly engaged in excessive use of force when dealing with Naxalites. On July 3, 1995, four Party Unity members were killed and eight arrested. The following month, the police fired into a crowd of 500 people gathered at a CPI(M-L) Liberation office in Begusurai town soon after they lathi-charged a peaceful protest on land reforms. Five people were killed, and one was seriously injured. Sixty-five people, including twenty-nine women, were arrested on charges of rioting and illegal assembly.

Three people were additionally charged with murder and attempted murder. All those arrested were severely beaten in police custody. In this incident, as in the two described above, the police claimed to have fired in self-defense, while villagers and other eyewitnesses claimed that the firing was one-sided. Post mortems were conducted immediately, and the bodies were quickly disposed of, eliminating any possibility of independent autopsies for verification of the manner of death.

Police raids

Under the pretext of seeking out Naxalite militants police have conducted raids on Dalit villages and falsely arrested those accused of harboring Naxalites. In some cases, federal paramilitary forces have been deployed. Like the private militias, police have sexually assaulted women and attacked children who remained behind after the men fled the villages. Women have also been arrested and taken into custody in order to punish their families and force their male relatives to surrender. After the Ekwari village massacre of April 1997, police conducted search operations in neighboring lower-caste hamlets. Women were molested and beaten, and local residents alleged that police took Rs. 5,000 (US$125) from them. As noted in a PUDR report:

> The loot of property and molestation of women by policemen in the course of [the post-Ekwari] search is a fairly common feature of routine police searches in poor settlements. So searches end up as punitive measures inflicted upon a section of the populace already targeted by the Ranbir Sena. Search operations in upper caste localities are not only rare but also very cursory.

A ten-member team comprising members of seven civil liberties organizations visited sixteen villages in Patna and Jehanabad district, Bihar, in February 1998. Their mandate was to investigate reports of abuses committed by Bihar police deployed to protect Dalits in the aftermath of the 1997 massacres. The team's report described the raids:

> In the course of the raids, the police routinely abuse women in the most vulgar and offensive language... [T]here are no women police at all in the raid. It is the male police [who] enter the houses without consideration for the woman's privacy. They abuse the women whose sons/husbands they are looking for. One frequent [accusation] is that the woman has sent her husband away "so that she may sleep with the extremists." Women who are going to the fields in the early morning cold are forced to remove the chaddar [blanket] so that the police may see whether they are hiding any arms or ammunition underneath. These "suspicions" are only meant to insult and humiliate women.

The report added:

> The raids are frequent and create fear and terror among the poorer classes who are suspected of harbouring Naxalites. These raids are common in villages where the landless agricultural labourers organised by the various sangathans [meetings] of the CPI(M-L) organisations have fought for wage increases and occupation of gair mazarua [government] land. In some villages the raids are very frequent. Jhunauti [Jehanabad district, Bihar]

> was subjected to at least twenty raids in the last two months. In Andhrachak, Jehanabad district, Bihar, there is one raid every week. Sevanan, Jehanabad district, Bihar, is subjected to at least two raids a week.

Raid in Andhrachak

On February 10, 1998, some 300 police officers, including members of the Special Reserve Police Force, surrounded fifty homes and arrested six people in In Andhrachak village. The eyevitness says:

> The first time they came at 4:30 p.m., they didn't take anyone. They came into all the houses. They took my friend's torches, his tobacco box and Rs. 500 out of the money box. They ransacked all the rooms and broke the pots and doors. We ran because we were afraid of being beaten... They also beat my brother's wife with the butt of their gun. They hit her on her backside; she had to seek treatment. The second time they came it was 4:00 a.m. The people they arrested were also beaten with sticks. They were charged under Criminal Procedure Code 107 [preventive detention]. I went to jail to get them released. They said they would only give bail after [national parliamentary] elections. They say it is Rs. 1,000 (US$25) for bail. We will have to get a loan or a bond.

The police told villagers upon arriving that they came in search of guns and that they suspected Naxalite activity in the area. But as sixty-year-old Sona Devi explained, "Where are we going to get guns from? We don't even have money for food, clothes or a home." Devi complained that the police never went to the landlords' houses: "They are the ones that have guns." She claimed that the Ranvir Sena was operational in Kayal, an adjacent village where Dalits laborers worked. "The Kayal people call the sena in to scare us and threaten us. We are afraid of them. They will kill us. They have already killed two Dalits in the field before... The Kayal village people tell police we are Naxalites, but no one goes and sees their Ranvir Sena activities."

Devi also reported that nine to ten days before the police raid, Bhumihar men came to the village to threaten its residents. "They said if you touch us, harm us, or don't work in the fields, then we will send the Ranvir Sena to set fire to the villages and kill everyone." The villagers did not go to the police, explaining that they "are afraid of them also, they [the sena and the police] are all together." Other women in the village claimed that members of the Sena had "misbehaved" with them. "They come in the night and beat the men and rape the women. It has happened many times. They beat the women too and rip their clothes off. The police don't do anything."

Raid in Jhunauti

The village of Jhunauti in Jehanabad district, Bihar, has over 190 Dalit households. Over one hundred Bhumihar families live adjacent to them in the same village. Since 1997, police have raided the village more than five times. According to a fifty-five-year-old Dalit agricultural laborer in the village:

> "The raids take place mostly at night. Once it happened during the day. Two times they took people away; once they misbehaved with women; usually they break everything and take our chickens. In December 1997 they came at 7:30 p.m., there were thirty-five to forty police. That is when they misbehaved with the women and broke everything. Everyone runs away when they come.

The village school teacher, who was present during the December 1997 raid, explained the reason for it:

> There is no Ranvir Sena in Jhunauti, but the police harass us. They found a gun at one laborer's house so they bothered all of us. In January 1998 they also went to Bhumihars for a raid. During the Kodihara "encounter," CPI(M-L) party people were killed. So they came here for a raid and then to the Bhumihars. In December during the bad episode [Bathe] they only came here... CPI(M-L)) stole a rifle from a landlord, which is what started the raid. But the party does not live here.

The school teacher also asked the police why they were searching the village. They told him they were looking for rifles, guns, and Naxalites and proceeded to enter his house.

Dacoity is defined under Section 391 as robbery committed by five or more persons. Thirty-eight days later, the court was asked for a bail order. The families had to pay Rs. 1,000 to Rs. 5,000 (US$25 to $125) each and were forced to sell their chickens and belongings and to ask for contributions from the village. Most villagers earn only one and a half to two kilograms of rice per day as agricultural laborers.

Many villagers had left their homes out of fear of another raid. Most other villagers had little to say to the fact-finding team as they feared a backlash from the police. One resident explained, "The police harm us so much, that is why they are not talking to you. They beat down the innocent and we can never ask why. They say we are Naxalites. They are only after the Dalits. They do not to this with Bhumihars."

Extortion and looting

Police throughout India engage in extortion, motivated in part by their need to pay off debts incurred for securing their positions through bribes—a cycle that has been documented both by Indian civil rights organizations and by the government's National Police Commission reports. In 1996 it was reported that police inspectors in Bihar were made to pay a bribe of Rs. 100,000 (US$2,500) before being recruited. It is not anomalous, therefore, that raids by the police in the aftermath of massacres have often been accompanied by looting and extortion.

According to the ten-member team's report, on January 6, 1998, police raided the village of Makarpur in Jehanabad district, Bihar. The villagers mistook the police for the Ranvir Sena and began to run. Seven young men were arrested and, after three days of illegal detention, were released after paying a Rs. 5,500 (US$138) bribe. They were threatened with further detentions and beatings if they refused to pay the money. In Nagwan village, Patna district, Bihar, two people were taken to the police station and threatened with being booked for a crime unless they paid Rs. 900 (US$22.50).

In several villages, under the pretense of kurki-japti (attachment of movable property), police have seized the property of those "absconding" in criminal cases. In so doing, they followed none of the legal procedures for seizure, including presentation of a court order and list of materials to be seized, and seizing in the presence of two witnesses. As the report noted of the pattern of behavior:

> The material seized in this looting is of varied kind, and appears to be aimed at destroying the livelihood of people. Grain or rice stored in the house, all possible utensils, chairs, cots and tables, door frames, etc. are taken away. Buffaloes were taken away in Uber village in Jehanabad [district, Bihar]. Goats were also taken away in some villages... In Uber, not satisfied with having taken away the buffaloes, the police asked the householders to give them Rs. 100 (US$2.50) a day to feed the buffaloes.

In some cases, police abandoned the pretense of seizure or attachment of property and engaged in outright looting. In Kodihara village in Patna district police stole jewelry, clothes, Rs. 2,000 (US$50), and consumables collected in preparation for a marriage from a villager's house. The raids have had a devastating effect on the livelihood of villagers who earned two kilograms of rice or less than Rs. 25 (US$0.63) a day.

Police Abuse against dalits

Police abuse against the urban poor, slum dwellers, Dalits, and other minorities has included arbitrary detention, torture, extrajudicial executions, and forced evictions. Because they cannot afford to bribe the police, Dalits and other poor minorities are disproportionately represented among those detained and tortured in police custody. Although the acute social discrimination characteristic of rural areas is less pronounced in cities, Dalits in urban areas, who make up the majority of bonded laborers and street cleaners, do not escape it altogether. Many live in segregated colonies which have been targets of police raids.

July 1997 incident in Bombay in which police opened fire on a crowd of Dalits protesting the desecration of a statue of Dr. B. R. Ambedkar in their settlement. The firing, which killed ten and injured twenty-six, was in direct violation of international standards on the use of firearms by law enforcement officials and of Bombay Police Manual guidelines. According to human rights groups and colony residents, the firing was unprovoked and caste-motivated.

On July 11, 1997, residents of Ramabai Ambedkar Nagar, a predominantly Dalit-populated urban colony in Bombay, woke up to find their statue of Dr.Ambedkar desecrated by a garland of sandals around his neck. The placing of shoes or sandals around the neck of the likeness of a person is taken as a sign of extreme disrespect and is usually an attempt to denigrate that person and his or her beliefs. When residents complained of the desecration to Local Beat No. 5 Pantnagar Police, located ten feet away from the statue, they were told to lodge a complaint at the Pantnagar police station. By 7:00 a.m. the growing crowd began protesting and blocked the Eastern Express Highway in front of the colony. Within minutes, members of the Special Reserve Police Force (SRPF), led by Sub-Inspector M. Y. Kadam, arrived in a van and stopped in front of the colony, hundreds of meters away from the statue and the protests on the highway.

SRPF constables opened fire on pedestrians on the service road in front of the colony and later into alleys between colony houses. The firing lasted for ten to fifteen minutes and killed ten people. Most of the victims were shot above the waist. Sub-Inspector Kadam and his SRPF constables left soon after the firing, only to be replaced by the city police and other SRPF members. Four hours later, at 11:30 a.m., at a site 150 meters away from the firing and 300 meters away from the desecrated statute, an angry crowd set fire to a luxury bus. At 2:00 p.m. twenty to twenty-five police officers entered Ramabai colony, started spreading tear gas, and began lathi-charging residents in their homes. At 4:00 p.m. they lathi-charged again. By late afternoon, twenty-six people had been seriously injured, and Local Beat No. 5 had been destroyed by protesters. Sub-Inspector Kadam, who ordered the firing, had a number of cases of "atrocities" against Dalits pending against him. Kadam's former supervisor and SRPF commandant Vasant Ingle had previously charged Kadam with being "anti-Dalit": he had accused Kadam of mistreating a subordinate for "casteist reasons" and had ordered his suspension for violating the Scheduled Castes and Scheduled Tribes (Prevention of Atrocities) Act, 1989. Ingle has also charged that Kadam's excessive use of force in dealing with Ramabai residents was a direct result of his caste prejudice. Kadam has denied this charge.

The Ramabai incident led to significant unrest throughout the state of Maharashtra, including rioting and social boycotts against protesting Dalits. A two-member team of the Indian People's Human Rights Commission (IPHRC), a Bombay-based NGO, visited the districts of Nagpur, Amravati, Yavatmal, and Wardha in October 1997 to investigate violence against Dalits in the wake of disturbances related to protests against the Ramabai incident. According to an article in the *Times of India*, the team concluded that in various villages, "the police had abetted supporters of the ruling Shiv Sena-BJP alliances... in committing atrocities on Dalits and terrorising them" and that "the people owing allegiance to the ruling alliance parties had made determined efforts to terrorise and punish the Buddhists [converted Dalits] for having dared to protest against the shameful act of desecration of the Ambedkar statue." According to IPHRC, such efforts included the stripping and parading of a Dalit woman in Karanja-Ghadge village in Wardha district. She was later reportedly framed for murder by the police after she complained of her ill-treatment.

Soon after the firing, the Maharashtra state government appointed a commission of inquiry, headed by Justice S. D. Gundewar, to determine whether "the steps taken by the police to deal with the large crowd and to disperse it were adequate, in accordance with the procedure established for riot control," or if the force used was excessive. The commission was also asked to report on measures, general or specific, "which are required to be taken by the police and the administration to avoid such occurrence in the future."

According to several eyewitness accounts and fact-finding reports, including that of the Indian People's Human Rights Commission, the National Alliance of People's Movements, and the Air Corporation SC/ST Employees Association, the firing went on intermittently for at least fifteen minutes. In a statement of claim submitted before the Gundewar Commission of Inquiry, an eyewitness described the manner in which the police began firing. Before firing they "did not lathi-charge, burst tear gas shells, fire a few rounds in the air or... make any serious, positive efforts to disperse people" but instead, "in a designed manner, deliberately, intentionally opened fire on innocent masses."

Monk Kashyap also witnessed the shooting of Sukhdev Kapadne, Kaushaliyabhai, Amar Dhanawade, Vilas Dodke, and Anil Garud, all of whom "died on the spot." After the initial firing, police charged forward into the housing areas. Once they were fully inside the colony, the firing continued. Most residents were caught completely by surprise. One of the bullets hit Bablu Verma and killed him: "He trembled like a fish and died. If someone tried to help him they would shoot at him too. He was twenty-six years old." Shridevi Giri was also injured by bullets. "I was hit in the arm twice," she said as she showed us her scars. Another woman stepped into the alley and saw her husband shot: "I was standing outside my door and saw the bullet hit my husband in the stomach." Babu

Phulekar was also standing in the alley and was also injured. V. S. Khade, a prominent member of the community, confirmed the manner of attack: "They did not say anything. There was no lathi-charge, no tear gas, no bubble bullets, just a direct firing." Khade lost his nephew's son in the firing.

He used to stay with us more after his mother died in 1994. On that day he was going to work. The crowds wouldn't allow him to cross the highway. So he came back and told my wife and my daughter not to go outside. Then he went to inform his father, who was one kilometer away. Before he could get there he was shot and killed. His brother and uncle went to pick him up, but the police shouted, "Don't touch him or we'll shoot you too." I heard the shots. When I arrived he was already dead. He was only seventeen.

Soon after the incident took place, colony residents proceeded to the Pantnagar police station to lodge a complaint against the police involved in the firing. The police refused to record or register a complaint. By 11:00 a.m. all the bodies had been transported to the hospital, though none had been taken by the police. Colony residents described the scene later that day:

> There were hundreds of officers. They tried to keep everyone quiet. There was no firing and no lathi-charge. Then at 2:00 p.m. twenty to twenty-five police came in the colony and started spreading tear gas. They shouted, "Close your doors and windows and don't come out." People went back inside. One person was injured from the tear gas. He was burned from the thighs down. The police left soon thereafter, but people were still going to the hospital until 11:00 p.m. that night. Everyone who died on the spot. On the spot they killed ten people.

National and International Standards on the Use of Firearms

The indiscriminate use of lethal force against unarmed demonstrators contravenes key provisions of the United Nations Basic Principles on the Use of Force and Firearms by

Law Enforcement Officials, which *inter alia* states: Law enforcement officials, in carrying out their duty, shall, as far as possible, apply non-violent means before resorting to the use of force and firearms. Whenever the lawful use of force and firearms is unavoidable, law enforcement officials shall: (a) Exercise restraint in such use and act in proportion to the seriousness of the offence and the legitimate objective to be achieved; (b) Minimize damage and injury, and respect and preserve human life ....

With respect to the policing of unlawful assemblies, Article 13 of the Basic Principles dictates that, "in the dispersal of unlawful assemblies that are unlawful but non-violent, law enforcement officials shall avoid the use of force or, where that is not praticable, shall restrict such force to the minimum extent necessary." Article 14 adds that, "in the dispersal of violent assemblies, law enforcement officials may use firearms only when less dangerous means are not practicable and only to the minimum extent. Law enforcement officials shall not use firearms in such cases, except under conditions stipulated in principle 9." Principle 9 allows for the use of firearms in cases of self-defense or defense of others against the imminent threat of death or serious injury.

The Basic Principles also state that: "Governments shall ensure that arbitrary or abusive use of force and firearms by law enforcement officials is punished as a criminal offence under their law."

Many of the steps taken by the Special Reserve Police were also in clear violation of the Bombay Police Manual provisions on riot control. Relevant provisions and the police's defense before the Gundewar Commission of Inquiry are outlined below. According to Rule No. 59 of the manual: It should be accepted as a cardinal principle that troops of armed police engaged in suppression of disorder should in no circumstances be brought into such close contact with a hostile mob which greatly outnumbers them as to lead to the risk of their being committed to hand-to-hand struggle. Apart from the danger of their being rushed or deprived of their arms, it is impossible in these circumstances to exercise adequate fire control and the effect of fire at such close quarters is, therefore, likely to be unnecessarily severe.

By its own admission, the state reserve police present at the scene brought itself into close contact with the crowd, fired shots in the air, and, according to several eyewitnesses and a fact-finding report, all but one person killed had bullet wounds above the waistline. Even assuming that there was a "riotous mob" in need of control, SRPF forces seemed to have reversed the conventional riot control protocol. Rather than proceeding from a lathi-charge to tear gas, firing in the air, and firing below the waist, they first fired above the waist, then administered tear gas, and on two occasions in the afternoon, lathi-charged residents in their homes after beating down their doors.

The lathi-charge included severe beatings of two women both of whom "bore the marks of lathi-charge on their hands and feet." In a statement of claim submitted on behalf of the police department to the Gundewar Commission of Inquiry, the police claimed that a total of fifty rounds were fired: four in the air and seven just north of the first firing. They did not account for the remaining thirty-nine rounds. Witnesses have challenged the police's claim that only fifty rounds were fired.. As Khade explained: "They fired for fifteen minutes_ But ten people were killed and so many were injured. A few people were shot two or three times. So how could it be that only fifty bullets were fired?"

The police's statement claims that a mob had set a luxury bus on fire and had stoned several tankers, and that an explosion of those tankers was imminent. According to the police, Sub-Inspector Kadam ordered one of his officers to fire warning shots in the air and upon realizing that the warning shots had no effect on the crowd, he "ordered his rifle section to aim and fire at arsonists and rioteers." They claimed, however, that the firings had no effect on the "mob."

During his deposition before the Gundewar Commission on February 18, 1998, Sub-Inspector Kadam admitted to ordering his subordinates to fire in the air, even though he was aware that the Police Manual prohibited such actions. When asked why he decided to ignore police procedures, Kadam replied that he had read in a newspaper that firing in the air was an effective way to disperse a mob. Rule No. 60 of the Bombay Police Manual, on the use of firearms in dispersing an unlawful assembly, instructs that whenever firing becomes "unavoidable to unruly mobs, it should be ensured that the aim is kept low and directed against the most threatening part of the crowd. Care should be taken not to fire upon persons separated from the crowd nor to fire over the heads of the crowd as thereby innocent persons may be injured. Under no circumstances, should firing in the air be resorted to as experience proves that this leads ultimately to greater loss of life."

The rule goes on to state that "it is impossible to pick out and put out of action individual leaders of a mob" and that "ineffective fire against a really determined mob is likely to influence it further so that the attack will be pressed home and the police overwhelmed." Sub-Inspector Kadam disregarded explicit procedure and ordered his officers to "aim and fire at arsonists and rioteers." The police claimed that the situation was unavoidable and that Kadam's orders needed to be looked at "in light of the situation that [was] faced by the officers on the spot."

Finally, in reference to medical aid during riots and disturbances, Rule 62 confers upon officers the obligation to "do the best they can do to provide medical aid to persons injured on such occasions and, when necessary to convey them to hospitals as quickly as possible." None of the bodies that were taken to the hospital that day were taken by the police. Moreover, anyone attempting to administer aid to the injured was immediately ordered to step away or face the same consequences.

An amateur video of the events was submitted by the police as documentation of the department's claim that the firing was necessary to control a mob on its way to setting gas tankers on fire. The video, the police claimed, "vividly depicts the incidents of arson, the black billowing clouds emanating from the rear of the LPG [liquefied petroleum gas] tankers, the northward movement of the police party and subsequent arrival of fire brigade and dousing of fire."

The authenticity of the video, however, has been called into question. A human rights NGO that examined the video concluded that the tape was doctored. It pointed to the video's choppy editing and the presence of two different backgrounds for incidents that police claim took place at the same scene. Closer examination of the video, eyewitness reports, and NGO fact-finding missions all confirm that the burning of public property that the police use as justification for their actions at 7:00 a.m. in fact took place much later in the day at a site hundreds of meters away.

The Indian People's Human Rights Commission issued a scene-by-scene analysis of the two-minute video, exposing inconsistencies between shots. Background scenes in the video provide evidence of two separate locales: Ramabai Colony and Nalanda Nagar, which is located some 150 meters away from Ramabai and approximately 300 meters away from the agitation around the statue. Although a luxury bus was set on fire, this occurred at around 11:30 a.m., more than four hours after the Ramabai firing began. Moreover, according to eyewitnesses, two seemingly empty tankers were brought in by the police themselves and placed behind the burning bus in order to "hide their blunder" and to fabricate a defense to the firing.

In its response to allegations received from the United Nations Special Rapporteur on Contemporary Forms of Racism, Racial Discrimination, Xenophobia and Related Intolerance, the government of India put forward the same defense: The gathering became violent and started damaging private and public property. It also tried to set fire to a LPG gas tanker. In order to discourage the mob from doing so (which otherwise would have resulted in extensive damage to human life and property) and for self-defence, the Police resorted to a "Cane-Charge" and subsequently, having failed to control the mob, opened fire. Unfortunately, 10 persons died and 24 persons were injured in the firing 8 police personnel were also injured.

The government also asserted that allegations such as those received pertaining to caste "do not fall within the mandate" of the special rapporteur. On August 7, 1998, the Gundewar Commission report was presented to the Shiv Sena-Bharatiya Janata Party government. In December 1998 the report was tabled in the state legislative assembly. The commission held Sub-Inspector Kadam responsible for an "unjustified, unwarranted and indiscriminate firing which [took place] without warning." It further recommended that the government terminate his services.

The Shiv Sena-BJP government accepted the report and declared that Kadam would be suspended. Many activists have protested the suspension and have demanded that Kadam be dismissed and charged with murder under Section 302 of the Indian Penal Code. As of February 1999 he had not been charged. Given the police action and the resulting loss of life and injuries, it is incumbent upon the government of Maharashtra to prosecute officers responsible for the attack.

7

Dalit Women and Human Rights Violations

Descent based discrimination based on caste imposes social exclusion on persons belonging to Dalit castes, and their physical separation from the dominant castes in housing patterns, strict enforcement of the prohibition of inter dining at public places, seating arrangements in educational institutions, particularly schools and forces the performance of degrading occupation like manual scavenging and carrying of night soil by women. Descent based discrimination based on caste results in the violent appropriation and sexual control over Dalit women by men of the dominant caste, evident in systematic rape of Dalit women and perpetuation of forced prostitution in the name of religion through Devadasi system.

Indian government figures shows the Dalit women constitute 49.96 percent of the 200 million of Dalit population, 16.3 of the total Indian female population. The Dalit women literacy rate in India was only 23.76 percent (1991), 7.07 percent in Bihar, 8.31% in Rajasthan and 10.69 in Uttar Pradesh showing distinct biases that state structures and contingent biases have that directly exclude the Dalit women. One of the major reasons for the high dropout rate among Dalit women in primary school is the discriminatory and insulting treatment that they receive first from their non-dalit teacher and form their fellow students.

That the Dalit women labour force constitutes the backbone of Indian agricultural economy is an open secrete. Although the Indian state consistently defaulted over the fast 55 years in not recognizing this truth by its abject neglect of their right to livelihood and education. 32-40 percent of the household sector and large number of them employed as unorganised labour in the urban areas. Feminisation of labour and poverty amply illustrate in the light of Dalit women due caste system which has strong hierarchic and patriarchal bias discriminate against Dalit women denying them just and equal wages, fare share in economic distribution, maternity benefits, the security and protection of property rights etc.

Redressal of Justice to the Victims

Caste, like race is exploitative, discriminatory and anti-developmental. The discriminatory nature of caste as well as race is duly recognised by the Indian constitution. Article 15 (which outlaws discrimination on grounds of religion, race, caste, sex or place of birth) and Article 17 (which in effect accepts the existence of caste based discrimination and its effects of untouchability as racial discrimination) are instances in point. But the major Institutions of our society and culture are being ideologically colonised, policies and priorities are being tilted in favour of the upper caste and to the disadvantage of the dalits. The rights and guarantees enshrined in the constitution are being eroded.

The Indian Govt. has passed two legislation namely Protection of Civil Rights Act (PCRA) 1955 and Prevention of Atrocities against Scheduled Caste/Tribe in 1989 to enable the dalits to enjoy human rights on par with other sections of Indian society. This is a positive factor for the potential to dispense justice to the Dalits. One of the fundamental reasons for this general apathy towards Dalit's sufferings, is due to the fact that there is a systemic flaw in the law itself. Despite the preamble which resolves to usher in a society where there is justice, social, economic and political, to We The People of India, the law lacks in providing for a dynamic programme of positive action to raise the levels of Dalits to the rest of the We People of India with out which "discrimination based on descent" is ever possible.

In an increasingly hostile environment, conflicts between men of Dalits and dominant caste men often results in the rape of sexual abuse of Dalit women. In 1991 the number of women were faced the torture of rape was estimated at 2 million and majority of the victims were tribals and Dalits.

Devi 17 old girl from Gunwanpoondi, with a promise of marriage raped and made pregnant, Amuda was raped in order to grab her piece of land from her, economic boycott threatening women in the villages of sexual assault in Tamilnadu, Barathamma, raped and strangle to death demanding return of loan, Krishnamma violently raped while collecting firewood (Mahabubnagar, Andhra Pradesh). In Rajashtan endless gory of atrocities and rape of women in communal phenomenon. Geeta Devi raped in Jaipur when she was taking bath, Narbada, 18 year old while she crossing the revier, Taradevi raped on 3rd February 2002, Mohini Devi Jatav wife of Lakshman Singh was raped on the issue of wages.

> "Beginning with the lodging of the First Information Report (FIR) at the local police station through to the Judge's opinion, should a case reach that far, the women in India are faced with daunting obstacles in prosecuting cases of rape. If a woman is poor, belonging to a lower caste, and lives in a rural area, it is even more difficult for her to gain access to the justice system. Those who are able to pursue cases of sexual assault have to battle entrenched biases at every stage of the process: With the police, the doctors, the Judges and even their own family members".

Lack of Law enforcement leaves many dalit women unable to approach the legal system to seek redress. Women are often also unaware of law, their ignorance is exploited by their opponents, by the police, and by the judiciary. Even when cases are registered, the lack of appropriate investigation or the judge's own caste and gender biases can lead to acquittal, regardless of the availability of evidence or witnesses.

The Government's two-pronged strategy to improve the socio-economic status of dalits and to provide them with legal protection in the form of social welfare legislation has been underminded by a lack of political will to ensure its implementation. Though employment of manual scavenging was abolished by statute in 1993, 7.9 lakh Dalits are still forced to continue as manual scavengers. Most state government, do not seem to know of even the existence of the Act and many others are not aware of the provisions of this Act. Manual scavenging is the worst form of negating human rights and the dignity of Dalits.

The fundamental lacunae in effectively implementing such laws like PCRA, SC/ST (prevention of atrocities) Act explains the lack of political will of the Government. The police do not deliberately register the offences promptly, and invariably they do not register the case under the Act. This is being done deliberately to connive at the law. Social exclusion, lack of effective legal protection and socio, economic and sexual exploitation have kept the dalit at sub human living condition for centuries. The state's complicity and its organs such as police, judiciary and government servant's caste bias the constitutional and other statues are followed in contravention. The civil actors (upper caste) act with impunity violating domestic and international human rights law.

It has been observed by the Jury of Public hearing (2000) on Dalit atrocities states that "we found that for Dalits the rights are non-existence and are invisible to say the least". "it is the law of caste Hindus that prevails and that the state law are subverted by the very authorities who are mandated and meant to enforce these laws. The conviction rate in India in criminal cases does not exist 4%. Many a times the courts have acquitted the accused merely on the grounds that the investigation of the case was carried by the officer of the low rank than one ought to have investigated. When non-dalits rape dalit women the honourable judges time and again determines the rapist acted out of lust, and the incident is nothing to do with the victim being a Dalit.

Caste status is decided by the birth and is therefore irreversible. The caste status of Dalit as outcaste or the untouchable is thrusted upon them and it is involuntary. There is inseparable relationship between caste status, occupation and discrimination. The Dalit women faces triple discrimination because she is poor, she is a woman, she is an untouchable. The discrimination inflicted on her because she is born as an outcaste. She cannot raise her voice. She is considered as loose and immoral. Her body and her humanity can be violated by the upper caste men. Instead of dispersed inequalities, we find in "caste system" an accumulative inequality where social and political power is concentrated into the hands of the same group. The best proof of descent-based discrimination is that only Dalits are untouchables.

The CERD should clearly reiterate that discrimination according to caste is included in definition of descent-based discrimination and therefore fall under the purview of racial discrimination as stated in Article 1 of ICERD.

Affirmative action be taken in Asia and Africa including India to end caste based discrimination. The committee should take note of the statement made by the National Commission on Human Rights, India at the WCAR, Durban. "(The NCHR) is convinced that discrimination on any grounds contained in the constitution of India, and these include race, caste and descent, constitute unacceptable assault on the dignity and worth of human person as a egregious human rights violation.

The gender perspective should be incorporated in all aspects of the convention, and inter sectionality of race/caste, and gender must be addressed. The state must recognize Dalit women as distinct social group and make special provision for Dalit women in planning programmes, allocation of finances etc.

Protective Discrimination

Equal protection of law and equality before the law are two of the most important values of a just society. Usually constitutions of democratic countries provide these guarantees and forbid discrimination between people. The failure of non-discrimination perse ineliminating inequality, however, is as old as the principle itself. Constitutional law, therefore, embodies the principle of reasonable classification of persons for different treatment.

The Constitution of India provides specific prohibitions against discrimination on the ground of religion, race, caste or sex but also for affirmative action in favour of groups who had been historical victims of the traditional social system. This is known as reverse discrimination or protective discrimination - empowering the state to secure the entitlement for such disadvantaged sections by special provisions.

The Untouchability Offences Act in was amended and rechristened in 1976 as the Civil Rights Act, and latter as the Scheduled Castes and Scheduled Tribes (Prevention of Atrocities) Act which make acts of tyranny against these groups punishable. These penal sanctions have helped to delegitimate the practice of untouchability, but not to eliminate it. Affirmative actions, particularly reservations of jobs and seats in educational institutions have triggered a fierce debate.

The Supreme Court has made a distinction between SCs and STs and the other backward classes. While SCs and STs are identified exclusively by caste, the backward classes (BCs) cannot be identified by caste alone. The Backward Class Commission under the Chairmanship of Mr. Mandal had determined backwardness by applying various social and economic criteria, of which caste was only one. The Supreme Court while upholding the Mandal Commission's recommendations observed that although caste could be one of the criteria, it could not be the exclusive criterion of backwardness. Another disputed question is on the extent of reservation.

The Supreme Court held that total reservation should not exceed 50 per cent of the total number of posts available for recruitment. The Supreme Court further held that there should be no reservation in promotion. The Court has also held that there should be no reservation in super-speciality courses in medicine or engineering. The Supreme Court has also laid down that along with the reservation strategy, the de-reservation strategy also must be employed. The Court held that 'creamy layers' among the BCs must not get the benefit of reservations. Reservations as a resource must be used economically and must be conserved for the have-nots among the BCs.

Affirmative action has doubtless benefited the SCs, STs and BCs. Without reservations, persons from these sections could not have competed for government jobs or access to higher education. Studies of SC students seeking admission to higher education shows that there has been marked improvement in their performance during last 50 years. The difference in the marks obtained by the last general candidate and the first reserved candidate has narrowed down over the years. There have been several SCs and STs who have secured admissions on merit.

The contention that there should be no reservation for higher courses of study has no substance because ultimately the passing standards for the general and the reserved candidates are not different. The argument that reservation would help incompetent people become doctors is based on bias and not on facts. But without a dent into poverty, reservations will benefit only the better-off sections among the Dalits. Without free and compulsory elementary education, large number of SCs, and STs and BCs are eliminated from educational opportunities from the earliest stage.

The result is that there are reservations in higher education and government service but there are not enough people to take advantage of it. The seats or posts remain vacant and since they are not available to others generated. Although individuals continue to suffer from social prejudice, SCs and STs as groups have now become political forces. The Mandal Commission's report was accepted and reservations in government jobs were extended to other backward classes, only because of the political mobilisation of the BCs. When the Supreme Court declared that reservations should in no case exceed 50 per cent of the total number of jobs to be given, Tamil Nadu government severely protested and its law allowing more than 50 per cent reservation was inserted in the Ninth Schedule of the Constitution so as to make it immune from judicial veto.

When the Supreme Court held in Indra Sawhney v. India that there shall be no reservation in promotion, the Constitution was amended to specifically empower the State to provide for reservation in promotion also. How far has protective discrimination benefited the SCs and STs as a group, beyond enabling a majority of them to access educational, economic and political power? Without drastic and effective reduction of poverty, majority of SCs and STs also cannot benefit in a substantial manner.

The leadership, however, regards reservations as a panacea for their ills. Without sustained anti-poverty and ant-illiteracy measures, reservations per se would increase the already widening inequality within these groups - especially on regional, class and gender lines. We illustrate a representative example of the use of protective discrimination in response to changing contexts - dealing with women's rights to equality, dignity and justice. As in the case of other groups, the high visibility of a few women in important positions of power and influence had fostered a belief amongst the middle class, the political leadership as well as women's organisations that the women's question in India had been resolved.

All that women needed - it was believed - was the spread of education and other aspects of modernisation to achieve what the Constitution promised - until the Report of the Committee on the Status of Women in India (CSWI) revealed some of the grassroot realities in their stark colours. A new wave of the women's movement and the critique of the 'dominant development paradigms' by feminist scholars - (themselves 'beneficiaries'), but who had opted to view the processes of change from the perspectives of the 'victims' appeared on the scene. Pressure groups - new and old - debates, studies and new data unearthed by adoption of innovative research methodologies armed the movement with new intellectual vigour, and internationalisation of the issue during the Women's Decade called for substantial changes from below. It found allies inside the government and in sections of academia to begin dialogues and a search for alternative strategies.

Development Planning and Women's Rights

The contemporary global debate on human rights for women was anticipated in India decades ago and was an intrinsic part of the freedom movement.

Constitutional Provisions

The ethos of the Preamble is both liberal, in terms of individual rights and liberty - and redistributive, in terms of the freeing of large groups of citizens from the distortions of the past. The extent to which the concept of rights has influenced 'women's development' in the post- Independence period is, however, contingent on the functioning of the policy and institutional framework, its structures, its mechanisms, its processes over time and its perception of the political will of the governments of the day which it attempts to translate into practice.

The State's choice of using the development policy and institutional framework to implement this directive has shaped the nature of the links between 'women's development' and 'women's rights' both in discourse and in practice. While concepts and approaches to women's development have emerged, modified and changed quite speedily, the changes in institutional structures, processes and thinking have not kept pace, leading to a mismatch between policies, plans and implementation in the field."

— The imperative for women's equality is rooted in Part III (Fundamental Rights) of this document.

— Articles 14 and 15 pronounce the right of men and women to equality before the law and the prohibition of discrimination on the basis of sex by the State.

— Article 15 forbids the State to subject any citizen to any disability, liability, restriction or condition, on the basis of sex, in the access to, or use of, any public place or service.

— Article 16 promises to both men and women, equality of opportunity in matters relating to employment under the State.

— Taken collectively, these provisions spell out the basic right to equality of Indian women as individuals.

The Fundamental Rights are individual rights. Sixteen years before India won independence from the British, the Karachi session of the Indian National Congress adopted the resolution on Fundamental Rights, which incorporated within it, the concept of equality of the sexes. Women's emancipation, through their right to equality, was thus a part of the new social order.

Directive Principles

Article 37 includes the right to an adequate means of livelihood for men and women, equal pay for equal work, protection of the health and strength of workers - men, women and children - from abuse, just and humane conditions of work, raising the level of nutrition, free and compulsory education to children up to the age of 14, maternity relief and conditions of work ensuring a decent standard of life and full enjoyment of leisure. Many of these provisions find place in the Convention on the

Elimination of All Forms of Discrimination against Women under Articles 11 and 12. Indian women have, historically, questioned double standards of morality in marriage and other dominant value systems perpetuating unequal gender relations in society periodically - some openly, others covertly.

The process accelerated during the freedom struggle - and had Mahatma Gandhi's support. The inclusion of equality between the sexes in Part III of the Constitution is therefore the logical sequel to the participation of women in the joint struggle for Swaraj and their own emancipation. Yet, when the CSWI completed their extensive review of the situation of women in India in the mid-1970s, their finding was that for the vast majority of Indian women, the Constitutional guarantee of equality of legal status and opportunity had remained an unrealized dream. Was there a grey area, an absence of a matching policy and institutional framework that was responsible for the very large gap between precept and practice?

Dr. Ambedkar valued the Directive Principles above all because they lay down that our ideal is economic democracy. Without them, he felt, a parliamentary form of government could have come into being, but with no direction as to what the country's economic ideal or social order ought to be. While Fundamental Rights are personal rights, the Directive Principles are the ingredients of State policy and are intended to guide the State as a whole. In fact, an amendment was suggested by Shri B. N. Rao (the Constitutional Adviser to the President of the Constituent Assembly), to make the Directive Principles enforceable in a court of law, 'to make it clear that in case of conflict between the rights conferred by Chapter III,......which are for the most part, the rights of the individual, and the principles of policy set forth in Chapter IV, which are intended for the welfare of the State as a whole, the general welfare should prevail, otherwise it would be meaningless to say that the principles are fundamental, and it is the duty of the State to give effect to them in making laws.'

This amendment was not carried out, as it did not find favour with the majority in the Constituent Assembly. The content of this argument is relevant when we pose the question-in what policy and institutional framework did the Indian State operate to carry out the pledge of gender equality in the Constitution? Did the lawmakers and the policy makers see the mandate for gender equality as part of the overall mandate for economic and social justice? Did failure to give 'teeth' to the Directive Principles result in dereliction of this charge? Was law the prime mover or instrument to bring about equality between the sexes?

These questions arise in the context of the findings of the CSWI in 1974 that neither the norms nor the institutions are in place which would enable women to fulfil the multiple roles that they are expected to play in India today. Rights can only build a foundation, a basis on which to build structures to provide women with opportunities. But who will monitor the State's observance of the obligations to which they have committed themselves? Rights granted by law need an organizational as well as a policy infrastructure or framework to enable women to exercise them. The mode of redressal of individual grievances of violations of basic rights is insufficient to challenge structural and policy-related discrimination. Women's studies scholars and feminist lawyers have differentiated between the 'formal' and the 'substantive' approach to equality. Whereas the formal model has been used in political and constitutional discourse, there is increasing concern that it cannot eliminate discrimination against certain marginalised groups and therefore the impact of the law or the justice redressal system will not have a favourable effect. In other words, 'equality sometimes requires that individuals be treated differently'.

Development Planning in India

Development planning was the pride of the new nation, borrowing from the Soviet model; and involved a massive investment of financial and physical resources. The Five- Year Plans disaggregated and allocated the total resources amongst various development sectors. The State's main emphasis was on achieving economic growth. The professed aims of centralized planning included achievement of self-sufficiency in food, creation of a strong industrial base in the public sector, including infrastructure, and generation of employment opportunities.

In the long term, these growth processes were supposed to improve the life of the common man. But in the short and medium term, the State, in pursuit of "social justice" objectives, to protect those who would not immediately benefit from the growth processes, had to provide a certain welfare orientation to the planning process and content. This dictated the creation of social development planning, with its own objectives such as the satisfaction of basic needs. This was done through direct interventions in certain sectors, even while the engine of economic growth was revving up to attain the "growth" objectives. Gender equality as the right of an individual woman therefore had to be fought for within a social structure which is itself based on an unequal power and resource base. The preoccupation of the State was to move ahead quickly through higher growth, modernization and industrialization. Social development was subsidiary, if not subordinated, to this goal and was left to the social welfare institutional framework to work on the Directive Principles to reduce them to a set of policies and strategies.

Social Welfare Services

However, early development planning identified social welfare services as appropriate interventions to tackle the basic problems of certain target groups of which women formed a part. Even as late as 1976, when the government prepared its National Plan of Action - which had the Mexico Plan of Action as well as the report of the CSWI for reference and guidance - this approach to women's issues found a clear articulation in the National Plan of Action.

Welfare services are intended to cater for the special needs of persons and groups, who by reason of some handicap-social, economic, physical or mental-are unable to avail of, or are traditionally denied the amenities or services provided by the community. Women are handicapped by social customs and social values and therefore Social Welfare Services have and should specially endeavour to rehabilitate them.' The NPA went on to say that since the developmental needs of these categories are unlimited and the resources are finite, 'priorities have necessarily to be assigned'. So amongst women in general, certain sub-categories were singled out, such as working women, women who were handicapped, destitute, widowed, in conflict with law, unmarried mothers and others similarly exploited.

A good deal of attention was paid to describing, analysing and finding solutions for the widows' problems, which were seen as social disabilities rather than economic, especially amongst the older widows. Even when young widows' economic vulnerabilities were described, marriage was held to be the appropriate response. When schemes and programmes were drawn up, they were not based on or linked to rights. In the Chapter 'Legislative Measures' the NPA does give a number of useful recommendations on laws relating to marriage, divorce, dowry, inheritance of property, nationality, adoption, etc., it refers to women in the abstract, and does not visualize the legal problems of any set of women nor attempts to design any mechanisms to actually reach legal services to the women who have been described as 'handicapped' in the chapter on Social Welfare, even while it accepts that because of their situation, they need special interventions to access the legal system.

This excerpt from the National Plan of Action has been dealt with in somewhat elaborate detail to highlight a recurring feature of the design of development programmes for women-a strong 'social welfare' bias, identifying women as victims or as vulnerable, oppressed, handicapped individuals, with the State providing services of a compensatory or ameliorative nature which are not seen as 'rights' accruing to them as citizens; and a corresponding failure to include legal rights in these programmes and services to help these women to fight for their rights. Institutionalization, for example, became one of the preferred modes of protecting such women, as it kept them safe from the depredations of the outside world Recalling the men and women who fought for freedom and successfully placed gender equality within the Fundamental Rights, a wide gap does seem to appear between the notion of legal rights, entitlements, legal processes and safeguards on the one hand, and of social welfare services of ameliorative and compensatory nature, on the other.

The Five-Year Plans and Women

The Five Year Plans were the instruments for planning in India, which emphasized and reinforced the concept of schemes and programmes denoting 'development'. Though production of food, industrial output, creation of infrastructure etc. were always given a higher development priority, sectors such as health, education, nutrition, sanitation, etc., were also seen as important, though as 'non-productive', 'social' sectors involving 'consumption expenditure'. Upto the Fifth Plan, (1974--1979), there was little or no effort to see women as human or productive resources nor in terms of their roles in production sectors. The 'statistical purdah' concealed the full extent of their participation in these sectors and their contribution to the domestic product, and this made them invisible to the policy planners. It was only in the Sixth Plan that a change took place.

The National Machinery

The institutional framework for women's development grew in size and complexity over the years, starting from the initial phase of planning in the 1950s. The delivery of social welfare services to women and children was carried out by the agencies created within the government as well as the organizations of the voluntary and non-government sector. These bodies were strongly shaped by the social welfare mode of planning and development.

The central social welfare board

The Central Social Welfare Board, (CSWB), a Gandhian experiment in harnessing women-power for all weaker sections created in 1953, involved women in income-generating activities, which was an innovation in the 1950s, especially when the funds were given to the women not as grant-in-aid, but as interest-free loans. The primary objective of the Board was to mobilise voluntary effort mainly by women's organisations in the task of improving the condition of women, children and other handicapped groups. Nurturing of women's leadership through the non-government route could be done with assured funding from the central government.

From the sector of 'social welfare services' and 'social services', the planning framework opened out to include the schemes of the Community Development sector, mainly in applied nutrition, food production within the household, crafts, and later, training in agricultural production for farm women. Health, especially maternal and child health, followed by family planning and family welfare also became new priorities. Policy emphasis on education for women and girls - demanded in a report by the National Committee on Women's Education in the late 1950s, a number of interventions including undifferentiated curriculum for girls and boys, financial incentives for parents of girl students and higher resource allocations to states for achieving girls' enrolment at 80 per cent of that of the boys.

The National Committee suggested a permanent institutional mechanism within the Ministry of Education - a National Council for Women's Education - [and similar bodies at the state level] for continuous review, monitoring and evaluation of girls' education. Though restricting its interest to the formal sector, the Second Five Year Plan looked at the plight of women workers and recommended that facilities such as creches, maternity benefits, training, equal pay for equal work, protection against injurious work, etc., should be made available to them. Legalisation of abortion [medical termination of pregnancy] was done in the early 1970s, family planning services [with focus on women] started getting a bigger and bigger share of the health budget and child health received a fillip with the launching of the Integrated Development of Child Services (ICDS).

Most important of all, the mega-programmes and projects such as Community Development, ICDS, etc. created large cadres of women whose presence in the villages gave a new meaning and significance to the concept of involvement of women functionaries in development.

Search for New Institutional Mechanisms

Mechanisms for institutional coordination needed to be put in place, however, to ensure that these expanded planning initiatives were conceived and implemented holistically. Existing mechanisms had to be revamped and new structures put in place, depending on the need.

The structures and institutions had to internalise the emerging needs and values, to see women in a more holistic and multi-dimensional light. The situation called for a paradigm shift. The CSWI's Towards Equality, found neither the norms nor the institutions to be in place. The 'special provisions' that the Constitution talks about have to be understood to mean the enabling mechanisms to help women to come out of their traditional modes of thinking and ways of carrying out their day to day duties. These provisions were to help women to step out from their subordinate/unequal status to access the equality rights without adverse consequences. They were not an end in themselves, but only a stepping stone to substantive equality. The absence of a mechanism created a void.

The Ministry for Social Welfare continued to co-exist in an uneasy relationship. The other Ministries whose portfolio was of vital importance to women such as Education, Rural Development, Health, Labour and Employment, etc. did not invest their resources in institutional innovations for women at policy and strategy level. Large cadres of women at village and cutting-edge levels were recruited but their own personnel and working problems did not attract much attention.

Mobilisation of women under the Mahila Mandal programme became a part of the Community Development plans, but no attention was paid to the task of converting them from status-quo groups to critical partners in change and development.

Women's Bureau as a 'Nodal' Agency

With the publication of the CSWI report and the launching of the International Women's Decade (IWD), things began to move comparatively faster. The National Plan of Action drew inspiration from the CSWI report as well as the World Plan of Action which had emerged from the Mexico World Conference on Women. The institutional mechanism of the Women's Bureau came as a consequence of these events. It was again, located in the under-resourced Ministry of Social Welfare. The clout possessed by it was not considerable, as compared to the other larger Ministries. It remained a discrete entity, not a cross cutting one.

The early 1990s saw the setting up of the National Commission for Women. The impetus behind this venture was the motivated lobbying of the women's groups. The Act provided a specific mandate to the Commission to study and monitor all matters relating to the Constitutional and legal safeguards provided for women, review the existing legislation to suggest amendments and look into the individual and collective complaints involving the deprivation of the rights of women. Commissions have also been set up at the State level along the same lines. While the statute has been drafted in such a way to ensure the maximum autonomy to this body, as per the insistence of the women's groups, in practice, it has functioned administratively as a part of the governmental configuration'.

Substantive work done by the Commission includes a solid review of the existing laws for women and recommendations to plug loop holes and frame new laws. In this endeavour, it was able to count on the committed work and contribution of many of the women's groups, women lawyers working on these issues and others. It was also able to coordinate, to some extent, its working with that of the National Human Rights Commission. In seeking to redress individual and collective grievances of women, the Commission has put in the best efforts, but has not been as successful mainly because of its subordinate, and marginal status in the government.

Panchayati Raj

The most recent entrant to the constellation of institutional mechanisms for women's advancement are the Panchayati Raj bodies at district, block and village levels. Tracing the course of State planning and development interventions for women in India, one cannot but be struck the range of theories and approaches, from welfare to development, from anti-poverty, equity and efficiency to empowerment. There is a distinct forward and positive movement towards creating women's agency, an emphasis on rights. The women's movements played a major role in urging along these changes, whether in theory or in practice. The Beijing PFA asks 'to include all institutional mechanisms and processes that facilitate, as appropriate, decentralised planning, implementation and monitoring, with a view to involving non-governmental organisations and community organisations from the grass roots level upwards'. It talks of 'relationships....with centres of women's studies and research, academic and educational institutions...the media...women's organisations and all other actors of civil society'. Following such a more inclusive definition, especially in the context of the changes in local governance wrought by the Panchayati Raj, would seem to be a logical step to follow in the search for women's rights to equality.

Empowering Dalit Women

In December 1992, India's parliament passed the 73rd amendment to the Indian Constitution with near unanimity in both houses. In four months the legislatures of more than the required 50 per cent of the state legislatures passed resolutions for its adoption to enable the President of India to give his assent to fully make it a constitutional amendment, effective from the 24th of April 1993. This amendment to revitalise local village councils called panchayats (which literally means an assembly of five persons) throughout the country constitutes one of the most significant systemic transformations of the Indian polity and an instrument for bringing democracy and devolution to the grassroots levels in the Indian countryside. It is an important step towards promotion of the human rights and opportunity of every citizen to take part in the conduct of public affairs, to vote and to be elected and to have access on general terms of equality to public services of the country as enshrined in Article 25 of the International Covenant on Civil and Political Rights.

Despite a federal structure, the Indian nation-state has shown a centralising tendency in its political, administrative and development paradigms. Consequently, the needs and concerns of the large masses in the rural areas have remained neglected despite many poverty alleviation initiatives and other developments. The need for democratic decentralisation with a three tier rural local councils to ensure people's participation was realised in the early years. The issue of representation of the rural local councils of panchayats with respect to weaker sections of SCs and STs had been addressed in the country even before this amendment and panchayat legislation in a number of states included reservation for these sections in the membership and sometimes among the chairpersons of these panchayats.

The national parliament and state legislatures already have reservations for these sections as mandated in the Constitution, which was originally included for 10 years but reviewed and extended further. The new amendment's significant contribution was to ensure this reservation uniformly throughout the country [except the tribal concentration areas - in the 5th and 6th Schedules. But most importantly it provided reservation of at least one-third membership and chairpersons at the three levels for women, and that too not only generally but across caste and class (the state can include even higher reservation in their legislation). It, therefore, brought a critical mass of women to these institutions and to that extent it is the most exciting enterprise undertaken so far and it is this aspect that we intend to look at here.

The Constitutional amendment was followed by state legislations to bring their panchayat laws in conformity within one year. The year 1994 and 1995 saw panchayats' elections across states and women's entry in a critical mass for the first time. Women have always and everywhere been on the fringe of political and social power. Has the formal change brought by this intervention adequately addressed women's marginality or has it just led to their numerical strength? What is its impact on women and on panchayats? Has women's presence transformed these structures, made them more responsive to women's needs and concerns or has the intention of the amendment been defeated by powerful interests? CWDS sought answers in the experience of women who have entered these panchayats, through a major study of women's experience in rural local councils in three northern states of India - Madhya Pradesh, Rajasthan and Uttar Pradesh in 1996.

The project was completed in 1999, capturing women's experience of the first half of their first tenure in these institutions. These states are low on most indicators of social development and gender, and it was felt that it would be possible to see what women's entry in these democratic structures had achieved despite the socio-political and economic odds stacked against them. These states accounted for 80 million (almost one-third) of India's rural poor in 1993-94, and 30 per cent of India's rural population. Here we see the experience of a socially and politically most marginalised group across caste, class and region. The three-year study included interviews of 1199 respondents, 843 of whom were elected women in panchayats, and 180 were community members. There were also 60 case studies.

Awareness is the first step towards participation and empowerment and we explored these women's awareness level about panchayats, about participation levels of men and women and about development. About 64 per cent to 92 per cent of the women have shown high awareness levels on each of the issues - of reservations, panchayats' responsibilities, meetings, attendance in meetings, panchayats' resources and success of government's development schemes and programmes. For first time entrants, in their first term and with 70.5 per cent of them illiterate or just literate without completing even primary level education and still subject to multiple social, economic and cultural constraints this can be seen as an excellent beginning. They are not significantly more ignorant about panchayat matters than the male members of their class, general impressions and sweeping statements being made about them notwithstanding.

Women's effective participation and leadership in panchayats would require not only physical presence but articulation, joining discussions, taking up issues and solving problems. Doubts have been expressed about these women participating in panchayats. These impressions, perceptions and biases are reflected in describing them as only proxy, 'namesake' members or illiterate, ignorant, absentee members and the new appellations of 'Sarpanch pati' and 'Pradhan pati' to describe the husbands of chairpersons, and members of village panchayats imply that only they perform the panchayats' work on behalf of their wives.

Significantly, these doubts and designations are focussed only on women in village panchayats where a large number of women from poor and weaker sections have entered and not on women in the higher tier of panchayats, that is, at block/district level. Women's experience and participation would vary in different groups and local contexts. It would also depend on a number of factors including the historical context, the social base and available supports. They have also to use the new political space despite the unspoken opposition or at least reservation on this change. These new women in panchayats have reported increase in self-confidence, change in life style, awareness about critical need of education and increased concern for village development. There are positive changes which they have seen in their own attitudes and consequent impact on the family with shifts in various social practices.

The amendment has begun a process of legitimacy and mandatoriness to women's new non-traditional role in panchayats which helps the supporting husbands to share responsibilities without the fear of ridicule and makes others to, at least, reconsider and think about women's new public role. We must also see this as a refreshing contrast to women's non-entity in pre-amendment panchayats. The pre-amendment studies on 'all-women' panchayats reports the repeated affirmative response of the gram sevak (the village extension worker) to the query 'Does everyone attend the gram sabha (the general meeting) of the village?'

However, when pressed further, he replies 'Men-Yes. Women-No'. He could not even see the anomaly of an all male sabha (meeting) in a village with an all women panchayat. One of our collaborating researchers observed that a major socio-political change has been seen there when a powerful Thakur (upper caste) male has to seek redressal/development work from the SC woman sarpanch. Women in our case studies have been seen to be effortlessly aware of women's most crucial needs, whether of drinking water facilities or measures against alcoholism. They have also brought out the serious social and political constraints they face and how they have coped with them.

Women's voices articulate their new found confidence, their successful attempt at combining continuity of traditional practices like Ghoonghat (veil) and change in its discarding it in formal public offices, in and outside the villages. They also express how they have successfully coped with the threats of the opponents from entrenched powerful elements. There is helplessness and frustration where their own illiteracy and poverty and the rural power structure in pockets of strong feudal social order with continuing culture of the gun can still successfully prevent them from being in control in the panchayats where they are in formal positions. Even with strong forces working against them, the women have not lost their initiative and urge to do something for the village and for women whom they have identified for their support and advocacy.

Women have shown their enthusiasm, capacity and will to do something despite the odds against them. It is the state and various actors in civil society who have to enable them to pursue this process further. Training programmes for these new women have so far not measured up universally in their quantitative coverage or in their contents and approach, as they tend to address procedures and programmes rather than politics, process and critical issues. The national consensus and commitment inherent in the amendment, therefore needs to be followed up in support for training which women need - not only in skills and knowledge of panchayat law and procedures but also in respect of issues and concerns of women and how these can be effectively addressed. They need to learn innovative ways to organise, cooperate, participate, manage and build alliances, how to network with other women's collectives and how the social practices adversely affect women, how information and knowledge is to be sought, stored and retrieved.

National Movements against Social Inequality

Dalit Movement

Dalit literally means the oppressed, but has acquired a new meaning in the contemporary Indian context. During the latter half of the 20th century this term came to mean the ex-untouchable castes, i.e. the Scheduled Castes. Indian society is notorious for social inequality based on the caste system that views society as a hierarchical structure. Some castes were historically treated as polluting and therefore untouchable.

The practice of untouchability compounded social, educational and economic deprivation among the untouchables. The Constitution abolished the practice and since 1950 the Indian state has legislated punishments against the practice or atrocities against them or tribals and adopted laws enabling them to enhance their dignity and social-political rights.

Twentieth century witnessed rise of a widespread movement among the Dalits in their efforts to contest social inequality. Dr. B. R. Ambedkar was the most revered leader among the Dalits. Even before he embarked upon his political career in the 1920s, sporadic efforts for fighting against untouchability had already taken place. These included reform movements led or inspired by non-Dalits like Jotirao Phule and V.R. Shinde. More notably, resistance to inequality emerged from the Dalit community itself in Punjab, U.P., Andhra, Maharashtra, Karnataka and Tamil Nadu.

Most of these activities contested the claims of Aryan/ Brahmanical superiority by claiming that Dalits were the original inhabitants and the Aryan/Brahmans were intruders. There was also an emphasis on modern education and attempts were made to obtain administrative/military opportunities from the colonial government.

The leadership of Dr. Ambedkar changed the nature of the Dalit movement in two crucial respects. He gave a new intellectual and ideological thrust to the Dalit movement. Combining his modern Western training with the urge to intellectually confront the caste system, Ambedkar produced a devastating critique of the Hindu social order, and grounded the Dalit movement in the forefront of the anti-caste discourse. Thus the Dalit question did not remain confined only to Dalits; it belonged to the genre of anti-caste struggles, acquiring an ideology of human dignity and social equality. The other aspect of the Ambedkarite movement was its mass character. No longer confined to only the spread of education among Dalits, the movement encouraged Dalits to 'organise and agitate' against oppression and exploitation.

Ambedkar realised that both in the context of colonial rule and independent India, democratic politics would require mass struggles if Dalits were to assert their role in the sphere of competitive politics. For some time he concentrated his attention on the issue of Dalits' right to entry in Hindu temples, shifting his focus later to share in political power and equal political rights. He also organized Dalits on economic issues. Finally he aspired to mobilise Dalits for a mass exit from the Hindu fold. He made very skillful use of the mass media, floated various socio-political organisations, set up educational institutions and combined legislative-elective politics with mass struggles. In the pre-independence period, Dalits in Andhra, Karnataka and Tamil Nadu also organized themselves taking inspiration from Ambedkar, Gandhi or sometimes Marxism.

In independent India, the Constitution (of which Ambedkar was one of the major architects) has guaranteed abolition of untouchability, promised legal equality, and provided reserved seats (constituencies) in Union and State Legislatures (also in local government) for Dalits. Besides, the Constitution has empowered the State to implement various programmes of protective discriminatory action such as reservation of seats in government jobs and educational institutions, etc. for the Dalits. However, despite the reservation policy, and a network of welfare programmes and protective regulations, the Dalit question has not been resolved fully or satisfactorily. Their social existence is still marked by educational backwardness, economic inequality, nominal share in political power, frequent ostracization, discriminatory social treatment and violence by the wealthy upper castes.

The post-Ambedkar Dalit movement is thus faced with an apparently favourable legal structure and an adverse social and political context. Most followers of Ambedkar believe that share in power and control over state are crucial means of Dalit emancipation. This belief has pushed the movement to a constant search of a political apparatus. At the time of his death, Ambedkar had prepared an outline for formation of a new political party, that would not be an exclusively Dalit party. After his death, his followers formed the Republic Party of India (RPI). Initially, this party had a good following in Maharashtra, U.P. and Bihar. Soon, the RPI faced splits on ideological and leadership issues and became ineffective in North India.

After the 1970s, the RPI has been restricted only to Maharashtra and there too, it has been splintered into fractions. Contrary to Ambedkar's expectations, the RPI has always been confined to Dalit following alone. The 80s witnessed the rise of yet another Dalit party, the Bahujan Samaj Party (BSP). This party has considerable following in Punjab, U.P., Bihar, M.P. and some following in Maharashtra. The BSP has been trying to forge an alliance between Dalits and OBCs in order to broad-base itself. Many Dalit politicians have so far chosen to join non-Dalit parties like Congress, the left parties, Janata Dal, etc. in order to get better opportunities. There are instances when Dalit MPs across the parties came together on issues pertaining to Dalits. Yet, there is no Dalit lobby in Indian politics outside of the avowedly Dalit parties. While politics attracts Dalit activists, Dalit movement is constantly challenged by social ostracization of poor Dalits in different parts of the country.

The failure of RPI to tackle this situation effectively resulted in formation of more militant organizations since the 1970s. The more notable among these have been the Dalit Panthers in Maharashtra, the Dalit Sangharsh Samiti in Karnataka, Dalit Sena in U.P. and Dalit Mahasabha in Andhra Pradesh. Such organizations faced a dual problem. On the one hand, Dalit question consists of marginalization in the urban context and oppression and impoverishment in rural environs. Activity of the movement has to tackle this complex nature of the Dalit question.

On the other hand, this complexity forces an ideological dilemma before the Dalit movement. The Dalit question cannot be/should not be considered in isolation. Dalit movement has to forge alliance with other oppressed sections and take up broader issues of equitable access to material resources. The Dalit Panthers movement had taken this position and widened the scope of the term 'Dalit'. This widening implied a more left-oriented ideological position. This led to a split in the movement but since then the left movement in Andhra and Bihar has seriously taken up the Dalit question. Sections of Dalit movement in these states have been part of the radical left movement with Marxist-Leninist ideology. In Maharashtra, Prakash Ambedkar has been organizing the Dalits since 1980s on the broader issues of redistribution of agricultural land and control over common property resources. His faction of RPI has floated an organization of the OBCs known as Bahujan Mahasangh. The policy of reservations, with all its limitations, has given rise to a large section of white collar employees in government and public sector undertakings. This section is often organized separately, giving rise to many unions of SC/ST employees in the public sector.

BSP leader, Kanshi Ram, started his political career by organizing Dalit employees along with tribal and minority employees - Backward and Minority Classes Employees' Federation (BAMCEF). Even after he branched off to the more militant Dalit Soshit Samaj Sangharsh Samiti (popularized as DS4), the white collar Dalit employees continue to organize and protect their specific job related and reservation related demands. These limitations notwithstanding Dalit activists have always felt confident that the Dalit movement alone can lead the struggles against caste system as a whole. At the same time, there is awareness among younger activists about the need to broaden and deepen the social and cultural terrain of Dalit movement. As the writings of Ambedkar imply, the Dalit movement has to annihilate caste and aim at fighting exploitation because therein lies the true emancipation of the Dalits and other oppressed masses.

Narmada Bachao Movement

India has experienced a number of mass based initiatives where people have questioned the wisdom of priorities as well as strategies of development and have asserted their right to have a greater voice and active role in decisions in such matters as they affect their own lives - often negatively. The Narmada Bachao Andolan (NBA) - one such mass based movement fighting for the rights of the tribal and peasant population in the valley, addresses the wider issue of whether big dams are necessary for solving the problems of water as well as power. It also advocates a model of development, which will be more environment-friendly and consistent with human rights.

The movement has grown from opposing the haphazard rehabilitation policies of the three state governments of Gujarat, Maharashtra and Madhya Pradesh, to questioning the entire centralised model for development that the country has adopted since after independence and continues to espouse today. The Narmada River is 1300 kilometers long and passes through the states of Madhya Pradesh, Maharashtra and Gujarat and finally drains into the Arabian Sea. This river system being one of the earliest cradles of civilisation is home to about twenty million peasants and tribal populations that subsist on the lands, and other natural resources in the Narmada basin.

Early History and Landmarks in the Movement - Till the '80s, the submergence that this project would bring about and the massive displacement of people it would result in was little known. In April 1986 the Narmada Dharangrasta Samiti was formed at Dhulia in Maharashtra supported by Medha Patkar and other activists. In September 1987 the Multiple Action Research Group (MARG) of Delhi, based on their field studies in the Narmada valley, brought out a report entitled 'Sardar Sarovar Oustees in Madhya Pradesh - What do they know?' The report pointed out that the oustees had very little knowledge of what the government had planned for them and that the government had failed from giving complete and timely information to the oustees. Such findings and more by the MARG team through 1988 and 1989 led to protest from various sections of people that were to be affected by this project . The struggle since then has been to secure the right to life, right to information and the right to participation. On 30th January 1988·, over 4000 project affected people from Maharashtra, Gujarat and Madhya Pradesh protested at Kevadia Colony demanding detailed information about the submergence that the Dam would bring, the plans for rehabilitation and sources of funds for the project.

On 18th October, the Gujarat government came down heavily on the 12 villages surrounding the dam site by applying the Official Secrets Act. Activists arranged a conscientization march through fifteen affected villages. Various organisations, scholars and journalists joined in the struggle. The Narmada Bachao Samiti (Maharashtra), the Narmada Pariyojana Pratikar Manch (Gujarat), and the Narmada Ghati Navnirman Samiti (Madhya Pradesh) were formed.

On 28th of September 1989, the town of Harsud hosted a gathering of thirty thousand project affected people, tribals, members of the rural poor and the backward classes, pledged collectively to oppose development that was non-sustainable and engendered greater economic disparity. The Harsud rally, for the first time, provided a platform where people involved in various struggles united for a common agenda and could henceforth depend on the participation and support of each other. It also marked the growth of a new consciousness among people affected by mega projects in various parts of India, leading to strong mobilisation of people.

Many have taken recourse to legal battles in the courts for protecting their fundamental rights. In 1990 the World Bank, Independent Review Team began examination of fulfillment conditions prescribed for its loan. Its report stated that due to the noncompliance with the various stipulations and conditions of the Narmada Tribunal, the World Bank and the Ministry of Environment as the sanctioning authorities, the project was unviable and would lead to widespread violation of human rights. NBA and its supporters welcomed it, but it was strongly criticised by the development lobby in Gujarat.

In 1993 World Bank funding was discontinued as Government of India renounced one-third of the loan. The year 1993 saw one of the biggest submergence and also the Manibeli Satyagraha. The dam had reached a height of 80 meters, and flooded the village of Manibeli. Activists faced severe state repression. In Manibeli the Maharashtra police far outnumbered the inhabitants and any one associated or expected to be associated with the Narmada Bachao Andolan was not given entry. Issues Raised by NBA The Narmada valley struggle opposes big dams and the policy for centralised development, which denies any rights on the natural resources acquired from communities living on them, without giving the communities the right to know, the right to participate in decision making, a share in the benefits and the right to dissent.

The tribals threatened by eviction and submergence have demanded their right to development. The NBA has also used the judicial process through its writ petitions, bringing before the Supreme Court issues that include large scale human rights violations committed by the state, the noncompliance of the state with the conditions of the Narmada Water Disputes Tribunal for environmental protection and rehabilitation of oustees, and has questioned the very viability of the project.

The Narmada Bachao Andolan in its petition has highlighted the environmental impacts of the Sardar Sarovar Project. The impact of the project on the downstream of Sardar Sarovar has been totally neglected so far. It holds that the salinity ingress that has been checked so far will increase due to the storage of such large quantities of water. Since the project would submerge tens of thousands of hectares of forestland and displace lakhs of persons, an environmental clearance and forestland clearance was required from the Ministry of Environment and Forests.

Till 1985 the environmental clearance for the Sardar Sarovar Project was held up by the Ministry and only upon the intervention of the then Prime Minister Rajeev Gandhi and with approval of the World Bank conditional clearance was given, on the understanding that environmental impact assessment studies would be conducted simultaneously with the construction of the dam. However, while many studies are yet to be completed others have not even begun. In December 1993, Mr. Maudgal, advisor to the Ministry of Environment and Forests in his review of progress of the project, held that the policy for 'conditional clearance' had proved to be a complete failure.

The NBA has grown over the last 14 years and become a symbol for a variety of mass based non-violent movements that are fighting to secure the rights of the socially and economically disadvantaged groups. The movement has thrown up new and innovative themes for mobilisation and spearheaded the demand for substantive realisation of democracy by espousing Hamare Gaon Mein Hamara Raj or self rule at the village level. Thus the protest in the Narmada valley or at other project sites is not merely against the displacement of masses of people and inadequate compensation but also against the violation of peoples' right to life, callous decision making, denial of their right to participation, the submergence of not only their homes and farms but of ancient cultures. The protest is essentially an opposition to the entire model for development and while doing so has developed its own new paradigm for development, which is sustainable, and governance, which is participatory. The success of the Narmada Bachao Andolan need not be counted in terms of whether the dam comes through or not. It will have to be counted in terms of the new awareness it has generated among the poor and the disadvantaged people. It has also warned policy makers that hereafter it would be difficult to plan development without taking people into confidence.

Women's Movement

The women's movement in India too is one of reassertion of citizen's claims to participate as equals in the political and development process. In contemporary India, the post-emergency - related upsurge in assertion of democratic rights and the two following decades representing a deepening crisis of the state, government and society - marked an end of the age of complacency, apathy and acceptance of the existing social order. Undoubtedly, these stem from both problems of transition as well as the outcome of the world's largest experiment in democracy. Shifts in foci and awareness of problems that impinged on women's lives, the social construction of gender relations and the identity of women from different classes in their attempts to resolve the problems of the national economy and polity occurred during a period of dissolving certainties that characterised local, national or global systems. Within the movement diversities manifested themselves in many ideological cleavages and fragmented, regionally uneven growth. But the issues on which women first articulated their visible opposition covered a vast terrain - ranging from those which were gender-specific to those which impinged on citizen's rights, class formations, values and the direction of social transformation.

The main concerns of the movement, as it emerged, were laid out in the issues opened up by the report of the Committee on the Status of Women in India (CSWI) in 1975 which drew attention to the wide diversities in 'culturally' prescribed gender roles in India's plural society. The Committee raised serious doubts about the 'development' or 'modernisation' models that not only ignored the real differences that revolved round caste, class and ethnic history, but exaggerated the influence of religion, culture and 'social attitudes' on gender role prescriptions. The CSWI noted clear linkages between existing and growing social and economic disparities and women's status in education, the economy, society and the polity, putting the demand for equality on an actual historical terrain. It also formed a starting point for women's studies. Coinciding with the flowering of the 'second wave of feminism' in the West and the United Nations' International Women's Decade, the Indian women's movement developed international linkages from the beginning, laying itself open to charges of being 'foreign- inspired', especially from the newly consolidating forces of socio-political conservatism within various communities and classes.

The movement confronted such charges by locating its primary concerns, and eventually its identity - among the worst victims of poverty and oppression within most of these communities. What began as a critique of economic development policies pursued by the Indian State for the 'exclusion' of women historically deeply involved in the economy for their survival - the poor peasants, landless labourers and millions in multiple occupations in the uncounted, invisible, informal sector in rural and urban areas - soon joined hands with other critics of the dominant development model - inside and outside the country.

The CSWI's initial analysis was based more on inferences, the cries of thousands of poor women across the country voiced before the Committee, and demographic evidence of a secular trend of decline in women's value in the economy and society as a whole. Finding allies among increasing intensity of critiques of the dominant model of economic growth emanating from various parts of the third world, women's studies in India began and grew rapidly in its initial stages to study the interaction between macro-economic changes and issues concerning women's status. This focus not only fed new information to the movement but transformed many of the academics into active participants in the women's movement, where they exerted a definite influence in the choice of priorities and lines of advocacy for dialogues with policy-makers.

Two important influences on the movement's decision to anchor its own identity among the overwhelming majority of women deprived of basic rights (literacy/education, health, security) - even the dignity of social acknowledgement of their labour and contribution to the family and nation's economy were: a) the escalation of social and political violence against women and children at different levels of society, including the most sacred cow of India's ancient culture and civilisation - the family/the domestic unit; and b) the violence of unrecorded history - of Indian women's own perspectives on their past, present and future. Educated, urban, professional women - mainly the products of the 'respectable' middle class - found themselves ill-equipped to deal with violence - in their homes or in the workplace, in public or private, and recognized a shared world with their poor sisters. Some even found the latter emotionally and intellectually stronger and better equipped to deal or cope with violence as a fact of everyday life. The movement's own efforts to counter such violence through better/tighter laws having met with abysmal failure, the wise among the activists turned to their poorer sisters for strength, solace and lessons in preserving women's own sanity and dignity.

Realisation of their own ignorance (in spite of education) of the range and diversity of poor women's economic roles, problems and perspectives brought shame and a sense of intellectual purpose, especially among women in academia. Women's studies was not only studying other women, but a process of self discovery and consciousness transformation - a search for new strength and energy to create a different, more just social order. This oversimplified analysis of the rise of feminist consciousness in India and the movement's choice of a political identity and ideology for itself should not be viewed as independent of the interaction between the dynamics of democracy and India's diverse plurality discussed earlier. What is being emphasised here is a changed scenario - external as well as internal - for those involved in the movement. The choices made in the 80s and 90s were not possible for most women in earlier periods, divided as they were by their region, community, culture, caste and class. Nationalism, Gandhism and 'revolutionary' ideologies/ movements had temporarily brought some closer to each other, but the violence of the Partition had not allowed the closeness to find deeper roots and expand. The movement has adopted a multi-pronged approach on the issue of economic roles. While the specific skills of women's studies' scholars have been directed at evolving a critique of the macro-level policies of the government, grass roots level initiatives to develop alternatives have been stepped up.

One of the biggest mobilisations of women in Delhi from all over the country, in September 1989, was of over 20,000 women demanding the right to work. It is important to note that the few important concessionsf wrested from the government in the poverty alleviation through economic development programmes provided some space for poor urban and rural women to use the support to organise and articulate their demands. The movement's critique of the current economic growth policies has adopted three basic thrusts:

(a) that they are increasing inequalities among the people in general;

(b) that they make condition of the majority of women already struggling for survival still more vulnerable; and

(c) they are contributing to the social turbulence and violence, of which women and children are the major victims.

An important factor influencing the movement's shift of identity, concerns and ideology was the emergence of some large organisation of poor women in the urban informal sector from the 70s (SEWA, Working Women's Forum, Annapurna Mahila Mandal etc,) and new research documenting the dynamism in struggle demonstrated by them as well as their rural counterparts in various agrarian struggles through the 20th century. It provided a major focus to the movement's search for alternative strategies for development with organised groups from the grassroots as primary agents of change. Women have comprised a crucial component of those struggling for land and forest rights, against the havoc wrought by construction of large dams and ecological disasters, struggles for fishing rights in coastal waters, for recognition as workers in governmental networks of health and child care services, as urban unorganised labour, migrant labour and rural workers. In all these they have fought for basic rights as workers, for equal wages and better working conditions. Microstudies have highlighted the role women play in all these sectors. The great change in women's participation in the movements of earlier decades and now is an extension of identity and consciousness-blending occupational status with sisterhood as women. The increasing interdependence of poor women and educated women activists marks a process of mutually reinforcing empowerment and transformation of both.

Population Policy and the Women's Movement In confronting the use of sex-determination and sex-selection tests followed by abortion of female foetuses and female infanticide, the movement ran into resistance from (a) the very favoured and high priority policy of population control of the government; (b) the social impact of 30 years of the population debate on the better off sections of the Indian population, which included health professionals (doctors, medical education/research), development advocates, (scientists/social scientists, technologists, media etc.); and (c) some women's organisations - which had moved from the original demand for birth control services put forward by women in the 1920s and 30s as a women's right - to a wholehearted support for the government's policy for population control.

The CSWI had to confront two critical questions: (1) Health allocations indicated that from the Third Plan onwards the share of resources allocated for family planning was increasing at a much faster rate than all the other sectors of public health, including maternal and child health. Mortality statistics showed a widening gender gap between males and females across all age groups; (2) The Medical Termination of Pregnancy Act, 1972 legalising abortions. Consultations with many senior professionals convinced that while legalisation of abortion was necessary to save women's lives, its use as an instrument of population control had negatively affected medical ethics.

The debate was not pursued initially because feminists viewed abortion as a woman's right to voluntary maternity. Others who had tried to assist unmarried mothers after their rejection (or worse) by their families, also supported this view from humane convictions. The CSWI supported the strength of their argument that a large section of criminal abortions had belonged to this category. In the period after the Emergency, the practice of forced sterilization of men with small monetary compensation was abandoned but the population policy adopted during the Emergency remained, increasing pressure on the sterilisation of women. Within one year after the lifting of the Emergency, female sterilisation rose to over 90 per cent of the total. By the early '80s new reproductive technologies (NRIs) like amniocentesis had appeared on the scene.

During the last two decades both sex-determination and sex-selection tests and female infanticide has spread to many other regions, indicating a marked decline of the juvenile sex-ratio stimulating the demand for more studies and intervention strategies. Unfortunately public reaction remains muted and the movement's efforts weak/ineffective. The movement agitated against hazardous contraceptives (Norplant, Depo Provera, Quinacrine etc.), discovering that prescribed rules and procedures were being violated by government bodies with increasingly liberal import and marketing of dangerous drugs. Liberalisation of imports accelerated the spread of NRIs - for sex-determination in mobile vans providing tests and abortion - are reported even in rural areas. The movement's protests have forced the state and national governments into announcing various schemes of financial incentives to persuade families to save their daughters. The schemes suffer from the basic premise that the practice is primarily among the poor.

Women's groups are in touch with their counterparts outside the country to identify the role played by manufacturers of these products (mostly multi-nationals) and donor agencies from the developed countries who have aided and abated the government in its relentless pursuit of population control. Some population experts have always argued against the use of coercive methods for population control or using women's ignorance to promote use of hazardous contraceptives. It is against this background that the movement went into a confrontation with the Government of India to prevent a new population policy and some proposed Constitutional amendments that the movement considered anti- democratic, anti-women and anti-poor.

The 79th Constitutional Amendment Bill, 1992 proposed to deprive persons who do not voluntarily accept the two child family norm, of their democratic right to stand for elective offices. It was drafted on the recommendation of a Sub-committee of the National Development CouncilÄ in 1991. The Committee was headed by Bhairon Singh Shekhawat then the Chief Minister of Rajasthan - who promptly introduced the principle in the Rajasthan Panchayati Raj Amendment Act without waiting for the passage of the Amendment at the national level. The Government of Haryana followed suit, while the government of India - without informing the nation of the drafted Bill, appointed an Expert (Swaminathan) Committee to draft a national population policy towards the end of 1993. Some information regarding the proposed Constitutional change reached women's organisations and activists through allies within the government - beginning a direct approach to influence the Expert Group, and joint meetings to offer concrete suggestions for a more positive population policy which would promote more democratic, cooperative and egalitarian social development, abandoning the negative and coercive methods.

The Expert (Swaminathan) Committee's philosophical attempt to propagate a 'pro-poor, pro-women, and pro-nature' policy however foundered in the face of the lack of determination on the part of the government. Though the Committee did not directly support the Amendment already drafted - its reference to the Haryana and Rajasthan Acts as 'demonstrations of political will' enabled the Government of India to claim that its new draft policy, including the Amendment (and other proposed legislation) is based on the Expert Committee's Report, though the latter's entire analysis of the problem and related issues advocating a social development focused, rather than mere population control focused approach is missing from the new draft. In November 1996, a Cabinet Note enclosing the new draft policy suggested that the 79th Constitutional Amendment Bill was now ready for passage through Parliament.

Fortunately, a belated reference to the National Commission for Women for its comments - as required under the National Commission for Women Act, 1990 - brought forth a straight negative after consulting women's organisations and population experts. The Bill has not so far been passed but 'population control' figures in the present government's national agenda. It is reported however that the Bill has been rejected by members of the ruling coalition. Another proposed Constitutional Amendment being resisted by the movement is the 83rd, or the Fundamental Right to Education Bill

Another objectionable legislation proposed in the new population policy, which is also being resisted by the women's movement and the National Commission for Women, is a law to improve enforcement of the Child Marriage Restraint Act by disqualifying the victims of such marriage from all public employment. The contemporary women's movement in India spans a large canvas. There are small groups as well as large national organisations. While some are recent having been formed only over the last two decades, others go back to over 50 or even 100 years. Some organisations focus on single issues while the mass organisations cover a vast range.

The women's movement has undoubtedly grown. Its outreach is far beyond the figures of enrolled membership of organisations. These have now to take note of the increasing articulation of confidence by women at the grass roots level. Nothing illustrates this better than the response to the literacy campaigns in several states where earlier attempts to reach women had been abysmal failures. At a general level it is estimated that two-thirds of the neo-literate learners as well as two-thirds of the volunteers are women.

8

Conversion of Dalits

India's inter-religious violence now extends to Christians, and its underlying causes are the same as those promoting violence against Muslims, Dalits and other marginalized groups in the country-political and economic power struggles linked rhetorically to the creation of a Hindu nation. Attacks against Christians, which have increased significantly since the Hindu nationalist Bharatiya Janata Party came to power in March 1998, point to a disturbing trend of the assertion of Hindu nationalism by governments in power at the state and central level. They are part of a concerted campaign of right-wing Hindu organizations, collectively known as the sangh parivar, to promote and exploit communal tensions to stay in power-a movement that is supported at the local level by militant groups who operate with impunity.

Amounting to 2.3 percent of the nation's population, Christians nonetheless constitute the third-largest religious group in India after Hindus and Muslims. Though characterized by Hindu nationalist leaders as an alien faith or the religion of India's colonial rulers, Christianity took root in India almost 2,000 years ago when St. Thomas the Apostle evangelized in the south-home today to a majority of India's twenty-three million Christians.

In more recent years, missionaries have converted sizable majorities in three small northeastern states: Nagaland, Mizoram and Meghalaya. Today, close to 70 percent of India's

Christians are Catholic. Attracted by the church's emphasis on social service and equality, many tribals and Dalits ("untouchables") have converted to Christianity in an effort to escape their impoverished state and abusive treatment under India's caste system.

Most of the attacks against Christians have taken place in the country's "tribal belt," which runs from the Pakistani border in the west to Burma and Bangladesh in the east. The belt is home to eighty-one million indigenous people, whose ancestors inhabited India before the Aryan invasions of about 2,000 B.C. brought the country its dominant ethnic group. Animists or spirit worshippers by nature, many tribals do not practice Hinduism. Much like Dalits, they traditionally fall outside the Hindu fold.

Dalits, a population of nearly 160 million people, continue to suffer from extreme social discrimination, segregation and violence because of their rank at the bottom of India's caste system. Upon converting to Christianity, Dalits lose all privileges previously assigned to them under their scheduled caste status.

Until recently, Christians enjoyed a relatively peaceful coexistence with their majority Hindu neighbors. In the past several years, however, Christians have become the target of a campaign of violence and propaganda orchestrated by Hindu nationalist groups attempting to stem the tide of defecting low-caste and tribal voters. In 1996, two Catholic priests were killed in Gumla district, Bihar, their skulls crushed. In October 1997, the decapitated body of a third Catholic priest was found in a forest in Bihar.

According to the Indian Parliament, a total of 116 incidents of attacks on Christians across the country between January 1998 and February 1999. Most of the attacks have taken place in the north and the west where the Christian populations are smaller and Hindu nationalist sentiments are stronger. The increase in violence has paralleled the rise of the

Hindu right in India's political arena and the undermining of communal harmony by Hindu extremists, a trend that had been noted by the United Nations special rapporteur on religious intolerance in a 1997 report.

The number of Christians being attacked is still relatively small but has increased in the months preceding national parliamentary elections in September and October 1999. Corresponding closely to particular election contests in which Hindu nationalist groups have pursued major strategic goals, the attacks have continued in the periods following electoral victory. A majority of the reported incidents of violence against Christians in 1998 occurred in Gujarat, the same year that the BJP came to power in the state.

There are representative of anti-Christian violence in many other parts of the country. These include the role of sangh parivar organizations and the local media in promoting anti-Christian propaganda, the exploitation of communal differences to mask political and economic motives underlying the attacks, local and state government complicity in the attacks, and the failure of the central government to meet its constitutional and international obligations to protect minorities.

Between January 1998 and February 1999, the Indian Parliament reported a total of 116 incidents of attacks on Christians across the country. Unofficial figures may be higher. Gujarat topped the list of states with ninety-four such incidents. Attacks have also been reported in Maharashtra, Kerala, Madhya Pradesh, Bihar, Orissa, Andhra Pradesh, Haryana, Tamil Nadu, Karnataka, Manipur, West Bengal, Uttar Pradesh, and New Delhi. Attacks on Christians have ranged from violence against the leadership of the church, including the killing of priests and the raping of nuns, to the physical destruction of Christian institutions, including schools, churches, colleges, and cemeteries. Thousands of Christians have also been forced to convert to Hinduism.

In a pattern similar to the response to organized violence against lower castes, the tendency is for local officials under pressure to arrest a few members but not the leaders of the groups involved. The communities affected represent some of the poorest in the country and include Dalits and members of local tribal communities, many of whom convert to Christianity to escape abuses under India's caste system. In many cases, Christian institutions and individuals targeted were singled out for their role in promoting health, literacy, and economic independence among Dalit and tribal community members. A vested interest in keeping these communities in a state of economic dependency is a motivating factor in anti-Christian violence and propaganda.

These recent attacks fall into a pattern of persistent abuse against marginalized communities. They represent a clear failure on the part of both the central and state governments to ensure that such communities enjoy the full protection of their constitutional rights to freedom of religion and equal protection under the law. Despite the existence of comprehensive legislation to address the problem of religious intolerance and communal violence, the government has failed to prosecute offending individuals and organizations; instead, it has in many cases offered tacit support and indirect justification for the attacks.

Christians are not the only minority to be targeted by the sangh parivar. Violence against Sikhs in northern India in 1984 and against India's Muslim community nationwide in 1992 and 1993 also stemmed from the activities and hate propaganda of these groups. Members of the sangh parivar include the Rashtriya Swayamsevak Sangh, the Vishwa Hindu Parishad, and the VHP's militant youth wing, the Bajrang Dal. In the state of Maharashtra, the Shiv Sena political party has also been implicated.

The RSS seeks to promote a Hindu ethos within India and among Indians living abroad. Although an ostensibly cultural organization, RSS cells are involved in supporting political candidates for government, trade unions, and student organizations. The VHP was established in 1964 to unite Hinduism's regional and caste divisions under a single ecumenical umbrella. It is actively involved in Sanskrit education, the organization of Hindu rites and rituals, and the converting of Christians, Muslims, and animists to Hinduism. These organizations, although different in many respects, have all promoted the argument that although India is a democracy, because Hindus constitute the majority of Indians, India should be a Hindu state.

In the words of a sangh parivar activist in Gujarat, "The VHP is for the promotion of religion, the Bajrang Dal is for the protection of Hindus, and the BJP is for politics. The work systems are different, but the aim is the same. The Christian community also asserts that the situation has worsened since the Hindu nationalist BJP came to power in Delhi in March 1998. Although Prime Minister Atal Behari Vajpayee has publicly dissociated himself from the VHP and given assurances of safety to all Christians, his position has been ambiguous: while officially condemning the killing of Australian missionary Graham Staines in January 1999, for example, the prime minister called for a "national debate on conversions." Human rights groups criticized the move as legitimizing the motives behind the Staines attack.

In Gujarat's Dangs district, local officials, including police officers, have given outright support to rallies organized by groups that have fomented the violence. State and local officials have also attempted to downplay the destruction of Christian property, dismissing the burning of churches as attacks on mere temporary structures. Though authorities have characterized the violence as spontaneous eruptions or communal clashes between local groups, there is much evidence to suggest that they have been carefully organized by the leadership of extremist Hindu groups.

Local police have not provided adequate protection to villagers in the affected areas, even though there have been early warnings of violence. In some cases, police have refused to register complaints by members of the Christian community, whereas they have registered complaints by others against Christians. Some Christians who have filed charges with the police have been pressured to withdraw their complaints.

Officers who have taken action in response to anti-Christian attacks have been threatened with transfers. India's National Human Rights Commission has taken notice of recurring attacks in various states and has also issued notices to the chief secretaries of Orissa, Madhya Pradesh, and Gujarat, and to the Union home secretary seeking immediate and effective measures to prevent such events in the future. The National Commission for Minorities has also submitted several reports to state and central governments recommending prosecutions and accusing the government of willful neglect at all levels.

Religious Conversions and related Violence

Hindu nationalist leaders continually propagate the notion that Christians, despite their small numbers, could outnumber India's 82-percent Hindu majority early in the next century. Several state governments have threatened to ban Christian conversions altogether, while Hindu nationalists have launched their own "reconversion programs" and have called on the government to expel all missionaries from the country and stop the flow of foreign funding to "proselytizing agencies working under the various humanitarian garbs." Central secretary of VHP, has charged: "We were slaves for 1,000 years, and now we have opened our eyes." He demanded that the government "throw out these people who are out to convert Hindus and ruin our culture, language and attire." Onkar Bhave, also a VHP leader, announced: "We want to stop this conversion business.... They are not propagating religion; it is political slavery.... They want to turn the poor into Christians so together they can say to Hindus, 'Get out of India.' They want to break India into different pieces."

The RSS sees Christian missionaries as posing a threat to Hinduism, particularly in the northeastern part of the country where three tiny states have Christian majorities. The sangh accuses missionaries of being responsible for the insurgencies and separatist movements in the states of this region. It also blames the Indian government's "secular policy" which allowed these missionaries to continue their work even after the British left India in 1947. Of equal concern to the RSS is the work of missionaries in tribal regions.

The tribals, they claim, had always been a part of Hindu culture but had been alienated from the national mainstream by the British. Even after independence, they argue, the government followed the steps of the British and allowed missionaries to work in tribal regions. The RSS considers tribals to be particularly vulnerable to exploitation and conversions by Christian missionaries as they are largely illiterate and come from the weaker sections of society.

In 1998 the National Commission for Minorities conducted numerous investigations into attacks on Christian communities. The majority of its investigations took place in the states of Gujarat, Madhya Pradesh and Orissa. The National Commission for Minorities has been flooded with complaints from all over the country: Similar atrocities have taken place against Muslim communities in the past fifty years. Now there is a shift of focus to Christians. These are deeply sentimental issues. Stories of coerced conversions of low-caste and tribal Hindus to Christianity are doing much harm. Society has been poisoned and the central government has been a silent spectator.

Although the commission has submitted numerous reports on the incidents investigated, the government has done little to implement the commission's recommendations.

Commenting on the nexus between political parties and communal attacks, the chairperson added:

> The BJP talks of distancing itself from guilty bodies, but no action is taken in that direction. These are the very bodies that helped them come to power. How can they dissociate themselves from them?... This is what they said they would do before coming to power. Now they say they are secular. But they cannot stop state governments.... In Madhya Pradesh, Orissa, and Gujarat, even criminals are becoming communally selective thanks to the policies of the central government. There is a nexus between criminality and communalism, and the credit goes exclusively to the policies of the BJP. Someone has to take responsibility. Communalization of politics is not new. Communalization of crimes is a new phenomenon.

The Hindu organizations most responsible for violence against Christians are the VHP, the Bajrang Dal, and the RSS. According to a former RSS member, these groups cannot be divorced from the ruling BJP party: "There is no difference between the BJP and RSS. BJP is the body. RSS is the soul, and the Bajrang Dal is the hands for beating." The RSS was founded in the city of Nagpur in 1925 by Keshav Baliram Hedgewar with the mission of creating a Hindu state. Since its founding, it has propagated a militant form of Hindu nationalism as the sole basis for national identity in India. According to the RSS, both the leaders of India's nationalist movement and those of post-independence India failed to create a nation based on Hindu culture.

More than fifty years later, the RSS still sees itself as the antidote to what it considers the dangerous tendencies of modern-day India: "the erosion of the nation's integrity in the name of secularism, economic and moral bankruptcy, incessant conversions from the Hindu fold through money-power, ever-increasing trends of secession, thought patterns and education dissonant with the native character of the people, and State-sponsored denigration of anything that goes by the name of Hindu or Hindutwa." Western thought and civilization are perceived as enemies of Hindu culture. Religions such as Islam and Christianity are depicted as alien to India, as they are the religions of foreign invaders-the Mughals and the British.

The RSS believed that the liberation of the Hindu state required what it termed sarvangeena unnati, or all-round development of the nation. The RSS wanted "the entire gamut of social life" to be designed "on the rock bed of Hindu nationalism," a goal that inspired the creation of RSS political, social, and educational wings, a family of organizations that is now referred to collectively as the sangh parivar.

The Vishwa Hindu Parishad (VHP) was formed in 1964 to cover the social aspects of RSS activities. The VHP organizes and communicates the RSS message to Hindus living outside India and holds conferences for Hindu religious leaders from all over the country. The most publicized of the VHP's activities was its campaign to build a temple to the Hindu god Ram at the site of the Babri Masjid, a mosque in the city of Ayodhya in Uttar Pradesh.

The VHP, along with the other sangh organizations, claimed that the site of the mosque was actually the birthplace of Ram and that a temple at that site had been destroyed in order to build the mosque. On December 6, 1992, the mosque was demolished by members of the VHP, the Bajrang Dal, and RSS-trained cadres. The police did not intervene. The incident sparked violence around the country in which thousands were killed. Since then, the VHP has also organized a program to reconvert those who had been converted from Hinduism to other faiths.

The Bajrang Dal is the militant youth wing of the VHP. It was formed in 1984 during the Babri Masjid conflict, in order to mobilize youth for the Ayodhya campaign.. A young women's association, the Durga Vahini, was also founded at this time. Unlike other organizations affiliated to the RSS, the Bajrang Dal is not directly controlled by the sangh parivar. With its loose organizational structure, it initially operated under different names in different states. Its activists are believed to be involved in many acts of violence carried out by Hindutva organizations, including the recent spate of attacks against the Christian community in India.

The Jana Sangh Party was formed in 1951 as the political wing of the RSS. It was later replaced by the Bharatiya Janata Party (BJP) in 1980. The BJP is the largest of the nineteen parties that formed India's coalition government in March 1998. In addition to its important role in national politics, the BJP controls the state legislatures in Maharashtra, Gujarat, and Uttar Pradesh. On April 17, 1999, the BJP-led coalition was voted out of office, losing a motion of confidence by one vote.

The government had lost its majority in Parliament when a major coalition partner withdrew its support on April 14. Because the opposition was unable to come up with an alternative government, the BJP-led coalition was to act as the caretaker government until national parliamentary elections in September and October 1999. Founded by Bal Thackeray on June 19, 1966, the Shiv Sena is a Hindu party based in Maharashtra.33 Arising out of a campaign against the growing influence of non-Marathi speakers in Bombay, the Shiv Sena became a major force in Indian politics during the 1980s. The Sena is a close ally of the BJP and is part of the ruling central government coalition. An alliance of the Shiv Sena and the BJP, with the Sena as the dominant partner, has also been in power in the state government of Maharashtra since 1995. Leaders of both parties were implicated in the demolition of the Babri Masjid in Ayodhya and the ensuing violence in Bombay, the state capital.

BJP president and Home Minister L. K. Advani and Uttar Pradesh Chief Minister Kalyan Singh were among the forty people accused by the Central Bureau of Investigation (CBI) for the destruction of the mosque. Also on the list were Murli Manohar Joshi, the former chief minister of Maharashtra, and Bal Thackeray, the leader of the Shiv Sena. The CBI charged all of the accused with "criminal conspiracy, intentional destruction and defiling of a place of worship, criminal trespass and intimidation of public servants on duty." Advani and Joshi were present in Ayodhya when Hindu militants tore down the mosque.

The Srikrishna Commission was established in response to the notorious 1992-1993 Bombay riots that claimed the lives of 700 people, mostly Muslims, in the aftermath of the mosque's destruction.

In January 1999, members of the VHP reportedly drew up an elaborate plan to counter missionary activity by "reconverting" those who had adopted the Christian faith. The plan, conceived of during a nine-day meeting in Jaipur, Rajasthan, reportedly identified 200 "sensitive districts" in the country where missionary conversions had taken place. The "reconversions" were set to take place over a three-year period. A month later, during a three-day plenary session, the VHP demanded that the government ban religious conversions in the country. It claimed, however, that reconverting Christians to Hindus could not be equated with religious conversions as they were mere "home-comings" for those who had be induced out of the Hindu fold. VHP members also pronounced that the burning of churches and prayer halls in Gujarat's Dangs district, further described below, were part of an "international conspiracy" to defame BJP-led governments and to malign the VHP and the Bajrang Dal.

A majority of the reported incidents of violence against Christians in 1998 occurred in the western state of Gujarat, the same year that the BJP came to power in the state. The year began with an unprecedented hate campaign by Hindutva groups and culminated with ten days of nonstop violence against Christian tribals and the destruction of churches and Christian institutions in the southeastern districts at the year's end.

The events were preceded by escalating violence throughout the state in which many police and state officials were implicated. In February 1998 the heads of the village police attacked a prayer hall in Divan Tembrum village while prayers were taking place, and physically assaulted the worshippers.In April, a crowd of 400 used tractors and iron bars to destroy St. Antony's Catholic Church and several other affiliated structures in different stages of construction in Naroda, a suburb of Ahmedabad city.

The crowd smashed icons and stole the contents of the donation box. Witnesses said the crowd included members of the police, the VHP, and the local BJP government. In an interview, the head of the village council, Sumbubhai Maiatbhai, admitted to attending the demolition but claimed that the church was razed because it stood in violation of a local building code. Church officials said they were unaware of any such code violation.

In June several prayer halls were burned in Ahwa town, Dangs district. On July 8, a Methodist man's corpse was dug up in a Christian cemetery in Kapadvanj and dumped near his church. Witnesses said local VHP leaders led this desecration. Attacks and harassment of Christian-run schools were also on the rise. On July 16, the Shantiniketan High School in Zankhav village, Surat district, was broken into and stoned; its playground was ploughed by a tractor. The school was run by Jesuit priests of the Loyola Education Trust. The following day large numbers of "hooligans" from the neighboring village entered the market place in Zankhav, and violence ensued. Prior to the incident, two local language dailies, the *Gujarat Samachar* and *Sandesh*, had published a series of inflammatory articles charging that the Jesuit priests were engaged in forcible conversions of tribals to Christianity and that the school was admitting only Christian students.

On August 9, a church in Ahmedabad was demolished by RSS activists. On October 9, the Home Minister of Gujarat, Harin Pandya, threatened evangelist Roger Houstma with legal action if he continued to hold preaching and healing meetings in Gandhinagar. The next day Houstma's meeting in Rajkot was attacked. On November 11, in Dahunia village in the Dangs district, several Christian tribals, including an ailing woman, were beaten up.

Several Christian families in the village were forced to undergo a "conversion" ritual and bathe in Unai hot springs just north of the district. The village *sarpanch* (elected head of the village council) supported the attackers and said that Christians could not draw water from the village well or have their cattle graze with the animals of other villagers. The sarpanch also issued a decree preventing Christians in the village from working in any government or government-aided projects.

The state's chief minister, Keshubhai Patel, and VHP General Secretary Dr. Pravin Togadiya have both denied the involvement of sangh parivar activists in any of the attacks. Togadiya claimed that most of the incidents being blamed on VHP activists were "fits of imagination of a section of the media." "The provocations, if any," he added, "have come from the minorities, and the Hindus might have retaliated." Chief Minister Patel described the incidents as minor and isolated and, succumbing to VHP demands for immediate action against the "guilty minorities," ordered an inquiry into conversions activities at the missionary school in Rajkot where hundreds of copies of the Bible were burned in July 1998. In a clear indictment of Christian missionaries, Patel also threatened to ban conversions by "force or inducement." According to a report by the United Christian Forum for Human Rights, an ecumenical organization based in New Delhi:

> The constant effort of the state government, the political leadership, the senior administrators and police officers has been to dismiss the violence as minor, to describe the places of worship as "wood and mud structures" and to point out that there have been no deaths among the Christian tribals so far. The constant effort has been to make it seem like a communal clash between two communities.

Despite numerous arrests, the assaults continued through the end of the year and reached their peak during Christmas week 1998. The Hindu Jagran Manch (HJM), an offshoot of the sangh parivar consisting of people who belong to the Bajrang Dal, VHP and RSS, obtained permission to hold a rally on

December 25 in Ahwa town in the Dangs district. Over 4,000 people participated in the rally, shouting anti-Christian slogans while the police stood by and watched. After the rally, the attacks began on Christian places of worship, schools run by missionaries, and shops owned by Christians and Muslims. Between December 25 and January 3, churches and prayer halls were damaged, attacked, or burned down in at least twenty-five different villages in the state.

A Campaign of Hate

Several fact-finding missions to southeastern Gujarat by local and national human rights organizations have attributed the increase in violence to the growing presence and activities of sangh parivar groups in these areas. According to an October 1998 joint report by the Committee to Protect Democratic Rights and the Andhra Pradesh Civil Liberties Committee:

> A well planned strategy is being operated by the Hinduvata forces in Gujarat and it aims at communalising society at the grass root level. Youngsters belonging to the age group of fifteen to twenty-five are being recruited as activists of the Bajrang Dal for this purpose. They are taught to carry out operations covertly and deny any knowledge of those incidents where communal flare-ups do take place.... The VHP has also intensified its activities all over Gujarat. Activities such as the distribution of the idols of Hindu Gods, revival of Hindu festivals, conducting of 'Artis' [prayer ceremonies] etc., are on the increase in recent months.... A well planned program to "Hinduvise" the tribals is in full swing in the entire tribal belt of South Gujarat. The founding of the units of the VHP and the BD [Bajrang Dal] in each tribal locality, the regular visits and preaching of Swamis, the construction of temples for tribals, etc. are being pursued vigourously.

RSS and HJM fliers in August 1998 proclaimed, "India is a country of Hindus.... Our religion of Rama and Krishna is pious. To convert [or] leave it is a sin." Another flier by the VHP in Bardoli, Gujarat, warned, "Caution Hindus! Beware of inhuman deeds of Muslims.... Muslims are destroying Hindu Community by slaughter houses, slaughtering cows and making Hindu girls elope. Crime, drugs, terrorism are Muslim's empire." While a flier produced by the Bajrang Dal and VHP in November 1998 described the Bajrang Dal as a "wide organisation of youth," "working under the Vishva Hindu Parishad," with the objectives of "protecting mother India," "raising a loud voice against people who ignore Hindu Sabha assembly," raising people's awareness against the "trapping of Hindu girls by Muslims and anti-national activities of Christian missionaries," and working for the "protection of religion and culture." A parallel anti-Christian campaign was supported by the vernacular press that printed false reports of Hindu temples being destroyed, cited an increase in the percentage of Christians in the area, printed announcements for upcoming rallies, and repeatedly labeled the Christians as the main instigators of violence in December 1998 and January 1999.

While Hindutva groups have accused Christian missionaries of deceiving illiterate tribals, human rights activists argue that militant groups have long used Dalits and tribals as their foot-soldiers, preying on their social and economic "backwardness" and tempting them with money and alcohol. According to John Dayal, veteran journalist and national convenor of the United Christian Forum for Human Rights: "Dalits and tribals are used as instruments. They are paid, drugged, alcoholized, they are in a stupor." A local activist, who wishes to remain anonymous, expressed similar sentiments: "Hindu tribals are used to attack Christian tribals, Dalits are used to attack Muslims. High-ranking members of the RSS are never physically involved."

An increase in the number of Christians in southern Gujarat over the past ten years has also been used by RSS and its allies to support the accusation that tribals are being forcibly converted by Christian missionaries. Human rights activists contend that tribal conversions to Christianity must be placed in a social context. As noted by the Citizens' Commission report, "The question of conversion cannot be considered without taking into account the background of the people involved-particularly tribals in Dangs living in abject poverty, illiteracy, and with no facility for health care and comfort."

According to social workers in the region, tribals choose to convert for many reasons. As one social worker put it, "People go to Christianity because they believe they can be cured of disease. They give up drinking and other habits and thereby improve their financial position and their domestic relations. They also convert for literacy and education services." Although tribals are animists or spirit worshippers, Hindutva groups have been claiming that when tribals are converted to Christianity, they are being taken away from the Hindu faith. The term "reconversion" is therefore a misnomer:

> Since many of the adivasis tribals are not Hindu to begin with, though some have been "Hinduised," there can be no "reconversion" from Christianity to Hinduism.... As the sangh parivar's ideology treats Hinduism as the original and authentically Indian religion and tradition, for them any conversion from non-Hindu religion to Hinduism is "reconversion."

Focusing on conversions also deflects attention from other possible motivations underlying the attacks. As is often the case in organized communal incidents, the motivation is political in nature. As John Dayal noted:

> Tribals have been pauperized. Forests have been made into reserved forests. Tribals are denied the right to use forest produce. They go to work in the fields of the upper castes; women's sexual exploitation is endemic. Evangelical empowerment leads to education that tells them that they are equal. They are free. Still they are being exploited, they do not get decent wages, this is how they live despite the constitution. Not only does it rock the boat, it turns it upside down.

The activist also contends that these short- and long-term political objectives have the support of non-tribals in the area, in particular upper-caste Hindus. Over the last several years, tribals have been formulating a movement for self-rule through implementation of the fifth schedule of the constitution in the eastern belt. The fifth schedule calls for autonomous councils in tribal areas that would possess many decision-making powers and would exert control over development funds. Non-tribals whose authority is threatened by the movement are able to use the communal incidents and divisions among tribals on religious grounds to successfully undermine the movement.

Although the highest number of incidents took place in Gujarat, attacks have also been reported in Maharashtra, Uttar Pradesh, Kerala, Bihar, Orissa, Madhya Pradesh, Haryana, Andhra Pradesh, Tamil Nadu, Karnataka, Manipur, West Bengal, and New Delhi. Most of the states are not BJP-led, but many in the north and west of India have strong sangh parivar networks. Some of the attacks, including the killing of an Australian missionary and his two sons in Orissa and the gang rape of four nuns in Madhya Pradesh, are described below. While they represent only a portion of the many incidents reported throughout the country, they are included to demonstrate that the events in Gujarat were part of a much broader pattern.

A series of attacks took place between February 1998 and June 1999 in the state of Maharashtra. On February 14, 1998, a hospital run by the Catholic Hospital Association of India was attacked and ransacked, allegedly by members of the RSS in Latur, Maharashtra. On October 16, a prayer hall gathering in Kumbale village in Nasik was attacked. The prayer house was also destroyed. On December 25, armed activists from the Bajrang Dal accosted about 1,000 people attending a dance at the St. Francis School in Borivill, Bombay. The assailants were arrested and then released. In June 1999, the Shiv Sena launched a renewed series of attacks against Christian mission-run kindergarten schools, allegedly because they were not giving admission to the Shiv Sena activists' children. On June 26, suspected Sena members vandalized the Sacred Heart school in Worli, Bombay.

A similar pattern developed in Uttar Pradesh. On September 23, 1998, the same day four nuns were gang raped in Jhabua district, Madhya Pradesh, nuns in a Clarist convent in Bhagpat were attacked and robbed. The next day, a group of men smashed the front door of the F.C.C. Convent in Bhagpat, desecrated the chapel, assaulted several nuns, and ransacked all their rooms and belongings. On September 26, activists of the Hindu Jagran Manch, the Bajrang Dal and the Rana Tharu Parishad broke into the Union Church in Amaun in Udham Singh Nagar district. They placed an idol of the Hindu god Shiva in the church and conducted prayers for two hours.

Christians in India's southern states also came under attack. In Karnataka, a total of eleven Christian-run schools in Bangalore, Mysore, Hubli, Mandya, and Belari were attacked by Bajrang Dal activists on July 17, 1998. On November 22, the St. Thomas Evangelical Church of India in Kulai was attacked while a prayer service was in progress. The pastor and several worshippers were severely beaten.

In Tamil Nadu, a group of Christians in Ayyampalayam in Erode district, were brutally attacked in February 1998, and the Bethany Fellowship Church was destroyed. In April 1998, VHP activists destroyed the Gibson Central Baptist Church in the Kurnool district of Andhra Pradesh. In Kerala the same month the Little Flower Church was attacked and a crucifix was desecrated.

One of the most egregious incidents involved the gang rape of nuns in the state of Madhya Pradesh. At about 2:00 a.m. on September 23, 1998, four nuns who operate a medical clinic in Preetisharan Ashram in Nawapura village, Jhabua district, were gang raped by more than a dozen men. According to Father Lucas, secretary of Indore Diocese, a group of about eighteen or twenty armed men tried to enter the convent by pretending to be the relatives of a sick boy who needed medical attention. When the four nuns refused to open the gate, the men forced their way in and looted cash and valuables. They then proceeded to gang rape the four nuns who had taken refuge in a chapel inside the ashram. The district administration claimed that the incident was a random attack by local tribals, some of whom had criminal records. Tribals constitute 84 percent of the population of Jhabua district. The district collector stated that tribals often engaged in looting, theft, and dacoity, and that "there have been cases when they have committed rape. Only very often the rape cases have gone unnoticed." Others contend that tribals are often made the scapegoat in such cases because of their alleged "criminal inclination." Christian groups in India have also been reluctant to accept that the gang rape was merely a random attack by tribals and claim that the incident was part of a series of organized attacks against the Christian community throughout the country.

The BJP condemned the rapes as "outrageous" and called for the offenders to be punished on a "most immediate basis." The VHP, however, accused the nuns of trying to convert local Hindus to Christianity, while VHP secretary claimed that the incident reflected the "anger of patriotic Hindu youth against the anti-national forces." The BJP did not criticize such inflammatory remarks and instead accused opposition parties of giving the incident communal overtones.

Legal Measures to Protect the Rights of Minorities

Attacks on Christians, the destruction of Christian institutions, forced conversions to Hinduism and numerous other abuses constitute violations of domestic and international law. International human rights law, constitutional provisions, and domestic legislation together impose on the government of India a duty to guarantee certain basic rights to minority populations, to prosecute those who participate in communal violence, and to punish complicit state officials who, having the power and duty to stop the violence, do not intervene.

The preamble of the Indian constitution openly declares India as a "sovereign socialist secular democratic republic" which secures to all citizens "liberty of thought, expression, belief, faith and worship." Though many have debated the meaning of the term secular, in the Indian context it has come to imply equality of rights for all regardless of religion, the exercise of religious freedom and tolerance, and the rejection of discrimination based on religion or belief.

Under articles 14, 15, and 16 of the Indian constitution, discrimination on the grounds of religion is prohibited, and all citizens are guaranteed the right to equal treatment before the law and the right to equal protection of the laws. Article 25 guarantees the right to freely practice and propagate religion while articles 26, 28, and 30 ensure the freedom to manage religious affairs, to attend religious instruction or religious worship in certain educational institutions, and the rights of minorities to establish and administer educational institutions, respectively.

Select provisions of the Indian Penal Code make punishable acts of violence or discrimination based on religion. These include:

- Promoting violent attacks against groups on grounds of religion, race, place of birth, or language.
- Injuring or defiling a place of worship with the intention of insulting the religion
- Committing deliberate and malicious acts intended to outrage religious feelings of any class, by insulting its religion or religious beliefs
- Disturbing religious assemblies
- Trespassing places of worship or places set apart for the performance of funeral rites with the intention of

wounding the feelings of any person, or of insulting the religion of any person

— Promoting enmity between different groups on grounds of religion, race, place of birth, residence, language, caste or community, etc., see also committing such an offense in a place of worship, sec. 505(3))

Three other laws should also provide protection to religious minorities. The Religious Institutions (Prevention of Misuse) Act, 1988, prevents the misuse of religious places for political and criminal activities. It prohibits, among other things, the use of any premises of any religious institution for any act that promotes or attempts to promote disharmony or feelings of enmity or hatred between different religious, racial, language or regional groups. Violations under the act are punishable with imprisonment for up to five years and with a fine of up to Rs. 10,000 (US$238). The Places of Worship (Special Provisions) Act, 1991, prohibits the conversion of any place of worship of any religious denomination into a place of worship of a different religious institution and for the maintenance of the religious character of places of worship as it existed on 15 August 1947.

Violations under the act are punishable with imprisonment for a term of up to three years and also a fine. A person convicted of an offence under the said act shall be disqualified for being chosen as, and for being, a Member of either House of Parliament or of the Legislative Assembly or Legislative Council of a state. The Representation of the People Act, 1951, prohibits the use of religion or religious symbols to promote one's candidacy or to adversely affect the election of another candidate constitutes a corrupt practice that debases the election and is an offense punishable under the law.

International Law

In addition to its duties under domestic law, India is also party to several international treaties that impose human rights obligations. Article 18 of the International Covenant on Civil and Political Rights establishes the right to freedom of thought, conscience, and religion. It provides that:

1. Everyone shall have the right to freedom of thought, conscience and religion. This right shall include freedom to have or to adopt a religion or belief of his choice, and freedom, either individually or in community with others and in public or private, to manifest his religion or belief in worship, observance, practice and teaching.
2. No one shall be subject to coercion which would impair his freedom to have or to adopt a religion or belief of his choice.
3. Freedom to manifest one's religion or beliefs may be subject only to such limitations as are prescribed by law and are necessary to protect public safety, order, health, or morals or the fundamental rights and freedoms of others.

Articles 2 and 26 bar discrimination on the grounds of religion while Article 27 dictates that "[i]n those States in which ethnic, religious or linguistic minorities exist, persons belonging to such minorities shall not be denied the right, in community with the other members of the their group, to enjoy their own culture, to profess and practice their own religion, or to use their own language." The right to freedom of religion and prohibitions on discrimination on the grounds of religion are further elaborated upon in the Declaration on the Elimination of All Forms of Intolerance and of Discrimination Based on Religion or Belief.

Although not a treaty, this declaration, proclaimed by the General Assembly of the United Nations in 1981, provides authoritative guidelines to U.N. member states on ways to eliminate religious intolerance and discrimination. Article 4 of the declaration proclaims that, "All States shall take effective measures to prevent and eliminate discrimination on the grounds of religion or belief in the recognition, exercise and enjoyment of human rights and fundamental freedoms in all fields of civil, economic, political, social and cultural life," and that "all States shall make all efforts to enact or rescind legislation where necessary to prohibit any such discrimination, and to take all appropriate measures to combat intolerance on the grounds of religion or other beliefs in this matter."

Following the election of a Hindu nationalist government in India in February 1998, an environment of increasing hostility toward religious minorities has been fostered by elements closely aligned with those in power. The burning of churches and assaults on Christians, including priests and nuns, are not only tolerated but are tacitly supported by the government through anti-conversion rhetoric and a systematic failure to prosecute individuals and leaders responsible for fomenting the violence. As was the case with the Wadhwa Commission report, inquiries often stop short of blaming the groups involved and instead characterize the incidents as the isolated actions of misguided individuals who remain free to attack again.

Though eyewitnesses have identified politicians and local officials as participants in the attacks, the state administration and Hindu nationalist leaders continue to portray the incidents as actions instigated by minority communities. The chief minister of Gujarat and BJP spokesmen have even blamed the violence on an "international conspiracy" to defame the political party. The prime minister has called for a national debate on conversions, while the central and state governments continue to ignore the recommendations of the National Commission for Minorities.

The government's failure to protect religious minorities also raises serious questions as to its own commitment to abide by constitutional provisions, international law, and domestic legislation that together guarantee minorities the right to freely profess, practice, and propagate religion. Using Hindu nationalist sentiments to cultivate vote banks also runs counter to the principles of a secular democracy as enshrined in the Indian constitution.

Actions to be Taken

The government of India should demonstrate its commitment to protecting the rights of minorities by implementing the following recommendations at the earliest possible date. In compliance with the Indian constitution and the International Covenant on Civil and Political Rights, it should ensure that all citizens may equally enjoy freedom of conscience and the right to freely profess, practice, propagate, and adopt religion. In particular, it should commit to taking steps to prevent further violence and prosecute both state and private actors responsible for attacks on religious minorities.

Recommendations to the Government of India

- Provide adequate police protection to Christians and other minority communities in violence-affected areas, including, where necessary, an increase in the number of police stations and outposts in each district.
- Require that police register all cases of communal attacks, regardless of the religious background of the complainant, and enforce this regulation through frequent reviews of registers by a magistrate or other competent judicial authority and the establishment of a civilian review board mandated to investigate complaints. Police who violate the regulation should be dismissed.
- Investigate and prosecute state officials complicit in attacks on minorities. Police who are found to be complicit should be dismissed.
- End impunity for past campaigns of violence against minorities. That is, prosecute and punish all those found responsible for murder, rape, assault, and destruction of

property during the post-Ayodhya violence of December 1992 and January 1993. Police responsible for excessive use of force should be prosecuted; those who having the power and duty to stop the violence but did not intervene should be punished accordingly. Victims and family members should be paid compensation.

— Implement the recommendations made by the National Commission for Minorities in its reports on attacks on Christians in various states.

— Make public the recommendations of the Wadhwa Commission and prosecute those found responsible for the 1999 attacks in Orissa.

— Ensure speedy review and publication of findings by commissions of inquiry appointed by the state to investigate abuses against minorities.

— Strengthen the capacity of the National Human Rights Commission, the National Commission for Minorities, and the National Commission for Scheduled Castes and Scheduled Tribes to operate branch offices in all states with enough financial resources and powers to initiate prosecution of cases.

— Prohibit surveys by district administrations to assess the activities and whereabouts of minority community members and leaders.

— Launch a nationwide public awareness campaign regarding the dangers of communal violence. This campaign should explain in simple terms what actions are legally prohibited, what recourse is available to minorities, and what the procedures are for filing a First Information Report. It should also include a program of public service announcements in all states aimed at sensitizing the population against any form of religious extremism and creating awareness of minority rights.

— Implement the recommendations made by the U.N. special rapporteur on the question of religious intolerance in his report on his December 1996 visit to India. In particular, the following recommendations should be implemented:

— Increase awareness of the existence and dangers of extremism because, despite the fact that it is confined to a minority, its influence on the masses through political parties, places of worship, schools and even seats of power, could well destroy community and religious harmony in India.

— The Representation of the Peoples Act, 1951, should be scrupulously implemented and that in addition it should be speedily supplemented by a new act debarring political parties from the post-election use of religion for political ends.

— Places of worship should be used exclusively for religious, and not political, purposes. As places for prayer and meditation, they should be protected against tension and partisan struggle. The State should therefore ensure that places of worship remain neutral ground and are sheltered from political currents and ideological and partisan controversy.

— Education can play a vital role in preventing intolerance, discrimination, hate and violence (including violence motivated by extremism) by creating and disseminating a culture of tolerance among the masses and the most disadvantaged segments of the population. It can make a decisive contribution to the assimilation of values based on human rights by the use of school curricula and textbooks reflecting principles of tolerance and non-discrimination.

Recommendations to the International Community

— India's donors and trading partners should pressure the Indian government to implement the recommendations of the Srikrishna Commission on the 1992-1993 Bombay riots, and the recommendations of the National Commission for Minorities on attacks against Christians. They should urge the Indian government to prosecute those responsible for masterminding attacks on minority religious communities.

— India's donors and trading partners should provide funding for preventative measures to ensure that communal outbreaks do not recur. Such measures might include community education programs on communal issues and the establishment of a civilian review board to act as a check on the functioning of the police and other governmental institutions during communal outbreaks.

9

Issues of Dalit Muslims

Islam entered India almost immediately after its birth in the 7th century A.D and made its way into different parts of the country. In the south it entered through the present day state of Kerala situated on the Malabar Coast in South India. Its carriers were the Arab traders who had been involved in trade activities with India even before the times of Prophet Muhammad.

During their numerous voyages to the Malabar region, the Arab traders established matrimonial relationships with the local women and had many progeny from these marriages. This resulted in the spread of Islam to different parts of the region. Many Sufi saints accompanied these traders and under the influence of their preaching and the attraction of an egalitarian faith many local people, mainly from lower classes, converted to Islam. A major factor to be borne in mind here is that Islam's first step on Indian soil was not, as many would like to believe, riding on the wave of the sword.

In the North, Islam came along with the invasion of Muhammad bin Qasim, a general of Yusuf bin Hajjaj, the governor of Iraq during the Umayyad period. This was followed by the many invasions of Muhammad Ghori and Mahmud Ghazni, both interested merely in the enormous wealth and riches that India offered. The two were never interested in occupying and ruling the land of India. Their main focus was to plunder, pillage and transfer as much wealth as possible to their respective capitals since this was crucial for them to maintain their large armed forces and entourage used in their frequent military campaigns.

The history of Islam in India is well over a thousand years old today. It has blended beautifully into the background of its adopted land and contributed immensely to the formation of a composite Indian culture and the building of the Indian nation. But this Islam and its practitioners are not a homogeneous entity as is widely believed. In fact there is a great deal of diversity in the manner in which Islam is practiced and perceived throughout India.

This is hardly surprising considering the facts that Islam in India is almost as old as the faith itself and that its followers in different regions of the country represent a myriad of cultures. In this process of adapting to the variety of cultural milieus, Islam has acquired many hues and should not be considered as a monolithic entity. Nevertheless, Muslims in India have responded well to the challenges of living as a minority in a religiously plural society. But this process of assimilation into the Indian society has not been an easy one and the challenges that Muslims of India face today continue to exist with the constantly shifting national and international state of affairs.

Caste Inequality Among Muslims

Although the Qur'an insists on the radical equality of all Muslims, caste (zat, jati, biraderi) remains a defining feature of Indian Muslim society, with significant regional variations. While the severity of caste among the Indian Muslims is hardly as acute as among the Hindus, with the practice of untouchability being virtually absent, caste and associated notions of caste-based superiority and inferiority still do play an important role in Indian Muslim society.

In most parts of India, Muslim society is based on the existence of numerous endogamous and generally occupationally specific caste groups, that have their own caste appellations. This disjunction between Qur'anic egalitarianism and Indian Muslim social practice has been theorized by Muslim scholars in different ways. While some have sought to reconcile the two by interpreting the scripturalist sources of Islam to support social hierarchy, others have pointed out that the continued existence of caste-like features in Indian Muslim society is a flagrant violation of the Qur'anic worldview.

Most studies of caste in India deal with the classical Hindu caste system or with its present forms among the Hindus. Since caste is the basis of the Hindu social order and is written into the Brahminical texts, studies of caste have been largely Hindu-centric. Following from this, the existence of caste-like features among non-Hindu, including Muslim, communities in India is thus generally seen as a result of the cultural influence on these communities of their Hindu neighbours or of Hinduism itself. This claim is based on the untenable assumption of a once pure, radically egalitarian Muslim community in India later coming under the baneful impact of Hinduism.

However, as several studies on caste among the Indian Muslims have shown, while the influence of Hindu social mores on the Muslims might partially explain the continued salience of caste among them it does not fully explain how the Muslims of the region came to be stratified on the basis of caste in the first place. It also ignores the role of sections of the 'ulama, scholars of Islamic jurisprudence, in providing religious legitimacy to caste with the help of the concept of kafa'a.

The vast majority of the Indian Muslims are descendants of converts from what is today called 'Hinduism'. Individual conversions to Islam in medieval times were rare. Rather, typically, entire local caste groups or significant sections thereof underwent a gradual process of Islamisation, in the course of which elements of the Islamic faith were gradually incorporated into local cosmologies and ritual practice while gradually displacing or replacing local or 'Hindu' elements.

In other words, conversion was both a social as well as a gradual process. Because it was a collective social process, the original endogamous circle prior to conversion was still preserved even after the group undergoing the process had witnessed a significant degree of cultural change. Hence, even after conversion to Islam marriage continued to take place within the original caste group. This is how Muslim society came to be characterized by the existence of multiple endogamous caste-like groups.

Because mass conversion to Islam was also rarely, if ever, a sudden event, but, rather, generally took the form of a gradual process of cultural change, often extending over generations, many of the converts retained several of their local, pre-Islamic beliefs and practices. It was thus not the influence of Hinduism among a previously 'pure', 'uncontaminated' Muslim community as such, but, rather, the continued impact of Hindu beliefs and customs on the converts who still remained within a largely Hindu cultural universe and retained many of its associated beliefs and practices, that explains the continued hold of caste-related practices and assumptions among large sections of the Indian Muslim community.

Ashraf-Ajlaf Divide

Scholarly writings on caste among Indian Muslims generally note the division that is often made between the so-called 'noble' castes or ashraf and those labeled as inferior, or razil, kamin or ajlaf. The ashraf-ajlaf division is not the invention of modern social scientists, for it is repeatedly mentioned in medieval works of ashraf scholars themselves. To these writers, Muslims of Arab, Central Asian, Iranian and Afghan extraction were superior in social status than local converts. This owed not just to racial differences, with local converts generally being dark-skinned and the ashraf lighter complexioned, but also to the fact that the ashraf belonged to the dominant political elites, while the bulk of the ajlaf remained associated with ancestral professions as artisans and peasants which were looked down upon as inferior and demeaning.

In order to provide suitable legitimacy to their claims of social superiority, medieval Indian ashraf scholars wrote numerous texts that sought to interpret the Qur'an to suit their purposes, thus effectively denying the Qur'an's message of radical social equality. Pre-Islamic Persian notions of the divine right of kings and the nobility, as opposed to the actual practice of the Prophet and the early Muslim community, seem to have exercised a powerful influence on these writers.

A classical, oft-quoted example in this regard is provided by the Fatawa-i Jahandari, written by the fourteenth century Turkish scholar, Ziauddin Barani, a leading courtier of Muhammad bin Tughlaq, Sultan of Delhi. This text is the only known surviving Indo-Persian treatise exclusively devoted to political theory from the period of the Delhi Sultanate.

The Fatawa-i Jahandari shows Barani as a fervent champion of ashraf supremacy and as vehemently opposed to the ajlaf. In appealing to the Sultan to protect the ashraf and keep the ajlaf firmly under their control and submission he repeatedly refers to the Qur'an, from which he seeks to derive legitimacy from his arguments. His is not a rigorous scholarly approach to the Qur'an, however, for he conveniently misinterprets it to support the hegemonic claims of the ashraf, completely ignoring the Qur'an's insistence on social equality.

In the process, he develops a doctrine and social vision for the ideal Muslim ruler, which, in their implications for what Barani calls the 'low-born', are hardly different in their severity than the classical Hindu law of caste as contained in the Manusmriti, the Brahminical law code. As Barani's translator, Mohammad Habib, writes, 'Barani's God, as is quite clear from his work, has two aspects-first, he is the tribal deity of the Musalmans; secondly, asbetween the Musalmans themselves, He is the tribal deity of well-born Muslims'. Barani was not a lone voice in his period, however, for he seems to echo a widely shared understanding of ashraf supremacy held by many of his ashraf contemporaries, including leading 'ulama and Sufis.

Barani's disdain for the 'low' born is well illustrated in his advice to the Sultan about education of the ajlaf. While the Qur'an and the traditions attributed to the Prophet repeatedly stress the need for all Muslims, men and women, rich and poor, to acquire knowledge, Barani insists that the Sultan should consider it his religious duty to deny the ajlaf access to knowledge, branding them as 'mean', and 'despicable'. Thus, he advises the Sultan:

> Teachers of every kind are to be sternly ordered not to thrust precious stones down the throats of dogs or to put collars of gold round the necks of pigs and bears-that is, to the mean, the ignoble and the worthless, to shopkeepers and to the low-born they are to teach nothing more than the rules about prayer, fasting, religious charity and the haj pilgrimage, along with some chapters of the Qur'an and some doctrines of the faith, without which their religion cannot be correct and valid prayers are not possible. But they are to be taught nothing else, lest it bring honour to their mean souls.

As Barani sees it, if the ajlaf were allowed access to education, they might challenge ashraf hegemony. Therefore, he sternly warns the Sultan:

> They are not to be taught reading and writing, for plenty of disorders arise owing to the skill of the low born in knowledge. The disorder into which all affairs of the religion and the state are thrown is due to the acts and words of the low born, who have become skilled. For, on account of their skill, they become governors (wali), revenue-collectors ('amils), auditors (mutassarif), officers (farman deh) and rulers (farman rawa). If teachers are disobedient, and it is discovered at the time of investigation that they have imparted knowledge or taught letters or writing to the low born, inevitably the punishment for their disobedience will be meted out to them.

In order to bolster his assertion that the Sultan should ensure that the ajlaf remain subservient to the ashraf, Barani seeks appropriate religious sanction. Thus, he asserts:

> [.] to promote base, mean, low-born and worthless men to be the helpers and supporters of the government has not been permitted by any religion, creed, publicly accepted tradition or state-law.

He then goes on to elaborate a theory of the innate inferiority of the ajlaf, the superiority of the ashraf and the divine right of the Sultan to rule, based on a distorted interpretation of Islam. Thus, he writes that the 'merits' and 'demerits' of all people have been 'apportioned at the beginning of time and allotted to their souls'. Hence, people's acts are not of their own volition, but, rather, an expression and result of of 'Divine commandments'.

God Himself, Barani claims, has decided that the ajlaf be confined to 'inferior' occupations, for He is said to have made them 'low born, bazaar people, base, mean, worthless, plebian, shameless and of dirty birth'. God has given them 'base' qualities, such as 'immodesty, wrongfulness, injustice, cruelty, non-recognition of rights, shamelessness, impudence, blood-shedding, rascality, jugglery and Godlessness' that are suitable only for such professions.

Furthermore, these base qualities are inherited from father to son, and so the ajlaf must not attempt to take up professions reserved by God for the ashraf even if they are qualified to do so, for this would be a grave violation of the Divine Will. Likewise, Barani claims, God has bestowed the ashraf with noble virtues by birth itself, and these are transmitted hereditarily. Hence, they alone have the right and responsibility of taking up 'noble' occupations, such as ruling, teaching and preaching the faith.

Since God is held to have made the ajlaf innately despicable and base, to promote them would be a gross violation of the divine plan. 'In the promotion of the low and low-born brings', Barani argues, ' there is no advantage in this world, for it is impudent to act against the wisdom of Creation'. Hence, he insists that if the Sultan confers any post in his court or government service to the ajlaf, the 'court and the high position of the king will be disgraced, the people of God will be distressed and scattered, the objectives of the government will not be attained, and, finally, the king will be punished on the day of Judgment'. In this regard, he refers to a tradition attributed to the Prophet, according to which Muhammad is said to have declared, 'The vein is deceptive'.

Although this tradition might be interpreted to suggest that one's social status does not depend on one's heredity, Barani offers a novel explanation of the tradition to suggest precisely the opposite conclusion, that 'the good vein and the bad vein draw towards virtue and vice', and that 'in the well-born and the noble only virtue and loyalty appear, while from the man of low birth and bad birth only wickedness and destruction originate'.

Likewise, he provides a novel interpretation of a Qur'anic verse (xlix: 13) to support his claim of ashraf superiority. He quotes the Qur'an as saying that God honours the pious, a statement that has generally been read to suggest that superiority in God's eyes depends on one's piety and not birth, to arrive at precisely the opposite conclusion. The verse, he says, implies that '[.] it ought to be known that in the impure and impure-born and low and low-born, there can be no piety'.

As Barani's writings on the ajlaf so clearly suggest, many medieval ashraf scholars shared a common understanding of the 'low-born' as born to serve the ashraf. Accordingly, to leigitimize this claim they interpreted the Qur'an as sanctioning a sternly hierarchical social order, with the subordinate status of the ajlaf ascribed to the Divine Will.

As H.N.Ansari, a contemporary Indian Muslim scholar and an activist of a 'low' caste Muslim organization, remarks, this represented a profoundly 'un-Islamic' reading of the Qur'an, which stresses the equality of all Muslims and lays down piety as the only criterion for merit in God's eyes. Yet, Ansari adds, men like Barani exercised a powerful influence in their times with their wrong interpretations of the Qur'an, resulting in the 'complete betrayal of the Qur'anic precepts of brotherhood'.

To imagine, as some writers today assert, a solidly egalitarian Muslim community pitted against a sternly hierarchical Hindu community in medieval India is thus hardly convincing. Nor, for that matter, is the explanation of the existence of caste and social hierarchy among Muslims as a result of the baneful impact of hierarchical Hinduism on egalitarian Islam.

Although the impact of the wider Hindu society on the beliefs and practices of the Muslims is obvious, in the face of hierarchical notions of religion and the normative social order as reflected in the writings of Barani, it is obvious that the Muslim elite played an equally central role in promoting and preserving social hierarchy by seeking to provide it with suitable 'Islamic' sanction. The effort to legitimize caste in 'Islamic' terms was given further impetus by the 'ulama through the notion of kafa'a, to which we now turn.

Legitimisation of Caste by the Indian Ulama

The Qur'an and the genuine Prophetic traditions consider Muslims as equals, and hence allow for any Muslim to marry a suitable Muslim spouse. In deciding an ideal marriage partner the Qur'an suggests the criteria of piety (taqwa) and faith (iman), regarding these, rather than birth or wealth, as the only mark of a person's nearness to God. It is clear from the records of the Prophet and his companions that this principle was actually acted upon. Thus, for instance, we hear of instances of slave men or recently freed slaves marrying free women with the Prophet's consent.

Over time, however, as Islam spread to new regions outside the confines of the Arabian peninsula, the early egalitarian Muslim society was transformed into a complex, sharply hierarchical social order. This owed to several factors, including the 'feudalisation' of Islam accompanying the emergence of the Ummayad empire; the incorporation of non-Arab groups as subordinate 'clients' (mawali) of ruling Arab tribes; and the impact of other cultures, particularly Greek and Persian, in which social hierarchies were already deeply entrenched.

These developments exercised a propound influence on the emerging schools of Islamic law (mazahib). As a result, notions of social hierarchy based on birth that were foreign to the Qur'an and to the early Muslim community were gradually incorporated into the corpus of writings of Islamic jurisprudence or fiqh. One manifestation of this was the central importance that the fuqaha or scholars of the different schools of Islamic jurisprudence now began paying to the notion of equality of status in matters of marriage or kafa'a. Elaborate rules were constructed built on the notion of kafa'a that specified the 'equals' whom one could legitimately marry.

Taking a spouse from outside one's kafa'a was sternly frowned upon, if not explicitly forbidden by the fuqaha. In the face of Qur'anic and genuine Prophetic traditions that stressed that the only basis for selecting one's marital partner was piety, the scripturalist sources of Islam were suitably misinterpreted to provide legitimacy for notions of kafa'a based on wealth and birth, including ethnicity.

These debates on kafa'a have a direct bearing on how the Indian Muslim 'ulama have looked at the question of caste, caste endogamy and inter-caste relations. Since the vast majority of the Indian Muslims follow the Hanafi school, the opinions of the classical Hanafi 'ulama on kafa'a continue to determine the attitudes of the Indian 'ulama on the question of caste and social hierarchy.

Most Indian Hanafis seem to have regarded caste (biraderi), understood here as hereditary occupational group, as an essential factor in deciding kafa'a, and in this way have provided fiqh legitimacy to the notion of caste. The detailed debates among the fuqaha of the law schools about kafa'a need not detain us here, and it is sufficient to mention that they differed somewhat on the criterion for deciding it.

Abdul Hamid Nu'mani, a contemporary Indian Muslim scholar, writes that many classical fuqaha considered the following issues to decide one's kafa'a for purposes of marriage:

— legal status as free or enslaved (azadi);

— economic status (maldari);

— occupation (pesha);

— intelligence ('aql);

— family origin or ethnicity (nasb);

— absence of bodily defects and illness; and, finally,

— piety (taqwa).

All these are said to have been deciding factors for kafa'a for the Hanafis and the Hanbalis, while according to Imam Malik, the real basis of kafa'a is said to have been piety. Imam Shafi' is said not to have included wealth in kafa'a. On the whole, however, most fuqaha insisted on taking factors other than simply piety in deciding kafa'a.

In the Indian context, this expanded notion of kafa'a, representing a considerable departure from the Qur'an, was accepted as laying down the norms for deciding on the legality of a Muslim marriage. By restricting marriage to one's occupational and ethnic group, caste, which is, in theory, an endogamous birth-based occupational category, came to be regarded as essential to establishing kafa'a for purposes of marriage. In this way, the notion of kafa'a helped to provide legitimacy to the existence of caste among the Indian Muslims by effectively restricting marriage within the endogamous caste circle. This is readily apparent even in the fatwa literature produced by several recent Indian 'ulama, an issue that we now look at.

To illustrate the ways in which significant sections of the Indian 'ulama have sought to employ the concept of kafa'a to legitimize caste and social inequality we focus here on a slim Urdu tract on the subject penned by a contemporary Indian Muslim scholar, Maulana 'Abdul Hamid Nu'mani. A senior leader of the Jami'at ul-'Ulama-i Hind ('The Union of the 'Ulama of India), Nu'mani belongs to the Ansari caste of hereditary weavers, traditionally considered by ashraf Muslims as 'low' in social status. His tract is a modified version of a speech that he delivered in 1994 at the request of the Anjuman Khuddam al-Qur'an, a Muslim missionary organization based at the town of Vaniyambadi in the southern Indian state of Tamil Nadu.

The Anjuman had invited him to deliver a lecture on the subject of Islamic mission (tabligh) and the question of kafa'a, for the Anjuman had itself discovered that one of the major hurdles in its missionary outreach work among the low-caste Hindus of the area was that while the converts were readily accepted as religious equals by other Muslims, the latter were unwilling, on grounds of kafa'a, to intermarry with them.

For the Anjuman, this problem appeared as a central concern for, by making the life of the converts difficult, it made conversion to Islam an unviable option for many. Accordingly, in order to clarify the 'true' Islamic perspective on kafa'a and to oppose notions of kafa'a that legitimize caste and social inequality, the Anjuman requested Nu'mani to deliver a scholarly paper on the subject in the light of the teachings of the Qur'an. The speech was apparently very well received, and was shortly published as a booklet, suitably titled Masla-i Kufw Aur Isha'at-i Islam.

Nu'mani beings his tract by arguing that the single most important factor for the spread of Islam in India was the Qur'an's message of radical sccial equality (masavat) and respect for all humankind (ihtiram-i admiyat). This naturally appealed most to the downtrodden 'low' castes who were sternly oppressed by the Brahminical religion and the caste system on which it was based. The Sufis who propagated Islam among the 'low' castes are said to have been seriously committed to their welfare, but because their scale of work was so immense they were unable to properly tend to the proper Islamic instruction of their neophytes.

Therefore, Nu'mani says, the converts retained several of their pre-Islamic beliefs and practices, including notions of caste. Further, he writes, caste and related concepts of birth-based ritual status were given added legitimacy by Muslim rulers and missionaries who had come to India from the lands of 'ajam, Iran, Turkey and Central Asia, where concepts of social inequality were already well entrenched.

Nu'mani quotes extensively from Barani's Fatawa-i Jahandari to show how discriminatory attitudes towards low-caste converts were widely shared by medieval Muslim elites. He also comments on the absence of any effective opposition to such views. In fact, he goes so far as to claim that, 'From Barani's time till 1947 the notion of Muslim society being divided into ashraf and ajlaf, high and low, was continuously present'.

He refers to some twentieth century Indian 'ulama of his own Deobandi school as opposing caste-based inequality among the Indian Muslims but laments that 'this sickness has not as yet been fully eliminated'. He admits that although the caste system is less severe among the Muslims than it is among the Hindus, in that untouchability is absent among the former, with caste playing a determining role only in marriage among Muslims. Yet, he pleads for Muslims to combat notions of caste based superiority and inferiority, for only then, he argues, can efforts to spread Islam among 'low' caste Hindus be effective. For this purpose, he says, a radical revisioning of the concept of kafa'a is urgently required

In the process of developing a Qur'anic notion of kafa'a, Nu'mani surveys notions of kafa'a as developed by the classical fuqaha and further elaborated upon by various Indian 'ulama. Since his concern is to revive the original Qur'anic notion of kafa'a, which alone he sees as normative and binding, he engages in a process of ijtihad (although he does not refer to it as such), refusing to remain tied down by formulations of kafa'a as contained in the corpus of fiqh, including of the Hanafi school with which he is associated.In evoking what he calls the true Islamic position on kafa'a, he has four broad objectives. Firstly, to revive the original message of radical social equality of the Qur'an which he sees many later 'ulama as having distorted, willfully or otherwise. Secondly, to combat caste-based divisions among the Muslims and thereby to promote Muslim unity. Thirdly, to disprove claims of critics that Islam is not an egalitarian religion and that, therefore, it cannot provide equality to 'low' caste Hindu converts. Finally, to provide an understanding of kafa'a that, being liberated from notions of caste, can help in integrating converts into the mainstream of Muslim society through inter-marriage and thereby remove a major hurdle in the path of Muslim missionary work, particularly among 'low' caste Hindus.

In doing so, Nu'mani has to deal with reports attributed to the Prophet and some of his close companions that seem to legitimize social inequality, as well as the writings of the classical fuqaha on the subject of kafa'a. As regards certain hadith which seem to promote discriminatory attitudes towards people who follow certain 'low' professions, Nu'mani subjects the lines of transmission (isnad) as well as content (matn) of these reports to close scrutiny, concluding that they are fabricated. He explains some statements by the companions of the Prophet that militate against social equality by reading them contextually, and hence argues that they are not applicable for all time.

On the restrictive provisions related to kafa'a that the fuqaha have prescribed, Nu'mani insists that the Qur'an and the genuine Hadith should be the sole criterion for judging them. Since the corpus of fiqh is a post-Qur'anic development, and since the fuqaha were mere mortals, although they might have been well intentioned, Nu'mani suggests that Muslims should not blindly follow their prescriptions if they violate the Qur'an and the genuine Hadith. However, rather than opposing the opinions of the fuqaha directly he points to the differences between the different schools of fiqh, and within each school the varying opinions of different fuqaha, on the question of kafa'a, highlighting those views that support his own radically egalitarian understanding of kafa'a.

After providing a brief note on the varying definitions of kafa'a in different schools of Islamic jurisprudence, Nu'mani writes that according to the Qur'an, kafa'a is based only on piety. Hence, the only criterion for deciding a marriage partner should, ideally, be his or her personal character and dedication to the faith. In other words, he suggests, there is no religious bar for a Muslim man from a low caste or a low caste Hindu convert to Islam to marry a Muslim girl from a high caste or vice versa. This, of course, goes completely against dominant notions of kafa'a. Nu'mani does not openly question the schools of fiqh as such. Rather, he points to possibilities within the existing schools and to differences among the fuqaha of the different schools as well as within each school to press his claim for an egalitarian reading of kafa'a.

In arguing the case for an egalitarian interpretation of kafa'a Nu'mani has to contend with traditions that have been used by many scholars to insist on the need for people to marry within their same social class. He does not deny the veracity of such claims but interprets them in a novel way to bolster his argument that cross-class marriages are to be regarded as legitimate as well.

Thus, for instance, he refers to a tradition according to which the third caliph, 'Umar, refused to let a girl from a rich family to marry a man from a lower class. Nu'mani does not say that the caliph was wrong in his pronouncement. Rather, he says, his opinion was correct because it might be difficult for such a girl to live in poor family without the comforts to which she was used to before marriage. Hence, for marital compatibility a rough equality of economic status is indeed preferable. However, Nu'mani argues, this does not mean that a girl from a rich family cannot marry a poor man or that equality in economic status is an absolute necessity in marriage. Nu'mani recognizes that rough equality of economic status is preferable in marriage partners, but insists that it is not absolutely essential. To use 'Umar's decision to argue the case that marriage must take place only within one's social class or caste, is therefore, untenable. Nu'mani here quotes another, conflicting report attributed to 'Umar, according to which the caliph declared that in deciding a man's marriage partner he did not consider her ethnic or economic status.

Likewise, on the question of occupation (pesha) in determining kafa'a, Nu'mani writes that many 'ulama have adopted what he calls an 'unnecessarily restrictive' attitude, which has led to notions of caste superiority and inferiority since caste is, in theory, also an occupational category. Nu'mani remarks that this is particularly unfortunate, given that Imam Abu Hanifa, whose school of jurisprudence most Indian Muslims claim to follow, did not himself consider occupation as a factor in determining kafa'a.

This is because one's occupation does not always remain the same and can, in theory, change. Nu'mani also refers to some Hanafi jurists who placed knowledge ('ilm) above profession in deciding kafa'a, thereby allowing a learned Muslim from a family following a 'low' profession to marry a woman from a 'respectable' family. On the other hand, Nu'mani notes that some Hanafi 'ulama, including Imam Abu Yusuf, a student of Abu Hanifa, did include occupation in deciding kafa'a, going so far as to single out the profession of weavers, barbers and tailors as 'despicable'.

On the basis of this, Nu'mani says, numerous Hanafi 'ulama have issued fatwas declaring weavers, barbers and tailors to be outside the kafa'a of those who pursue other, more 'respectable', professions. He notes that some fuqaha have adopted a somewhat less severe position on the matter by declaring that if a weaver gives up his profession and takes to trade, then he can be considered the kafa'a of a trader and can marry a trader's daughter. Not all Hanafi 'ulama were ready to provide this concession, however. Nu'mani refers to Ibn Najim who opined that even if a person were to abandon a 'low' profession he would not be able to remove the 'stains' that, allegedly, inevitably form on his character from such an occupation and hence he cannot be considered as the kafa'a of a person from a family that follows a 'respectable' profession.

Closer to our times, Nu'mani notes, Ahmad Raza Khan, the founder of the Barelwi school, is said to have declared that weavers, cobblers and barbers, even if learned in religion, could not be considered the kafa'a of those following 'respectable' professions. Hence, Nu'mani remarks, the notion that one should not marry outside one's occupational group, which in India is generally the caste group, is widely accepted by many Indian Hanafi 'ulama.

In discussing the Hanafi position on kafa'a being determined, among other factors, by one's profession, Nu'mani writes that Hanafi 'ulama have resorted to two sources to legitimize their argument. Firstly, popular custom or 'urf. By regarding caste-based occupation as a legitimate 'urf they have sought to incorporate it into the corpus of fiqh. This, however, says Nu'mani, is a gross violation of Islam and 'a conscious or unconscious imitation of the Indian Brahminical social system'.

The other source that the fuqaha have invoked to support their claim of kafa'a being dependent on occupation is a single hadith attributed to the Prophet. According to this narration, the Prophet is said to have declared that weavers and barbers are not to be considered as the kafa'a of others. This means, therefore, that weavers and barbers cannot marry people who belong to families that follow other professions.

Nu'mani remarks that this hadith is 'very weak' (intihai za'if) and adds that numerous scholars of Hadith have argued that it is a later fabrication wrongly attributed to the Prophet. How could the Prophet, who is considered as a source of mercy for all, consider any members of his community as despicable simply because they were weavers or barbers, Num'ani asks. Indirectly critiquing these anti-egalitarian reports, Nu'mani here refers to several prophets before Muhammad as well as numerous companions of Muhammad who engaged in occupations that some later fuqaha wrongly described as 'low'. Thus, he notes that the prophet David was an artisan and that numerous companions of Muhammad were weavers and carpenters.

Nu'mani writes that all legitimate occupations are noble and praise-worthy in God's eyes, and hence to claim that weaving, barbering and other such trades are 'despicable' as some fuqaha have done, is completely against basic Islamic teachings. Therefore, he argues, from a strictly Qur'anic perspective, a person pursuing any legitimate profession may be considered the kafa'a of any other similar person for purposes of marriage.

In this regard he quotes Mufti Kifayatullah, a leading Indian Deobandi scholar, whom he singles out as one of the few Indian 'ulama to have taken a correct position on kafa'a, as having declared in a fatwa that 'To consider someone inferior simply because he follows a legitimate is profession is opposed to the teachings of Islam'.

In approvingly quoting Mufti Kifayatullah here Nu'mani does not deny that several other leading Deobandi scholars, such as Ashraf Ali Thanwi and Mufti Muhammad Shafi, had adopted a divergent stance by supportingthe dominant Hanafi position on kafa'a as being determined, among other factors, by occupation. He also admits that Thanwi had gone so far as to declare weavers and oil-pressers as 'low' castes. Yet, he claims, in contrast to their Barelwi opponents, the Deobandi 'ulama have never hesitated to correct each other's views. Indeed, he does this himself explicitly in critiquing the views of his fellow Deobandis, renowned 'ulama such as Thanwi and Shafi, on the matter of kafa'a.

Family, tribe or ethnic group (nasb) have also been considered by several classical fuqaha as well as Indian 'ulama as an essential basis for deciding kafa'a. Yet, Nu'mani writes, not one of the several traditions attributed to the Prophet that have been adduced for this purpose have been proved to be fully genuine (sahih). They are all said to be 'very weak' and even 'fabricated' (mauzu).

Nu'mani examines five traditions attributed to the Prophet that are generally used to argue the case for nasb to be included in kafa'a. All of them, he contends, are fabricated, have weak chains of narration (isnad) or else do not have any direct bearing on the question of nasb in marriage. To illustrate his argument, he focuses on one particular tradition, according to which the Prophet is said to have laid down that all members of his Qur'aish clan are of the same kafa'a; that all Arabs belong to the same kafa'a; that members of one tribe are the kafa'a of each other; and that all people are of the same kafa'a except for weavers and barbers. Like other similar reports, this one, too, Nu'mani claims, is not to be regarded as absolutely authentic for it has a weak narrative chain. Indeed, several Islamic scholars have insisted that it is 'completely fabricated'.

The Qur'an repeatedly stresses that all Muslims are equal, and one such Qur'anic verse, Nu'mani writes, is said to have been specifically revealed to the Prophet to refute the belief that people should marry only within their own tribe. Likewise, numerous genuine Prophetic traditions are said to directly oppose the belief in nasb being essential to kafa'a. Thus, several companions of the Prophet are said to have married outside their tribe with the Prophet's consent.

The Prophet advised one of his followers, an Ansar from Medina, to give his daughter in marriage to one of his closest companions, Bilal, a freed black slave. Abu Bakr, the first caliph, accepted the marriage proposal of Salman Farsi, a Persian companion of the Prophet, to marry his daughter. All this very clearly proves, Nu'mani writes, that it is indeed legitimate to marry outside one's ethnic group or caste and that the bar on such marriages placed by numerous fuqaha is not Islamic.

Despite the clear evidence in the Qur'an and the Hadith that nasb is not to be included in kafa'a, Nu'mani notes that several fuqaha have expressed contrary opinions. However, he writes that there is no complete consensus among the fuqaha on the matter. Thus, Imam Malik as well as some Hanafi 'ulama did not include nasb in establishing kafa'a, while Imam Abu Hanifa and Imam Shafi' did so.

There are conflicting views on Imam Ahmad ibn Hanbal's opinion. According to one report he ignored nasb in establishing kafa'a, while according to another report he regarded all Arabs as being equal for marriage purposes, and all non-Arabs ('ajamis) as equal, thus forbidding marriage between Arabs and non-Arabs.

Nu'mani argues that those fuqaha who included nasb in kafa'a probably did so because of the particular social conditions prevailing at their time. However, he adds, because of the 'unnecessary importance' which the contemporary Indian 'ulama give to nasb, 'numerous social problems have been created' and non-Muslims are 'getting a wrong message' about Islam. Hence, he appeals for 'serious thinking' on the matter of nasb in establishing kafa'a. A mark of the remarkable flexibility of Nu'mani's approach to fiqh is his approval of the few Indian Hanafi 'ulama who have adopted the position of Imam Malik on the question of nasb in kafa'a in their fatwas instead of blindly following the dominant Hanafi position.

Further on the question of linking nasb to kafa'a, Nu'mani deals with the distinction that many Hanafi scholars have established between old Muslims (jadid al-islam musalman) and new Muslims (jadid al-Islam musalman), and arguing that the two may not intermarry because they are not the kafa'a of each other. According to these scholars, a man who converts to Islam cannot marry a woman who was born to a Muslim father. The son of a convert to Islam cannot marry a woman whose paternal grandfather and father were Muslims, but the grandson of a convert can marry a woman from an 'old' Muslim family. Accordingly, a convert to Islam can only marry a fellow convert. This holds true only for non-Arabs, there being no distinction between 'old' and 'new' Muslims for Arabs.

Nu'mani sees this restrictive provision as making life for converts to Islam even more difficult and, therefore, making conversion to Islam a difficult choice for non-Muslims. By making this distinction between 'old' and 'new' Muslims, he says, 'rather than welcoming our new guests we are insulting them',

Accordingly, he fervently appeals to his fellow 'ulama to relax or abandon this rule, which in any case he sees as having no sanction in Islam. He reminds them that because they insisted on this un-Islamic provision, a large group of Hindus of the Tyagi caste in northern India who were ready to convert to Islam finally decided not to because the Muslim Tyagis refused to intermarry with them on the grounds that 'old' Muslims could not establish marital relations with converts. Likewise, Nu'mani writes, it was because of the discriminatory and anti-Qur'anic rules that the 'ulama have devised on kafa'a that Dr. Ambedkar, the leader of the 'low' caste Dalits, declined to convert to

Nu'mani admits that some of his fellow Deobandis have argued that 'old' and 'new' Muslims are not of the same kafa'a and so cannot intermarry. In addition, he notes that they have also argued that Muslims from different castes cannot marry on the grounds of not belonging to the same nasb. Yet, Nu'mani refuses to be bound by their views.

In order to press his claim that nasb should not be regarded as an essential factor in determining kafa'a he points to alternate opinions within the broader Deobandi tradition. Thus, he refers to fatwas by such scholars Mufi Kifayatullah and Sayyed Sulaiman Nadwi asserting that nasb was not to be considered as essential component of kafa'a, and that a convert could indeed marry into a family of 'old' Muslims on the grounds that all Muslims are equal. Nu'mani notes the existence of what he calls 'very weak' prophetic traditions stressing nasb in kafa'a, but says that in their light 'at the most' what can be said is that it might be better to marry within one's ethnic group or caste (biraderi) than outside. However, he says, this clearly does not mean that marriage must only take place within one's caste but only that marrying outside one's caste is not disallowed by the shari'ah. If marriage outside one's caste were thus to be recognized, Nu'mani suggests that it would promote Muslim unity, help converts to Islam find spouses within the Muslim community, and counter the perception among non-Muslims' of the existence of caste discrimination among Muslims.

After reviewing the writings of the classical fuqaha and some influential twentieth century Indian Hanafi scholars on kafa'a being determined by wealth, occupation and ethnicity, Nu'mani writes that, notwithstanding their differences, all the schools of Sunni jurisprudence are agreed that piety should be a determining factor in deciding kafa'a in marriage. 'It should not be', he writes, 'that a pious girl who regularly says her prayers and keeps her fasts should be married to a criminal' simply because he belongs to the same ethnic or occupational group. He approvingly refers to some classical fuqaha who opined that the piety was to be the only determining factor in selecting a marriage partner.

In order to further support his contention that piety alone should be the criterion for kafa'a he quotes a Prophetic tradition to the effect that a marriage proposal from a man of high morals should be accepted, otherwise it would lead to strife. In another hadith the Prophet is said to have warned against marrying a woman simply because of her beauty or wealth. Her good looks might lead her to evil ways, while her wealth might make her rebellious and proud. On the other hand, a pious black slave girl, Muhammad declared, made a much better marriage partner. Thus, Nu'mani concludes, the

Qur'an and the genuine prophetic traditions clearly suggest that it is piety alone that should be basis of kafa'a, with other factors 'having no real importance'.

In effect, then, by subjecting the existing corpus of fiqh and the writings of the classical and later Indian 'ulama to a critical reading, Nu'mani argues for the need to go back to the Qur'an and the genuine Prophetic traditions to develop a new fiqhi perspective on kafa'a and caste. By appealing to the radically egalitarian social ethics contained in the Qur'an and the genuine Prophetic traditions, by subjecting some traditions that seem to promote social inequality to a critical contextual reading, by dismissing anti-egalitarian traditions as inauthentic, and by pointing out the divergent views of the fuqaha and 'ulama of different schools of jurisprudence and within each school on the matter of kafa'a, Nu'mani argues that piety alone should be considered as the essential basis of kafa'a. In this way, he critiques both the notion of caste as well as the arguments of the fuqaha who have sought to incorporate caste as a major factor in deciding kafa'a and thereby grant caste a certain religious legitimacy.

Recognizing the Issues of Dalit Muslims

The Dalits and Adivasis have close relations with the Christians but not with the Muslims. The service of several Christian missionaries operating in our country has ensured the strengthening of the Dalit-Christians tie. But despite sharing a certain strong historical connection with each other, no such common ground could be forged between the Dalits and the Muslims, which has only resulted in the lack of intimacy between the two.

Many Muslim and Dalit activists have also come to recognize how both the sections of society continue to be exploited by the Hindu fundamentalists and instigated to kill each other at the time of the so-called communal riot. They have realized the need for a strong Dalit-Muslim tie in order to counter the fundamentalsits' ulterior motives in pitching the two against each other at the time of communal violence. Such organizations as the Jamat-ul-Ulema-I Hind, the All India SC/ST Federation and the Muslim United Morcha have recently come up with the innovative ideas of organizing Dalit-Muslim Community Dinner, etc. that has helped provide the two communities enough ground to understand each other.

Media has reacted passively to any event of such enormous significance. Its preoccupation with many other trivial issues leaves no room for its engagement with issues like this. We must recognize the harm entailed in such Media passivity.

Coming back to the issue of Dalit-Muslim unity, for any such venture to succeed, one should first stress on the need for the recognision of the caste dynamics operating in Islam, the understanding of which we have been deliberately denied by several Islamic religious institutions and 'English-speaking Muslim intelligentsia', who find it safe to propound the false idea of an egalitarian Islamic society. By doing this they consolidate the Muslim population and make them serve their private political purposes.

Shocking it might be for many, around 85% of the total Indian Muslim population are Dalits who have been denied access to those Constitutional provisions that their Hindu counterparts have enjoyed. Despite this being by and large a common knowledge that these Muslims are the converts of the Dalit Hindus, we necessarily ignore the fact that they are very much in the same social trap as Dalit Hindus are. Even the most strident advocates of the caste identity have refused to acknowledge the undercurrent of castes running in Islam.

The real state of affairs of the majority of Muslims is betrayed by the notion of pan Islamic identity that does not stand true in the context of Indian society where majority of Muslims are the Dalit converts. The Dalit Muslims are today victims of a large political and religious conspiracy unleashed on them by the religious leaders like the ulemas of the madrassas and the English speaking intelligentsia among the Muslims, who constitute just a fraction of the total Muslim population in India.

A few organizations have come up to struggle for the rights of the Dalit Muslims. Among them, the All India Backward Muslim Morcha has raised strong voice against discrimination inflicted on the Dalit Muslims. Sociologists have recently made many studies dedicated to the understanding of the same caste dynamics at play in Indian Muslims.

Muslims in India are divided into two broad categories, Ashrafs and Non-Ashrafs. Ashrafs are upper castes by virtue of their foreign descent. And Non-Ashrafs, being the alleged converts, constitute the lower castes. Further, while the Ashrafs are divided into four castes, Sayyads, Sheikhs, Mughals and Pathans, the Non-Ashrafs are divided into a number of 'occupational castes'. In Non-Ashrafs, writes Bhatty, 'the superiority or inferiority of a caste is determined by the relative pure or impure nature of the occupation associated with each.' It must also be mentioned alongside that despite being in an overwhelming majority, the Non-Ashrafs have no particular voice of their own; their social and political situations are largely determined by a handful of upper caste, English-speaking elites, who in order to keep the whole Muslim community together, have consequently done away with their identity as Dalits, thereby depriving them of their claim to social justice and political privileges.

Whatever sociological research has gone in finding caste dynamics in either Hindu or Muslim community is itself debatable. Questioning the integrity of Indian sociologists, Gail Omvedt writes in her essay entitled, 'Caste and the Sociologists,' that 'the most haunting lacuna of contemporary Indian sociology remains the lack of data...the apparent lack of concern for even gathering data.'

It is in fact this lack of understanding among Indian sociologists that has for long put the idea of the existence of something called "Dalit Muslims" under the cover. However, the recent study in the field has given all those activists who want a separate Dalit identity to the Muslims a much-needed shot in their arm. A clear identification of Dalit Muslims and recognition their political and social needs will help bring together Dalit Muslims and Hindus, which can prove strong bulwark against the fundamentalist force working against them.

All-India Backward Muslim Morcha

Forming almost a fifth of the Indian population, the Scheduled Castes or the Dalits, a conglomeration of numerous caste groups considered as untouchable, by caste Hindus, are victims of the most sternly hierarchical social order that human beings have ever devised. Since the social and economic oppression of the Dalits has been so closely intertwined with the Hindu religion, over the centuries many Dalits have sought to escape from the shackles of the caste system by converting to other religions. Consequently, a considerable majority of India's Muslims, Buddhists, Christians and Sikhs today consist of descendants of Dalit and other 'low' caste converts.

Recent decades have witnessed a remarkable upsurge in radical Dalit assertiveness. This resurgence of Dalit consciousness has not been limited to those defined according to the law as Scheduled Castes, though. Rather, the Dalit struggle for human rights has had a profound impact on other communities as well, most particularly the large category of castes, the Other Backward Classes (OBCs), who form over half the Indian population, as well as the Christians and Muslims, most of whom who share, in terms of social and economic background, much in common with the Dalits.

Most Indian Muslims are descendants of ' untouchable and 'low' caste converts, with only a small minority tracing their origins to Arab, Iranian and Central Asian settlers and invaders. Although the Qur'an is fiercely egalitarian in its social ethics, Indian Muslim society is characterised by numerous caste-like features, consisting of several caste-like groups (jatis). Muslims who claim foreign descent claim a superior status for themselves as ashraf or 'noble'. Descendants of indigenous converts are, on the other hand, commonly referred to contemptuously as ajlaf or 'base' or 'lowly'.

As among the Hindus, the various jatis among the ajlaf Muslims maintain a strong sense of jati identity. The emergence of democratic politics is, however, bringing about a radical change in the manner in which this sense of identity is articulated. Aware of the importance of numbers in order to acquire political power and the economic benefits that accrue from it, the Dalit movement has sought to establish a wider sense of Dalit identity that transcends inter-caste and inter-religious divisions and differences among the 'lower' caste majority.

This wider Dalit identity does not seek to deny individual jati identities. Rather, it takes them into account but seeks to subsume them within the wider collective Dalit identity, based on a common history of suffering as well as common racial origins as indigenous people. This seems to have been a crucial factor in the emergence of a specific 'Dalit Muslim' identity that the AIBMM seeks to articulate. 'Lower' caste Muslim ideologues and activists in the AIBMM are now in the process of fashioning a new 'Dalit Muslim' identity, seeking to bring all the 'lower' caste Muslims under one umbrella, defined by their common identity as Muslim as well as Dalit.

The AIBMM was set up in 1994 by Ejaz Ali, a young Muslim medical doctor from Patna, capital of the eastern state of Bihar, belonging to the Kunjera caste of Muslim vegetable-sellers. Bihar, India's poorest state, is notorious for its acute caste problem and for its frequent anti-Dalit pogroms. Consequently, the Dalits in Bihar have been among the first to take to militant forms of struggle.

The Muslims of Bihar, who form over fifteen per cent of the state's population, are also characterised by sharp caste divisions. The plight of Bihar's Dalit Muslims, whom the

AIBMM estimates at forming almost ninety per cent of the state's Muslim population and consisting of twenty-nine different caste groups, is particularly pathetic. 1 Most Bihari Dalit Muslims work as daily wage labourers, manual workers, artisans and petty peasants, barely managing to eke out an existence.

According to Ali, the plight of the overwhelming majority of the Muslims of Bihar, as well as an acute awareness of the limitations of the traditional Muslim leadership, suggested to him the need for the establishment of the AIBMM to struggle for the rights of the Dalit Muslims. He regards the destruction of the Babri mosque at Ayodhya in 1992 as a landmark event in this regard, seeing the traditional, and largely 'upper' caste, Muslim leadership as having only further complicated matters by playing into the hands of Hindu militants and as 'misleading' the Muslim masses for their own petty gains.

In less than a decade of its founding, by early 2001 the AIBMM had emerged as an umbrella group of over forty organisations claiming to represent various different Dalit Muslim castes. It now has branches in the states of Uttar Pradesh, Madhya Pradesh, West Bengal, Delhi, Rajasthan and Maharashtra, in addition to Bihar, where it has its headquarters.

The foremost priority for the AIBMM is to get recognition from the Indian state for the over 100 million 'Dalit Muslims' as Scheduled Castes so that they can avail of the same benefits that the Hindu, Sikh and Buddhist Scheduled castes enjoy, including reserved government jobs, reserved seats in state legislatures and in the Indian Parliament, special courts to try cases of atrocities against them as well as social and economic development programmes meant specially for them.

According to Indian law as it stands at present, only those Dalits who claim to be Hindus, Sikhs and Buddhists can be considered to be members of the Scheduled Castes and thereby eligible for the special benefits that the state has made available to these castes. The AIBMM sees this as violating the basic secular character of the Indian Constitution. It insists that its demand for Scheduled Caste status for 'Dalit Muslims' is fully in consonance with the spirit of the Indian Constitution.

Recognising the fact that demands for special legal status for Muslims have been viewed in the past as 'separatist' and 'anti-national' and even 'pro-Pakistan', the AIBMM is careful to project its demands as aimed at integrating the 'Dalit Muslim' into the 'national mainstream' by enabling them to progress economically and socially, along with other deprived sections of the Indian population.

Besides being considered 'anti-secular', the law as it stands today is also condemned by the AIBMM as a gross violation of human rights. Furthermore,it is seen as a ploy to keep the more than one hundred million Dalit Muslims in perpetual thraldom, a conspiracy in which both the Hindu as well as Muslim 'upper' caste elite are seen as being involved. Because they have been denied Scheduled Caste status and the benefits that accrue from such status, the Dalit Muslims are said to lag far behind the Hindu Dalits, who have been able to make considerable progress in all fields because of the special facilities that the state has provided for them.

The AIBMM prides itself in having coined the term 'Dalit Muslims', and in this it seeks to radically refashion notions of Muslim community identity. Deconstructing the notion of Muslims as a homogenous bloc, it brings to the fore the existence of caste distinctions among the Indian Muslims, which it sees as one of the primary and defining features of Indian Muslim society.

In articulating a separate Dalit Muslim identity it finds itself at odds with the traditional, largely 'high' caste Muslim leadership, which, in seeking to speak for all Muslims, sees the question of caste that the AIBMM so stridently stresses as divisive. Leading Muslim spokesmen have, not surprisingly, accused the AIBMM of seeking to create divisions within the Muslim community and of spreading 'casteism', and thus playing into the hands of militant Hindus.Ali sees as Islam as having historically played a key role in the emancipation of the Dalits, a role which, he says, was gradually watered down over time.

Islam spread in India principally through the agency of the Sufis, he says, whose teachings of love and social equality attracted many Dalits to the new faith, shackled as they were by the chains of the caste system and the Brahminical religion. 7 It was not by the sword but through the love and compassion that the Sufis exhibited in their behaviour towards the poor, principally the Dalits, that large numbers of Hindus converted to Islam. With the establishment of Muslim political power in various parts of India, however, he says, this radical egalitarianism of the early Sufis gave way to more institutionalised forms of religious expression.

'High' caste Hindus, in order to save their properties or to secure high positions in Muslim-ruled territories, converted to Islam, bringing with them notions of caste superiority that are foreign to pristine Islam. Doctrines were developed that sought to legitimise caste inequalities by suitably misinterpreting the Qur'an. Gradually, he says, the 'spirit of Islam' was replaced by the 'rituals of Islam'.

One of the crucial tasks before the Dalit Muslims, as Ali sees it, is to rescue Islam from the clutches of those who claim to speak in its name, the 'high' caste Muslim leadership. Thus, he calls for a revival of 'the true spirit of Islam', which fiercely condemns all caste and racial divisions. The practice of untouchability, which Islam roundly condemns, is still observed, Ali notes, to varying degrees, by 'upper' caste Muslims, who look down upon 'lower' caste Muslims as inherently inferior.

While Islam calls for Muslims to share in the plight of their fellow believers and to work for their social emancipation, the Muslim 'upper caste feudal lords' are said to be 'deaf, dumb and blind to the suffering of backward Muslims'. Ali is bitterly critical of the traditional, largely 'high' caste, Muslim leadership, both 'ulama as well as 'lay'.

Over the centuries of Muslim rule, he says, the ruling class among the Muslims displayed little concern for the plight of the Dalit Muslims, who remained tied down to their traditional occupations, mired in poverty and ignorance. The only concern of the ruling class Muslims, he writes, was to perpetuate their own rule, and for this they entered into alliances with 'upper' caste Hindus, keeping the Dalits, both Hindus as well as Muslims, cruelly suppressed under their firm control.

This disdain for the Dalits, he writes, carried down right through the period of Muslim rule, and continues till this very day. He accuses the present-day Muslim 'high' caste leadership of playing the 'minority card' and practising the politics of 'minorityism' to garner power for themselves while claiming to speak on behalf of all Muslims, the vast majority of whom are Dalits. They, he says, refuse to recognise the acute problem of caste within the community because 'they do not want to lose their jagirdari (power and privileges)'. Yet, the cling to their exalted caste titles simply to 'produce an impression of supremacy and to demoralise the backward caste Muslims'.

In their attitudes towards the latter they are said to be hardly different from the way Hindu 'upper' castes treat their own Dalits. He sees the Indian Muslim community as a whole as having 'all the ingredients of the Brahminical order'. The 'upper caste' Muslim leadership, he argues, thrives on championing such 'communal' 'non-issues' as the protection of the Muslim Personal Law or the Babri mosque, which have only helped militant Hindu 'upper' caste forces, resulting in terrible violence unleashed against Muslims and communal riots in which the major victims are the Dalits, both Hindu as well as Muslim. 'The time has now come', he declares, for the 'upper' caste Muslims to 'stop thinking of the entire Muslim community as they have been clearly reduced to their caste leadership, which they were doing from the very beginning under the pseudo-umbrella of Muslim unity'.

Given the stress that Islam places on radical social equality, on the one hand, and what he sees as the failure of the traditional Muslim leadership in championing the rights and interests of the backward caste Muslims, on the other, Ali calls for a 'power shift' from the 'Arab-origin ashraf' to the 'oppressed Muslims'. Denying that his struggle is aimed against the 'upper' caste Muslims, he says that it is directed principally at the government, to force it to grant Scheduled Caste status to the Dalit Muslims.

A new, Dalit Muslim leadership is called for, for it alone is seen as able to champion the rights of the oppressed among the Muslims. By taking up the interests of the Dalit Muslims, he argues, the AIBMM is not seeking to divide the Muslim community on caste lines, as some have accused him of doing. Rather, he says, championing the cause of the oppressed is what Islam itself calls for, a radical concern for the poor and the weak, which 'is repeatedly stressed in the Holy Qur'an and in the Hadith'.

The Prophet Muhammad's early followers, he notes, were largely poor and dispossessed people, and because he spoke out on their behalf, he was fiercely opposed by the rich Quraish of Mecca. Islam, he says, insists on a passionate commitment to the poor. Hence the accusations against the AIBMM of allegedly dividing the Muslims by taking up the cause of the poor Muslims alone are dismissed as baseless. If special facilities were to be provided by the state to the Dalit Muslims, they would, he argues, be able to advance economically and socially.

As a result, inter-marriages between them and the 'upper' caste Muslims would increase, and gradually the caste system within the Muslim community would begin to disintegrate, this being seen as working towards the fulfilment of Islam's vision of a casteless society. By denying the existence of caste within the Muslim community, he says, the traditional Muslim leadership is only helping to perpetuate it.

Ali calls for a struggle to be waged to fight for extending Scheduled Caste status to Dalit Muslims, and in this the Dalit Muslims would join hands with non-Muslim secular and progressive forces, in the face of the stiff opposition that is expected from many 'upper' caste Muslims as well as 'upper' caste Hindus. The struggle would need the help of non-Muslim Dalits as well, for if the Dalit Muslims gain Scheduled Caste status, they could join hands with Dalits from other religions and become one strong force, almost half the Indian population. They could, together, even capture political power, bring their interests and demands to the centre of the Indian political agenda and put an end to atrocities against them.

Ali sees the new Muslim leadership that he envisages as being drawn primarily from among the 'backward' Muslims, who form the vast majority of the Muslim population in India, for they alone can truly speak for their people. Since the primary concerns of the backward caste Muslims are sheer physical survival, jobs, wages and the like, this new leadership would seek to bring about a 'revolution of priorities'. Instead of taking up 'communal' issues that would further exacerbate Hindu-Muslim differences by playing into the hands of fiercely anti-Muslim Hindu zealots, which only works to further their interests of the Hindu and Muslim elites, this new leadership would focus on issues such as 'employment, food, housing and elementary education', issues which affect the daily lives of all poor people irrespective of religion. In this way, Hindu-Muslim antagonisms would fade away, the Dalits of all religions, the primary victims of the politics of communal hatred, would unite, and the conditions of the poor would improve.

Since the Dalit Muslims share similar concerns of sheer survival with Dalits of other religions, this new Muslim leadership would seek to build bridges between the Muslim Dalits and those of other faiths. All Dalits, irrespective of religion, belong to the same 'nation' (qaum), Ali says. Mere change of religion cannot wipe away the common blood that runs in their veins.

The Dalit 'nation', representing the indigenous inhabitants of India who today follow various different religions, has been fractured into various antagonistic groups, but they must be united. The 'divided Dalit nation', he writes, will be united once again when all Dalits, irrespective of religion, are granted the same status as Scheduled Castes.

Hence, in order to re-unify the Dalit 'nation' so that the Dalits emerge as a powerful collective force, all Dalits must unite to support the AIBMM's demand for Scheduled Caste status to the Dalit Muslims (as well, interestingly, to the Dalit Christians, who, too, are denied such status). By joining hands with Dalits of other faiths and jointly struggling to improve their living conditions, Ali writes, the Dalit Muslims would be able to join the 'national mainstream' of Indian society.

With a new Muslim leadership coming to the fore drawn from the Dalit Muslims, the community would turn its back to the communal antagonisms of the past rooted in a long tradition of exclusivism and separatism. The Dalit Muslims would begin to collaborate with other Dalits, with whom they have 'a great commonality of interests', pursuing the same occupations and facing the same economic and social problems. In this way, a joint struggle for social justice and inter-communal harmony can be launched for all Dalits, irrespective of religion.

Demanding Scheduled Caste status for the Dalit Muslims may, in itself, not be a very radical step, given the present climate of privitisation in the country, where government jobs are being sharply curtailed and public expenditure and subsidies drastically reduced. However, its wider implications are certainly more momentous in their probable consequences. The demands of the AIBMM, limited as they may well be, might actually help facilitate a radical shift in the very terms of Muslim political discourse.

Its stress on secularism and human rights, which it sees as being grossly violated by the present law related to Scheduled Caste status, its call for 'integration' of the Muslims into the 'national mainstream', its radical disavowal of communal politics,.and its appeal for building bridges and working in collaboration with other Dalits in order to reunify the 'Dalit nation' and working for inter-communal harmony, might well provide a key to what has so far seemed the intractable communal problem in India.

10

Legal Obligations to Protect Dalits

The Constitution of India proclaims the decision of the Constituent Assembly to provide social, political, and economic justice for all. To this end the constitution has several provisions to protect scheduled castes and to improve their position. The constitution affects social justice in two ways. First, it confers rights on men and women alike, through "fundamental rights" which can be enforced by the courts. Second, it directs the states to implement "directive principles of state policy." Although these are not enforceable in Indian courts, they are declared to be fundamental in the governance of the country and as such have moral and political value.

Scheduled Castes and the Constitution

Article 17 of the constitution abolishes the practice of "untouchability" and punishes the enforcement of any disability arising out of the practice. Article 21 guarantees the right to life and liberty. The Indian Supreme Court has interpreted this right to include the right to be free from degrading and inhuman treatment, the right to integrity and dignity of the person, and the right to speedy justice. When read with Article 39A on equal justice and free legal aid, Article 21 also encompasses the right to legal aid for those faced with imprisonment and those too poor to afford counsel.

Article 23 prohibits traffic in human beings and other similar forms of forced labor. Since the majority of bonded laborers belong to scheduled castes, Article 23 is especially significant for them. Similarly, Article 24 provides that no child under the age of fourteen shall work in any factory or mine or engage in any hazardous employment. Again a majority of children engaged in bonded labor in such hazardous industries are scheduled caste members. Article 45 charges that the state shall endeavor to provide free and compulsory education for all children until they reach the age of fourteen, while Article 43 calls on the state to secure to all workers, agricultural, industrial or otherwise, a living wage and conditions of work ensuring a decent standard of life.

Article 46 comprises both development and regulatory aspects and stipulates that: "The State shall promote with special care the educational and economic interests of the weaker sections of the people, and in particular, of the Scheduled Castes and the Scheduled Tribes, and shall protect them from social injustice and forms of exploitation." As the article falls under the category of directive principles and not fundamental rights, it cannot be enforced by the state's courts.

Article 15(4) empowers the state to make any special provisions for the advancement of any socially and educationally backward classes of citizens, or for scheduled castes and scheduled tribes. This particular provision was incorporated into the constitution through the Constitution (First Amendment) Act, 1951 and has enabled several states to reserve seats for scheduled castes and scheduled tribes in educational institutions, including technical, engineering, and medical colleges. It has also paved the way for reservations in police forces.

Article 330 provides reservations for seats for scheduled castes and scheduled tribes in the Lok Sabha (the House of the People), while Article 332 provides for reservations in the state legislative assemblies. Article 334 originally stipulated that the above two provisions would cease to have effect after a period of ten years from the commencement of the constitution. This article has since been amended four times, extending the period by ten years on each occasion. The provision is now set to expire in January 2000. Through Article 16(4) the state is empowered to make "any provision for the reservation of appointments or posts in favour of any backward class of citizens which, in the opinion of the State, is not adequately represented in the services under the State." The claims of scheduled castes and scheduled tribes, as per Article 335, shall also be taken into consideration, consistent with maintaining efficiency of administration, in the making of appointments services and posts in connection with the union or of a state.

In addition to constitutional provisions, the government of India has pursued a two-pronged approach to narrowing the gap between the socio-economic status of the scheduled caste population and the national average: one prong involves regulatory measures which ensure that the various provisions to protect their rights and interests are adequately implemented, enforced and monitored; the second focuses on increasing the self-sufficiency of the scheduled caste population through financial assistance for self-employment activities through development programs to increase education and skills.

The protective component of this strategy includes the enforcement of those legal provisions that make up the Protection of Civil Rights Act, 1955, and the Scheduled Caste and Scheduled Tribe (Prevention of Atrocities) Act, 1989; of other state and central government laws; and of "positive discrimination" through reservations in the arenas of government employment and higher education. These protective measures are monitored by the National Commission for Scheduled Castes and Scheduled Tribes. The development measures for the educational, social, and economic upliftment of scheduled castes are administered by the Ministry of Welfare through the state governments.

The National Commission for SC/ST

The National Commission for Scheduled Castes and Scheduled Tribes is a body set up pursuant to Article 338 of the Indian constitution. It has been entrusted with the responsibility of ensuring that the safeguards and protections that have been given to scheduled castes and tribes are implemented. As part of the National Commission, the Commission on Atrocities Against Scheduled Castes and Scheduled Tribes oversees implementation of the Prevention of Atrocities Act, 1989, and the Protection of Civil Rights Act, 1955, though does not have a statutory responsibility to do so.

The commission both receives complaints and proactively investigates matters that come to its attention through news reports or by any other means. Under the constitution the commission has the powers of a civil court and can call on anyone for evidence to ensure that the laws are being implemented. The commission lacks the powers of a criminal court, however, and therefore cannot enforce its findings.

The Protection of Civil Rights Act, 1955

With an eye to eradicating pervasive discrimination practiced against scheduled-caste members, the central government enacted the Protection of Civil Rights Act, 1955 (PCR Act) to enforce the abolition of "untouchability" under Article 17 of the constitution. The PCR Act punishes offenses that amount to the observance of "untouchability." These include, inter alia, prohibiting entry into places of worship, denying access to shops and other public places, denying access to any water supply, prohibiting entry into hospitals, refusing to sell goods or render services, and insulting someone on the basis of his or her caste. In 1973 the Protection of Civil Rights Cell was established to respond to a lack of convictions under the PCR Act. Chaudary added, "Society as a whole never accepted the PCR Act. No one ever thought that name-calling wouldn't be okay. Ill-treatment was very common." The act was also vulnerable to abuse. "It was easy to make an allegation that someone was called by his or her caste name."

The greatest deficiency of the Protection of Civil Rights Act was the fact that abuses against Dalits were not limited to name-calling or denial of entry into public spaces: violence was a defining characteristic of the abuse. Thirty-four years after the introduction of the PCR Act, the Scheduled Castes and Scheduled Tribes (Prevention of Atrocities) Act, 1989, was enacted to bring these other forms of abuse to an end. "In the Atrocities Act the complainant is given more weight... There are also stringent provisions against the police for negligence."

The promulgation of the act itself was an acknowledgment by the central government that abuses, in their most dehumanizing form, continue to take place against Dalits throughout the country. The Tamil Nadu nodal (implementation) officer for the Atrocities Act explained to Human Rights Watch: The Atrocities Act is very stringent. It is needed to eradicate the practice, not just control it. It is the second phase of the Protection of Civil Rights Act which is very soft. The 1989 [Atrocities] Act is grounded in the understanding that scheduled castes are being subjected to violence, not just the practice of "untouchability."

There was a long period of dialogue before its enactment. After forty years of India, people began to acknowledge that violence continued to be perpetrated and it needed to be stopped. The act presumes that if a non-scheduled-caste member harms a scheduled-caste member then it is because of the culpable mind of "untouchability" [a belief in the inferiority of lower castes]. They don't have to utter the caste name in the 1989 act; any humiliation is an offense.

Section 3(1) stipulates that the following acts, when committed by a person who is not a member of a scheduled caste or a scheduled tribe, are atrocities and thereby punishable by a term of six months to five years with a fine.

— Forcing a member of a Scheduled Caste or Scheduled Tribe to drink or eat any inedible or obnoxious substance (Section 3(1)(i));

— Acting with intent to cause injury, insult or annoyance to any member of a Scheduled Caste or Scheduled Tribe by dumping excreta, waste matter, carcasses or any other obnoxious substance in his premises or neighbourhood (Section 3(1)(ii));

— Forcibly removing clothes from the person of a member of a Scheduled Caste or Scheduled Tribe, or parading him naked or with painted face orbody, or committing any similar act which is derogatory to human dignity (Section 3(1)(iii));

— Wrongfully occupying or cultivating any land owned by, or allotted to, or notified by any competent authority to be allotted to, a member of a Scheduled Caste or Scheduled Tribe, or getting the land allotted to him transferred (Section (3)(1)(iv));

— Wrongfully dispossessing a member of a Scheduled Caste or Scheduled Tribe from his land or premises, or interfering with the enjoyment of his rights over any land, premises, or water (Section 3(1)(v));

— Compelling or enticing a member of a Scheduled Caste or Scheduled Tribe to do "beggar" or other similar forms of forced or bonded labour, other than any compulsory service for public purposes imposed by the Government (Section (3)(1)(vi));

— Forcing or intimidating a member of a Scheduled Caste or a Scheduled Tribe not to vote or to vote [for] a particular candidate or to vote in a manner other than that provided by law (Section (3)(1)(vii));

— Corrupting or fouling the water of any spring, reservoir, or any other source ordinarily used by members of the

Scheduled Castes or the Scheduled Tribes so as to render it less fit for the purpose for which it is ordinarily used (Section (3)(1(xiii));

— Denying a member of a Scheduled Caste or a Scheduled Tribe any customary right of passage to a place of public resort or obstructing such members so as to prevent him from using or having access to a place of public resort to which other members of public or any section thereof have a right to use or access to (Section 3(1)(xiv));

— Forcing or causing a member of a Scheduled Caste or a Scheduled Tribe to leave his house, village, or other place of residence (Section 3(1)(xv)).

The act also punishes public servants for committing any of the enumerated offenses. Specific offenses are also designed to protect Dalit and tribal women. Specifically, Sections 3(1)(xi) and 3(1)(xii) criminalize the assault or use of force on any woman belonging to a scheduled caste or scheduled tribe, "with the intent to dishonour or outrage her modesty," and the use of a position of dominance to exploit a scheduled caste or scheduled tribe woman sexually.

Section 3(2) of the act prohibits, inter alia, the fabrication of false evidence in cases against members of scheduled castes or scheduled tribes and defines punishments for public servants who commit any of the offenses enumerated in Section 3. In addition to providing for stricter punishments for various offenses, the act also imposes certain positive duties on state and central governments to ensure proper implementation of the act. Many of these duties are listed under Section 21 which, among other things, provides that the central government shall, every year, send to both houses of parliament a report on the measures taken by the center and the states in pursuance of the provisions of the act. The section also includes guidelines for:

— Providing legal aid to victims;

— Making provisions for travel and maintenance expenses for witnesses and victims;

— Providing prompt economic and social rehabilitation to victims;

— Appointing officers for initiating or exercising supervision over prosecutions under the act;

— Identifying areas where Dalits would be subject to periodic or large scale atrocities, and;

— Setting up citizens committees to assist the government in the formulation and implementation of measures under the act.

Offenses under the act are cognizable—an officer can arrest without a warrant—and non-bailable. Provisions of the Criminal Procedure Code regarding anticipatory bail do not apply. Property can also be attached, sold, or forfeited to recover fines imposed by the court. When serious crimes such as rape, murder, or assault are proved, the punishments meted out are much greater than those provided for under the Indian Penal Code.

In 1995 the government of India enacted accompanying rules for the Atrocities Act. The rules set out the amounts of, and timetables for, state-allotted compensations for victims of various crimes defined under the act. Rules 16 and 17 call for the constitution of state and district-level vigilance and monitoring committees comprising official and non-official members. The committees are responsible for reviewing, inter alia, implementation of the act, prosecution of cases, victim relief and rehabilitation, and the role of different officers and agencies charged with the act's implementation. The Atrocities Act, and its accompanying rules, could go far in promoting justice and human rights among members of scheduled castes and scheduled tribes, but only if they are properly implemented and those whom the act is meant to protect are made aware of its existence and the rights that they possess.

Higher-caste police already have a biased mind. They assume that complaints of [Dalits] are made up or bogus. It is with this mentality that they investigate. Any person who has already presumed something as wrong will ultimately prove the case wrong to prove him or herself right.

Although a potentially powerful piece of legislation, the Scheduled Castes and Scheduled Tribes (Prevention of Atrocities) Act, 1989 is hampered by the police's lack of willingness to register offenses or their ignorance of the terms of the act itself. Under Indian law, a police officer is bound to enter in the station diary all reports brought to him concerning all cognizable and non-cognizable offenses. Failure to do so, or entering a report that was not made to him, is punishable under Section 177 of the Indian Penal Code. In most cases, however, the offending officer escapes punishment. The police take on the role of the judiciary and determine the merits of the case even before pursuing investigations. Cases at all levels are influenced by caste bias, corruption and ignorance of procedures under the Atrocities Act.

The functions of the Indian police are governed by the Indian Police Act, 1861, the Code of Criminal Procedure, 1973, the Indian Penal Code, 1860, the Indian Evidence Act, 1832, the Constitution of India, and other state acts. The government of India has known about the extent of police corruption in the registration of cases at least since 1979 when the National Police Commission issued a devastating indictment of police behavior.

Two decades later, none of the police commission's recommendations have been adopted, and police continue to detain, torture, and extort money from Dalits without much fear of punishment. Police often escape liability for their own abuses of Dalits and are rarely punished for their negligence in the non-registration of caste-related cases. Even when cases are registered, the absence of special courts to try them can delay conviction for up to three to four years. Some state governments, including those of Maharashtra and Uttar

Pradesh, have come under upper-caste pressure to repeal the legislation altogether.

Most beneficiaries of the Atrocities Act know neither the content of the act nor which agencies are responsible for its implementation. In an interview with Human Rights Watch, the then-chairman of the National Commission for Scheduled Castes and Scheduled Tribes asserted, "Many states do not even have translated copies of the act or the rules. Station-house officers do not even know of its existence." In many instances, however, even knowledge of proper procedures has not led to registration or investigation of cases.

Because offenses under the Atrocities Act are non-bailable, the mere registration of certain offenses can result in fifteen to twenty days in jail for the accused. An activist in Tamil Nadu explained, "If any case comes under the Atrocities Act, the accused will go straight to jail without any bail. So caste Hindus cleverly use the police to avoid putting cases under the act." Police manipulate First Information Reports [FIRs] and charge sheets, charging the accused under sections of the Indian Penal Code or under lesser offenses of the Atrocities Act.

The police consider Dalits to be their enemies. They don't register cases. They just say, "Don't fight anymore. After all, they [caste Hindus] are taking care of you; they are giving you employment. They made a mistake, let it go." And in so doing, the Dalits are usually persuaded to let the case go. In rare cases where they make an FIR, they will turn it around in the charge sheet and say that after investigation, they found that the FIR was not true. This is all to try and help the accused escape.

Under Indian law if a police officer suspects the commission of an offense, he is obligated to investigate the facts and circumstances of the case. The officer must then send a report and a copy of the FIR to the magistrate empowered to take cognizance of the offense. If the officer-in-charge of the police station believes that there are insufficient grounds for investigation, then the reasons for non-investigation must be communicated to the complainant.

In the case of a cognizable offense, if the police officer does not take action on the basis of an FIR, the aggrieved person can submit a complaint to the magistrate having jurisdiction to take cognizance of the offense. Despite these stringent procedures, Dalits generally hesitate to approach the police with their complaints. According to National Commission Chairman Hanumanthappa, "Scheduled caste people hesitate because they feel vulnerable. Even if they do report something, there is a tendency not to register the case. Many times the station-house officer simply chases them away."

Due to the diligent efforts of many Dalit activists and lawyers in the past several years, police have begun to register more cases under the Atrocities Act but often only as a result of immense public pressure. Increases in registration, however, have not resulted in increased convictions. A Dalit lawyer who has been practicing in Tamil Nadu for seventeen years asserted that in his experience only 2 percent of cases end in conviction. "The investigating officers are upper-caste," he said, "and the accused pay large amounts to judges to get an acquittal in the case." The lack of convictions is a reflection of police and judicial corruption, of deficiencies in the investigation process, and of a lack of special courts to try Atrocities Act cases. Each is discussed in turn below.

In Tamil Nadu, from 1992 to 1997, some 750 cases of atrocities against Dalits were registered annually by the state police. However, the number of convictions secured by protection of civil rights cells established in each district to implement the Atrocities Act was very low. From 1992 to 1997 only four out of 1,500 cases led to a conviction, despite the fact that in 1997, as many as 118 villages were considered by the government to be "atrocity-prone." Police officers have attributed the problem to the lack of a supporting unit to investigate reported crimes and to the fact that "most police personnel come to the cells either because they are facing action for delinquency or inefficiency, or as punishment for refusing to toe the line of their political bosses."

A lack of witnesses can also hamper an investigation—they either do not exist or are unwilling to come forward out of fear or economic vulnerability. These cases take place in the privacy of rural areas where there are no witnesses available. The demand of Indian criminal law is that a witness must be available to prove the crime. Indian law does not accept circumstantial evidence easily. That is the basic crux of the matter. Also there is great distrust toward the investigating officer. Good persons do not come forward to become witnesses, only those who can be influenced by the police.

Local police biases are mirrored at the judicial level. Should a case even reach the trial level, the judge's own caste affiliations can color his or her perception of witness credibility: "Judges issue an opinion in favor of the accused because they belong to the same caste."

The backlog of cases is largely due to a lack of special courts and special prosecutors. Pursuant to the act, each revenue district within each state must designate a special court for the trial of such offenses. According to lawyers with the People's Union for Civil Liberties (Tamil Nadu), almost all Atrocities Act cases go to regular sessions courts, which are already overburdened with original and appellate jurisdiction over district-level civil and criminal cases.

Terrorism and Anti-Disruptive Activities Act (TADA) cases are also being sent to these courts. According to a PUCL attorney: One court has so many nomenclatures. The whole purpose of a speedy trial is defeated. Even with all these new cases, not a single extra typewriter is added. In reality there is no special court. Half the day goes into calling names, calling civil court matters, dealing with civil and criminal appeals, interim orders, and bail applications.

An activist who runs a legal aid organization in Gujarat claims that Atrocities Act cases can take up to three years to reach trial while all others "take only one year. Existing sessions courts are named as special courts, existing public prosecutors are named as special public prosecutors. Cases take so long that people are forced to compromise." Chairman Hanumanthappa confirmed that the problem persisted throughout the country: "In practice, sessions courts are designated as special courts. They are already overburdened. More than judges, special prosecutors are required. There should be exclusive special courts."

In 1997 and 1998 four special courts were created in Tamil Nadu, in the districts of Madurai, Tirunelveli, Trichi, and Kumbakanam, to try Atrocities Act cases. Human Rights Watch spoke to the judge assigned to the Madurai district court, which at the time was handling cases from five districts; hundreds of cases had already been transferred to his court. Compensation in these cases was handled by the district collector and the district magistrate, not by the court itself.

Without more special courts to share the caseload, the judge explained, the rate at which cases were tried would remain slow. Unless special courts are established in each revenue district in each state, and unless witnesses feel protected by the police, the backlog of cases will continue, and increases in case registration will not result in increased convictions. All states should ensure establishment of these courts and appoint special prosecutors for trying cases that arise under the act.

Under-reporting of Atrocities Act Cases

An investigation conducted by Navsarjan, an NGO that has been working with Dalits in Gujarat since 1989, exposed the under-reporting of Atrocities Act cases and the biases of officers charged with its implementation. The study covered eleven "atrocity-prone" districts between 1990 and 1993 and showed that 36 percent of atrocities cases were not registered under the Atrocities Act. Moreover, in 84.4 percent of cases where the act was applied, cases were registered under the provision for name-calling (Section 3(1)(10)). That is, in many cases the actual and violent nature of abuses was concealed. Martin Macwan, founder and director of Navsarjan, told Human Rights Watch that the under-reporting continues to be a problem in his state and throughout the country.

The police see their primary duty as the maintenance of law and order. An increased crime rate sends the message that they are not doing their job and can often lead to suspensions, demotions, and other punishments. To keep up the facade of lower crime rates, police send information on only a portion of cases to district headquarters. Under-reporting at the district level gets reflected in state-level statistics and presumably gets even more diluted at the national level. Ultimately, "there is no system for getting authentic information, and the public has no way of counter-checking the information that is there."

The Navsarjan study also interviewed ninety-eight police officers of all ranks in the eleven districts surveyed, on their knowledge of and attitude toward the Atrocities Act. Dalits constituted a minority of the officers interviewed. Several deputy superintendents of police (DSP) in charge of implementing the actviewed the act as an obstacle between caste communities. "Because of the act," one officer said, "Dalits have become more powerful, thus having an adverse impact on society." Another added that "Dalits are dependent on non-Dalits for economic reasons. Because of this act they are spoiling their own chances of employment." One DSP even complained, "We high-caste pay income tax which goes to the social welfare department that pays Dalits and they are the ones who make us accused and put us behind bars." According to the survey, 75 percent of DSPs charged that Dalits were misusing the act and filing false cases for monetary gain. A Dalit superintendent of police rejected that assertion, saying, "Almost all laws are misused, but this act is for harijans [Dalits] and has direct provisions for stringent punishment. Therefore even a little misuse creates uproar in society."

India's Obligations under International Law

As a party to these treaties, India is obligated to comply with their provisions. The Committee on the Elimination of Racial Discrimination (CERD) and the Human Rights Committee (HRC), monitoring bodies under the United Nations International Convention on the Elimination of All Forms of Racial Discrimination and the International Covenant on Civil and Political Rights, respectively, have both expressed concern over the severe social discrimination still practiced against members of scheduled castes and scheduled tribes. Both committees have also recommended measures that can be taken to ameliorate the situation.

International Convention on the Elimination of All Forms of Racial Discrimination, 1965

In the concluding observations of its forty-ninth session held in August 1996, as it reviewed India's tenth to fourteenth periodic reports under the convention, the Committee on the Elimination of Racial Discrimination (CERD) affirmed that "the situation of Scheduled Castes and Scheduled Tribes falls within the scope of" the International Convention on the Elimination of All Forms of Racial Discrimination, 1965. Article 6 of the convention provides that state parties shall "assure to everyone within their jurisdiction effective protection and remedies, through the competent national tribunals and other State institutions, against any acts of racial discrimination which violate his human rights and fundamental freedoms contrary to this Convention, as well as the right to seek from such tribunals just and adequate reparation or satisfaction for any damage suffered as a result of such discrimination."

The committee added that the provisions of Article 6 are mandatory and that "the State party [should] continue to and strengthen its efforts to improve the effectiveness of measures aimed at guaranteeing to all groups of the population, and especially to the members of the Scheduled Castes and

Scheduled Tribes, the full enjoyment of their civil, cultural, economic, political and social rights, as mentioned in article 5 of the Convention." It recommended that:

— special measures be taken by the authorities to prevent acts of discrimination towards persons belonging to the scheduled castes and tribes, and in the case where such acts have been committed, to conduct thorough investigations, to punish those found responsible and provide just and adequate reparation to the victims;

— a continuing campaign be undertaken to educate the Indian population on human rights, in line with India's constitution and with universal human rights instruments, including the International Convention on the Elimination of All Forms of Racial Discrimination, and aimed at eliminating the institutionalized thinking of the high-caste and low-caste mentality;

— legal provisions be adopted to make it "easier for individuals to seek from the courts just and adequate reparation or satisfaction for any damage suffered as a result of acts of racial discrimination, including acts of discrimination based on belonging to caste or a tribe."

International Covenant on Civil and Political Rights, 1966

In July 1997 the sixtieth session of the Human Rights Committee considered India's third periodic report submitted under Article 40 of the International Covenant on Civil and Political Rights (ICCPR). The committee made the following observations pertaining to caste: The Committee notes with concern that, despite measures taken by the Government, members of scheduled castes and scheduled tribes, as well as the so-called backward classes and ethnic and national minorities continue to endure severe social discrimination and to suffer disproportionately from many violations of their rights under the Covenant, inter alia, inter-caste violence, bonded labour and discrimination of all kinds. It regrets that the de facto perpetuation of the caste system entrenches social differences and contributes to these violations. While the Committee notes the efforts made by the State party to eradicate discrimination: it recommends that further measures be adopted, including education programmes at national and state levels, to combat all forms of discrimination against these vulnerable groups, in accordance with articles 2, paragraph 1, and 26 of the Covenant.

In addition to the violations outlined above, Articles 7, 9, 14, and 26 of the ICCPR are of particular relevance to the abuses against dalits. Article 7 prohibits the use of torture, or cruel, inhuman or degrading treatment or punishment. The right to liberty and security of person is guaranteed by Article 9 and includes freedom from arbitrary arrest and detention, entitlement to a trial within a reasonable time or to release, and compensation for victims of unlawful arrest or detention.

Illegal arrests and detentions are by definition "arbitrary"; such acts can also be arbitrary if not in conformity with international standards of human rights and procedural fairness, regardless of specific provisions of domestic law. While noting India's reservation to Article 9, the Human Rights Committee commented that this reservation, "does not exclude, inter alia, the obligation to comply with the requirement to inform promptly the person concerned of the reasons for his or her arrest."

The committee also added that: preventive detention is a restriction of liberty imposed as a response to the conduct of the individual concerned, that the decision as to continued detention must be considered as a determination falling within the meaning of article 14, paragraph 1, of the Covenant, and that proceedings to decide the continuation of detention must, therefore, comply with that provision. Therefore:

> the Committee recommends that the requirements of article 9, paragraph 2, of the Covenant be complied with in respect of all detainees. The question of continued detention should be

> determined by an independent and impartial tribunal constituted and operating in accordance with article 14, paragraph 1, [the right to equality before all courts and tribunals] of the Covenant. It further recommends, at the very least, that a central register of detainees under preventive detention laws be maintained and that the State party accept the admission of the International Committee of the Red Cross to all types of detention facilities, particularly in areas of conflict.

Finally, Article 26 of the ICCPR guarantees the right to equal protection before the law and prohibits discrimination on any ground including, among others, race, sex, religion, political or other opinion, social origin, birth, or other status.

International Covenant on Economic, Social and Cultural Rights, 1966

Article 7 of the International Covenant on Economic, Social and Cultural Rights (ICESCR) provides that state parties shall "recognize the right of everyone to the enjoyment of just and favorable conditions of work." These include "fair wages and equal remuneration for work of equal value without distinction of any kind," and "safe and healthy work conditions."

Succumbing in part to pressure from domestic human rights NGOs and the National Human Rights Commission, India signed the Convention Against Torture and Other Cruel, Inhuman, or Degrading Treatment of Punishment on October 14, 1997. The provisions of the convention will become binding upon its ratification.

The convention defines torture as:

> [A]ny act by which severe pain or suffering, whether physical or mental, is intentionally inflicted on a person for such purposes as obtaining from him or a third person information or a confession, punishing him for an act he or a third person has committed or is suspected of having committed, or intimidating or coercing him or a third person, or for any reason based on discrimination of any kind, when such pain or

> suffering is inflicted by or at the instigation of or with the consent or acquiescence of a public official or other person acting in an official capacity.

Severe beatings of Dalit men and women by the police fall well within this definition. Indian police routinely employ torture techniques in police stations, lock-ups, and detention centers throughout the country. The sexual abuse of women by state agents in a custodial setting amounts to torture if the agent uses force, the threat of force, or other means of coercion to compel a woman to engage in sexual intercourse. If the agent uses force or coercion to engage in sexual touching of prisoners, including aggressively squeezing, groping, or prodding women's genitals or breasts, and the acts cause severe physical and mental suffering, that too would amount to torture.

Acts that do not rise to the level of torture or cruel or inhuman treatment may nevertheless be classified as degrading treatment, which is defined a streatment that causes or is intended to cause gross humiliation or an insult to a person's dignity. The prohibition on degrading treatment also extends to the use of demeaning language where the employment of such language is intended to dehumanize and weaken an incarcerated person.

Convention on the Rights of the Child, 1989, and Forced Labour Convention, 1930

Finally, the Convention on the Rights of the Child, 1989 (CRC) and the Forced Labour Convention, 1930 mandate protections that are particularly relevant for bonded laborers. Article 32 of CRC dictates that states parties recognize the "right of the child to be protected from economic exploitation and from performing any work that is likely to be hazardous or... be harmful to the child's health or physical, mental, spiritual, moral or social development." Similarly, the International Labour Organisation (ILO) Forced Labour Convention requires signatories to "suppress the use of forced or compulsory labour in all its forms in the shortest period possible." In 1957, the ILO explicitly incorporated debt bondage and serfdom within its definition of forced labor.

More than 160 million people in the "world's largest democracy" remain at risk of systematic human rights violations on the basis of the caste into which they are born. Despite the fact that India constitutionally abolished the practice of "untouchability" in 1950, the practice continues in the constitution's fiftieth year, and violence has become a defining characteristic of the abuse. In 1989 India enacted the Scheduled Castes and Scheduled Tribes (Prevention of Atrocities) Act to prevent and punish state and private actors for abuses against Dalits, to establish special courts for the trial of such offenses, and to provide for the rehabilitation and relief of the victims.

However, without a serious and sustained commitment to implementing constitutional safeguards and other national and international legal protections, human rights abuses in their most degrading forms will continue against scheduled-caste community members. The response of state administrations to incidents of caste violence amounts to a failure to ensure equal protection under the law and exposes a pattern of complicity and collusion on behalf of police and local officials.

Despite ambitious calls for action by central and state governments in the aftermath publicity of massacres and police raids, the Indian authorities have shown little commitment to resolving the root causes of caste conflicts. In Bihar, Tamil Nadu, and other states where massacres and large-scale police attacks on Dalits in rural and urban settings continue to take place, state administrations should act swiftly and without bias to bring offending state and private actors to justice. They must heed calls for protection from Dalit communities and work to address those issues of inequity that are at the heart of the class-caste conflict.

To dismiss the violence as purely a "law and order" concern, or to depict it as the inevitable consequence of ancient feuds between caste Hindus and Dalits, or between the haves and the have-nots, is misleading and irresponsible. Such a characterization erroneously suggests that the state has no protective role to play, or that the state itself has not contributed to the abuse.

At the same time, other forms of human rights violations should not go unaddressed. The false arrests and detentions of social activists are insidious, as they punish those members of the population who attempt to peacefully and democratically claim their rights and protect the rights of others. The exploitation of agricultural laborers and the rigid assignment of demeaning occupations on the basis of caste keeps Dalits in a position of economic and physical vulnerability.

The triple burden of caste, class, and gender effectively ensures that Dalit women are the furthest removed from legal protections. Only with the honest implementation of laws designed to protect agricultural laborers and abolishmanual scavenging and forced prostitution, and the systematic prosecution of those responsible for attacks on Dalit men and women, can the process of attaining economic and physical security begin.

The Scheduled Castes and Scheduled Tribes (Prevention of Atrocities) Act has the potential to bring about social change by sending the message that human rights violations against scheduled-caste members will not go unpunished. The implementation of the Atrocities Act and other legislation, however, depends largely on the ability and willingness of the police to follow proper procedure and overcome caste biases, economic hurdles, and other obstacles.

More than twenty years ago, the Indian government set up the National Police Commission to examine the causes of police abuse and police negligence. The commission's 1980 eight-volume report, which followed a series of similar reports by state-level commissions, is a comprehensive account of police brutality and corruption, providing serious recommendations to address the problems. It documents deficiencies in training, salaries, and the de facto immunity from punishment that police continue to enjoy.

Civil rights activists and attorneys in India have argued that even partial implementation of the reports' detailed recommendations would substantially curb police abuses and improve their overall performance. The importance of implementing the recommendations was reiterated in a recent Supreme Court judgment. Despite repeated calls for reform from former Home Minister Indrajit Gupta, the National Human Rights Commission, and civil rights activists, little action has been taken.

Without an immediate and comprehensive commitment to police reform, abuses against the countries lowest castes, and indeed against all marginalized communities, will continue. India's emerging human rights discourse, and the innovative work of the women's movement and the Dalit movement, are already helping to generate solutions to the problem of police corruption and caste issues generally. The Indian government should solicit the participation of these local groups and of the international community in tackling the problem.

The government of India has also consistently refused to allow relevant U.N. bodies, including working groups and special rapporteurs, to gain access to the country. Simultaneously, the difficulty of slotting caste-based abuses into standard categories of human rights violations, as well as the prevalence of constitutional and legislative protections at the national-level, have allowed for these abuses to escape international scrutiny. As a signatory to several international human rights conventions, India is obligated to abide by their provisions.

The Indian government should enlist the support of the United Nations, multilateral financial institutions, India's trading partners, and national and international nongovernmental organizations to eradicate the pervasive problem of caste-based abuse. It should also place a priority on strengthening institutional mechanisms aimed at addressing issues of violence and discrimination. In 1997 India celebrated its fiftieth anniversary of independence from British rule. In 1998 the world celebrated the fiftieth anniversary of the Universal Declaration of Human Rights. The Indian government should mark these occasions by dismantling a system that in practice relegates millions of people to a lifetime of violence, servitude, segregation, and discrimination, all on the basis of caste.

Bibliography

Elliot, W., *Aboriginal Caste Book. 3 Vols.* Ms, c1829.

Hemlata Rao & Devendra Babu, M., *Scheduled Castes and Tribes, Socio-Economic Upliftment Programmes*. New Delhi: Ashish 1994

Jogan Shankar, *Devadasi Cult. A Sociological Analysis*. New Delhi: Ashish 1990 [G]

Karanth, G.K., *Caste after fifty years of Independence, Review of Development and Change* 2, 1997: 319-337

Kadetotad, N.K., "Caste hierarchy among the Untouchables of Dharwar", Eastern Anthropologist 19, 1966: 205-14

Laxminarayana, V., "Post-Independence Dalith Movement in Karnataka". *Report for ICSSR*, 1989

Mishra, R.K., *State level Scheduled Caste Corporations in India: promise and performance*, EPW 31, 33, 1996: 2217-9

Nagaraj, D.R., *The Flaming Feet: a Study of the Dalit Movement in India*. Bangalore: South Forum Press 1993.

Nair, J., *Badanavala killings: signs for the Dalit movement in Karnataka*, EPW 28, 1993, 19: 911-12

————————, *The devadasi, dharma and the state*, EPW, Dec. 10, 1994: 3157-67

Parvathamma, C., *Scheduled Castes at the Crossroads*. Ashish, New Delhi 1989

————————, *The glamour of clamour for reservation*. Mimeo. Madras: MIDS 1990.

Prabhakar, M.E. (ed.), *Towards a Dalit Theology*. Bangalore: CISRS 1988

Rajshekar, V.T., *Dalit: the Black Untouchables of India*, Atlanta: Clarity 1987

Rajshekhar Shetty, V.T., *Apartheid in India*. Bangalore: Dalit Sahitya Akademy 1983

Ramu, G.N., "Untouchability in rural areas", *Indian Journal of Social Work* 27, 1968: 147-55

Tharamangalam, J., "Caste among Christians in India", In M.N. Srinivas (ed.) *Caste, its Twentieth Century Avatar*. New Delhi: Viking (Penguin) 1996

Thurston, E., *Ethnographic Notes in Southern India*. Madras: Government Press 1906.

Trivedi, H.R., *Scheduled Caste Women: Studies in Exploitation*. Delhi: Concept 1976

Uplaonkar, A., "Scheduled Castes and social justice: a Karnataka case in point", *Indian Journal of Social Work* 53, 1992: 39-44

Venkatarayappa, K.N., *Slums: a Study in Urban Problems* Delhi: Sterling 1972

Index